Mark A. E. Williams may have found rhetoric's Ariadne's thread in his *Just Words*. This thread, Professor Williams maintains, does not glorify rhetoric as the definitive answer to the questions we face and it resists, rightly, the "present family of theories hovering around the humanities" that are linked "to the unchallengeable certainties of subjective experience." Rhetoric's Ariadne's thread, Professor Williams observes, honors, and critiques the theories set forth in the classical tradition, the Middle Ages, the Enlightenment, and the modern period. What sets *Just Words* apart from other struggles to understand rhetoric is its emphasis on the divine. Rhetoric's Ariadne's thread is marked by, in Professor Williams words, "the pursuit of the actual divine—while admitting that we will never fully comprehend it." This pursuit, one that threads between and among absolutes, "is the true rhetoric." *Just Words* is a provocative and insightful journey taking the "scenic route" through the rhetorical tradition.

—**David A. Frank**, PhD, University of Oxford Consortium for Human Rights, Professor of Rhetoric and Political Communication, Robert D. Clark Honors College, University of Oregon

With erudition, panache, and subtle wit, Mark Williams revives a neglected tradition of classical rhetorical texts, such as Plato's *Phaedrus*, and subverts subjective approaches to education, restoring both religion and rhetoric as foundational building blocks. Echoing C. S. Lewis's profound unraveling of modern pedagogy in *The Abolition of Man*, Williams critiques current power-based ideologies and celebrates the relevance of the past with his remarkable insights and wit in one of the most lucid, accessible, and stimulating books on religious communication in the last decade.

—**Terry Lindvall**, PhD, C. S. Lewis Chair of Communication and Christian Thought, Virginia Wesleyan University

In the tradition of C. S. Lewis, Professor Williams invites us to look at and along the intersections of ancient education, classical rhetoric, and the core tenants of religion to offer a fresh look at our present age. This book helps us connect the dots between words, meaning, and a better understanding of the challenges we face if we do not heed the lessons of the past. An important and thought-provoking book.

—**Steven A. Beebe**, PhD, Regents' and University Distinguished Professor Emeritus, Past President, National Communication Association

Mark Williams's fine book asks all of the right questions for a rhetorical time such as this. It is a bold, intellectually energizing exploration of both how we got to our current communicative mess and how we might move forward with honest, hospitable discourse. I recommend *Just Words* for its wit and wisdom amidst our contemporary period of cheapening rhetoric on all fronts.

—**Quentin J. Schultze**, PhD, Calvin University, Communication Professor Emeritus, founding member of the *Journal of Media & Religion*

If it is true that Western philosophy is a series of footnotes to Plato, we have become an academic and social culture so lost in footnotes that we've forgotten that there is a main text. Mark Williams's *Just Words* aims to remedy this by reminding us not just about the main text but also what is so vibrant, necessary, and basically undefeated about the arguments on truth, method, and meaning. Many treasures await careful readers of this book. Hardly a nostalgic call for a return to Platonism, *Just Words* nevertheless manages to highlight the degree to which a future society that aims for substantive practices of truth, justice, love, and meaning must largely rely on Plato's essential insights and arguments. Namely, that without a transcendent referent and conceptualization, we are stuck with the brutalities and whims of power and domination. *Just Words* is a must-read for everyone who cares about the myriad problems facing the world today.

—**Ryan Gillespie**, PhD, Study of Religion, UCLA

The subjective use of words to further one's own ends is not new. In this careful argument laced with fresh examples and asides, Professor Williams traces the relationship between rhetorical power and religious motivations in three Greek rhetoricians. Their understandings of the purpose of education and its relationship to the broader community vary, and that variation helps break up any monovocal stereotype of "the Classical world." But even more, these differing trajectories illuminate our own contemporary conflicts. Williams argues persuasively, but he doesn't leave us with mere abstractions. He leads us with hope toward the power of anchoring words to the divine in order to arrive at *just* words.

—**Annalee R. Ward**, PhD, Director, Wendt Character Initiative, University of Dubuque

Because our world is littered with injustices like human trafficking, the Trail of Tears, the deaths of civilians in wartime, or ecological racism, Mark Williams's analysis makes clear that neither the Modernist nor the Postmodernist—any more than the Conservative or the Liberal—have achieved the justice or better world that they promised. He rightfully argues, with insight, wit, and lucidity, that if we want justice, we will have to communicate and listen to each other in ways that our rhetorical, political, and educational systems have not prepared us for. We need meaningful alternatives, and *Just Words* lays out a compelling place to begin to imagine those alternatives.

—**Naaman Wood**, PhD, co-editor of *Humility and Hospitality: Changing the Christian Conversation on Civility*

In contemporary academic culture, particularly in the fields of rhetoric and education, characterizing someone's ideas as "Platonic" is usually seen as an insult or even as a *casus belli*. Not so with Mark Williams. Proceeding from the assumption that Plato didn't get as much wrong as is fashionable to think these days—and that he actually got more things right than we give him credit for—Williams makes a provocative case for reconsidering the connections among language, reality, and truth; and for reconsidering the consequences of fashionably subjectivist views of language and rhetoric in education and in public and political life. His argument is definitely countercultural. It will surely be difficult for many to accept. But we would do well to listen, and listen carefully.

—**Mark Allan Steiner**, PhD, Christopher Newport University

Mark Williams invites his reader on a conversational journey alongside the rhetoricians of the Ancient Greek world in pursuit of the pedagogy of the actual divine. Passionate, personal, and reformist, this book defines the calling of the educator in transcendent terms and stands with Plato that true rhetoric directs our vision toward the heavens.

—**Nathan Crick**, PhD, Texas A & M, author of *Rhetoric and Power: The Drama of Classical Greece*

Language has power. Words matter . . . but only so long as they are moored to meaning. Williams suggests that our words, stolen from substance and given meaning purely through the lens of subjective experience, fail to lead to the end we hope for and expect. Timely and important, this book suggests that by returning to the past, we might see and understand the present in an entirely different light. The answer to our present problems, he suggests, is not the work of modernity, but found hidden in the shadow of Gorgias and Isocrates. Come, sit in the shade and consider carefully . . . perhaps the old teachers have one last lesson for us.

—**Sean T. Connable**, PhD, co-editor of *Humility and Hospitality:*
Changing the Christian Conversation on Civility

Just Words

Just Words

Lessons of Ancient Education, Classical Rhetoric, and
Pagan Religion for a Post-Christian World

MARK A. E. WILLIAMS

Integratio Press

Pasco, Washington

JUST WORDS: Lessons of Ancient Education, Classical Rhetoric, and Pagan Religion for a Post-Christian World

This is a publication of Academe, a Division of Integratio Press.

www.integratiopress.com

Integratio Press is an Imprint of the Christianity and Communication Studies Network
11503 Easton Dr.
Pasco, WA 99301

www.theccsn.com

Cover design: Carol O'Callaghan Design
Interior design: Atritex Technologies
Image: Depositphotos (Apollo Drives his Chariot, Garden of Versailles)

PAPERBACK ISBN: 978-1-959685-11-1
EBOOK ISBN: 978-1-959685-12-8

Library of Congress Control Number: 2024935044

Dedication

For Dante and Vera

Et ad idem ipsum bonum est omni homini
toto corde, tota anima, tota mente
amando et desiderando nitendum.

Monologion lxxiii

Table of Contents

Acknowledgments

SOMEONE MUCH SMARTER THAN I am once offered me a bit of very simple advice: "Spend a lot of time with people who are smarter than you. It is the easiest way to learn things." I found the recommendation so inescapably compelling that I married the advisor. And my debts to her are only the first in a long string of debts that are so numerous and so deep as to be almost paralyzing. I have spent a lot of time with a lot of people who are, to put it bluntly, better than me.

For a decade before his death, I had the privilege of spending time with Jerry Murphy. We met at a symposium he had helped arrange at Oxford, and when he discovered we were only a few minutes apart in California (he was in Davis, and I was in Sacramento), we began meeting for lunch regularly. Those lunches were consistently the best part of my commute to campus, and usually the best part of my semester. When I first sketched out this book for him at one of our meals, he put his fork down, held up his hands and said, "Well it's *about time*." And the rest of that meal, and large parts of a number of others, were taken over by discussions of religion and rhetoric. But his first reaction has remained a touchstone of encouragement throughout this project. Jerry was almost preternaturally encouraging, as anyone who knew him could attest.

Much of the research for this book was done in Oxford, and Dr. Matthew Mills, then at Regent's Park, now teaching at Durham University and working in Durham Cathedral, was impeccably carefree and hospitable and possessed of a mind so unselfconsciously insightful and so casually deep that I sometimes did not fully realize the connections he had drawn between ideas until an hour after the pub had closed. He sharpened my thought in ways he never noticed. And sharing his company (within my mind at least) is Dr. Ryan Gillespie, a former student of mine who had outgrown his teacher before I met him. I have taken the liberty of our friendship to bounce a lot of the ideas in this book off of his golden soul and diamond intellect. Our conversations and correspondence are the backdrop to any number of the *topoi* found here, and those exchanges, not always agreements, have absolutely filled in a great number of uncomfortably deep potholes in my own thought.

Another Matthew, J. Matthew Melton, has served as a mentor and, more richly, a friend. He was President of the Religious Communication Association immediately before my term, and his guidance and encouragement were indispensable to me during those hectic days. Since then, Matthew has been a recurring voice of insight and wisdom in my life, on the topics here and other matters as well. He is the sort of character who is simply good for your soul.

And I could fill pages just with names of other folks who have stumbled into my life and done good and challenged ideas and structured my intellect. When, at one point late in the book, I talk about high school teachers who love their subjects and who inspire their students, I am thinking primarily of Ms. Stone—later, Ms. George—who certainly did more for me than she ever understood. And Eve Johnson, David Nelson, Harold Mixon, Andy King, and Ken Zagacki all continued that tradition. Every one of them took me as a student and sent my world spinning; when it stopped, it was larger than before, and richer. In my professional spheres, Annalee Ward, Naaman Wood, Sean Connable, Joy Andrick Qualls, Mark Steiner, John Hatch, Brandon Knight, and Robert Woods (without whom, absolutely not!) are all voices that have encouraged, challenged, and interrogated me, often directly about the ideas in this book, and whenever we arrived at disagreement in anything, they were exemplars of charity without condescension. That is only one of a dozen reasons I am so kindly affectioned toward them all.

I have also spent so many late nights and good scotches and even better conversation with my friend Michael Gillespie. We very often ended up talking around and about the various points in this book. He has been a godsend, calling my attention to relevant texts at exactly the right moment. I am richer for his friendship, and this book is better because of his intellect.

And then students of mine, undergraduate and graduate. So many who sat in seminars and discussions as we worked out confusions and ideals and ideas and relationships between action and thought. Miles Cochran, Nathan Thompson, Andrea Terry, Miles Coleman, Hannah Edwards, Paul Parkin, Chris Maben, Bethany Davis—all of these graduate students (several of them now professional colleagues across the country!) pushed me toward considerations of religious life, education, moral choice, and rhetorical thought that I might never have seen without them.

There are more amorphous and less personal debts, too, but no less important. I owe a very great debt to the librarians and staff of the Bodleian in Oxford where much of the heavy lifting in this book took place. While there, I have frequently been hosted by the Middlebury Centre for Medieval and Renaissance Studies, and the directors and staff have made the place a delight: St. Michael's Hall is as accommodating and heuristic as one could hope for. The faculty at Regent's Park College, Oxford, have also welcomed me on occasion and shared their Faculty Common Room and granted me access, as well, to the impressive collection in their Angus Library and Archive, for which I am deeply grateful. And I am also thankful to my own deans at California State University, Sacramento, Dean Meyer and Dean Bellon, who have consistently supported my travel and research time.

All this, and I have not even started on authors and artists and poems, much less those friends, less directly related to this book but no less central in my understanding of the ideas here: Derek Peterson and Rob Bell and Steve Johnson and Kevin Johnson. *Iter longum ambulavimus sed in bono comitatu.* And who would have it any other way?

I am a man of more debts than I can name, or even remember, much less repay. That said, none of these folks here should be assumed to agree with any specific part of any argument or conclusion in this book. But they have each been gracious when disagreeing and always encouraging.

All these debts I wear openly and acknowledge gratefully.

Foreword

CICADAS ARE AMONG NATURE'S MOST curious creatures. In spite of all the natural science brought to bear on them over the centuries, aspects of their existence remain mysterious, such as how or why one breed is able to remain in stasis below ground for up to 17 years awaiting their debut above ground. Recent research has also found that the astonishing nanostructure on the surface of cicada wings kills deadly bacteria, prompting an investigation into broader applications.[1] In this book, Mark Williams tells us how centuries ago, Socrates, in Plato's *Phaedrus*, claimed cicadas were the opposite of the Sirens whose seductive songs brought unsuspecting sailors to shipwreck. The cicadas, Socrates said, were once people who lived at the dawn of creation and could not stop singing about the wonder of it, so the gods gave them prolonged life, and now their songs report the creative words and works of humans to the Muses, who inspire these things.[2]

Socrates's account of cicada song has that touch of the "madness of the gods" that the *Phaedrus* tells us is necessary for Truth to imbue human discourse and allows words to participate in the kind of meaning that sticks, that changes things.[3] Before reading Socrates's explanation of the cicada song, I viewed the shrill sound as a nuisance akin to the high-pitched whine of power lines. But I smiled on reading about the Muses and their ancient connection to these insects. And now I cannot help but think more favorably of the constant summertime hum, which I can hear out my window as I write this.

That marked change in perception, in a very reduced nutshell, may very well be at the heart of Prof. Williams's fascinating exploration into the beginnings of the study of *just words*.

---

[1] Jillian Kramer, "Structure and Chemistry Dictate How Cicada Wings Repel Water and Kill Bacteria," *The Scientific American*, September 1, 2020. https://www.scientificamerican.com/article/structure-and-chemistry-dictate-how-cicada-wings-repel-water-and-kill-bacteria/.

[2] Robin Waterfield, *Phaedrus* (Oxford: Oxford University Press, 2009), 259c-d.

[3] Waterfield, Phaedrus, 244a-245e

Persuasion is partly about changing perceptions. It suggests that, while the world around us, what we call "reality," is phenomenologically present, it arrives in our minds through our senses and is interpreted by us with the aid of constructed frameworks of thought and value. These frameworks are subject to change, to maturity, to "epiphanies" that create paradigmatic shifts. We do not arrive as squalling infants possessed of fully developed interpretive frameworks. Our valoristic interpretations of what we sense is largely gifted to us by others, whether it be those who serve in the role of parents, guardians, teachers, mentors, or one of thousands of online proxies. David Hume argues in his *An Enquiry Concerning Human Understanding* that, as we grow older, we begin to do a lot of inferring about the nature of things around us.[4] Sometimes experience serves to adjust our inferential matrix. My father, for example, told me never to run my finger along the edge of a blade to test it when sharpening it but to try it against some other surface instead. As a boy, I ignored that advice once—and learned experientially why it was a sound view of things. I inferred from this experience that my father's warnings about other things had a strong likelihood of being equally true. As Aristotle suggests, persuasion taps many tools to adjust our interpretive framework, potentially saving us a lot of experiential trouble.[5]

In *Just Words*, Williams nudges us toward the notion that words, and their potentially staggering consequential contingencies, have much more sheer power than we have given them credit for, especially lately. Words have the potential, he argues, not only to transform but also to transcend our interpretive frames, creating an entirely fresh encounter with what is real and an entirely fresh understanding of one another. If this transcendent work can rise to the level of reframing the constructs shared among groups of people (Cicero's *communitas*, perhaps[6]), the possibilities are even more consequential. A legitimate question at this point would be: have we all but surrendered to cultural white noise? Words are yet with us. Their power as tools of craft and action is not diminished. As Neil Postman noted in his discussion of communication technologies, a clock or a microscope

---

[4] David Hume, "An Enquiry Concerning Human Understanding," sec. 4, part II, 29, in *Locke, Berkeley, Hume*, ed. Mortimer J. Adler, *Great Books of the Western World*, vol. 35 (Chicago: William Benton).

[5] See, e.g., Aristotle, *Art of Rhetoric*, trans. J. H. Freese, Loeb Classical Library 193 (Cambridge, MA: Harvard University Press, 1975), book II.

[6] Cicero, *De Officiis*, trans. Walter Miller, Loeb Classical Library 30 (Cambridge, MA: Harvard University Press, 1990), II.73.

are not neutral tools. They generate very specific consequences.[7] The same is true of words. They are not neutral tools. They still bring consequences.

Kenneth Burke's celebrated definition of humanity claims, "Humanity is the symbol-using (symbol-making, symbol-misusing) animal, inventor of the negative (or moralized by the negative), separated from his natural condition by instruments of his own making, goaded by the spirit of hierarchy (or moved by the sense of order), and rotten with perfection."[8] Humans, by Burke's fallen standard, are anti-natural beings, averse to mutuality with nature. But what if Burke's definition is itself an anti-definition? In other words, maybe Burke is not wrong, but perhaps the opposite side of the Burkean coin reveals a potential for humanity, especially on his last three points. Might there be a redemptive (in the Latin sense of "buying back") purpose for human symbol making? He hints at this in his *Rhetoric of Religion*. Might a redemptive framework employ the principle of the negative as the mortar between the bricks of mutuality, commonality, human agency, and equity? Are we limiting ourselves?

A true creator of *just words*, according to Plato, holds a power that others do not possess. When we speak of the cicada, as when we speak of other things, words can spin a weave around them, around any insect or creature or thing. Yes, we can speak of things with a clinical interpretive framework, as if sterile scientific terms were somehow "pure" and untainted by metaphor (they never are). But in speaking of cicadas, amazed scientists in their approach to the 17-year cycle creature faltered after Cicadettinae Lamotialnini . . . and decided upon *Magicicada*. Why?

Argentinian poet Maria Elena Walsh wrote a song in 1973 called "*Como la Cigarra*—Like the Cicada," with the following first verse:

> *Tantas veces me mataron, tantas veces me morí*
> So many times, they killed me, so many times I died.
> *Sin embargo, estoy aquí, resucitando*
> Yet here I am, rising again.
> *Gracias doy a la desgracia y a la mano con puñal*
> I thank the disgrace and the hand with the dagger.
> *Porque me mató tan mal, y seguí cantando*

---

[7] Neil Postman discusses at length the non-neutrality of communication technologies in the first chapter of *Amusing Ourselves to Death* (New York: Viking Penguin, 1985).

[8] Burke's definition was first published in his *Rhetoric of Religion* (Boston: Beacon, 1961) and subsequently expanded upon in *Language as Symbolic Action* (Berkeley: University of California Press, 1966), 3–24.

Because they killed me so badly; yet I kept right on singing . . .
Cantando al sol como la cigarra
Singing to the sun like a cicada
Después de un año, bajo la tierra
After a year, beneath the earth
Igual que el sobreviviente
Just like the survivor
Que vuelve de la guerra
Who returns from the war.[9]

The artist uses the cicada metaphor to refer to her own resilience in the face of many setbacks, but the song's first recording coincided with the Argentinian coup that overthrew an elected government and set up a brutal military *junta* in its place—and before long, these words became the Truth of the oppressed, the Voice of the resistance. The song was banned in the country, and those who sang it were jailed or exiled. When the *junta* was finally driven from power in 1983, the song was welcomed as the informal anthem for those returning from exile and for those enjoying freedom for the first time in a decade. Even today when the stylistically dated song is performed before a live audience in Argentina, the crowd spontaneously takes up the words, and tears are not uncommon.[10] How did these simple words acquire such power?

Since the 1960s, those who study persuasive discourse, discourse that reshapes shared realities, embarked on a paradigmatic shift that remains with us today, a drift away from *words* and into the broader world of symbolic action. There is no denying that there is a great deal of importance to those broader conceptions of discourse, even those that strive to unpack the symbolic priorities of theme parks, rock concert venues, and clothing fashions. Auto-ethnography has become an accepted term and area of study as well. The results of these studies can be illuminating and heuristic in the best scholarly tradition. So, there may be no compelling reason to set such studies aside.

Meanwhile, sitting on a dusty shelf in increasingly unvisited libraries are *just words*. Mark Williams, like J.R.R. Tolkien's wizard Gandalf among

---

[9] Walsh's first recording of this song was on her LP album *Como La Cigarra*, Track A5 (CBS), 1973, vinyl.

[10] Mariana Turiacci's article "'Como la Cigarra,' la icónica canción de María Elena Walsh que se convirtió en un himno nacional," *Billiken*, February 1, 2023, is one of many readily available pieces that discuss the history of Walsh's influential song: https://billiken.lat/interesante/como-la-cigarra-la-iconica-cancion-de-maria-elena-walsh-que-se-convirtio-en-un-himno-nacional/

the forgotten scrolls of Gondor, wants to bring words back into focus, to remind us that neglecting them is not really an option. But more than that, the living spark residing within words stands in need of fanning back into flame.

Williams peels away, almost like the archaeologists at the site of Troy, layer upon layer of time and technology and allows us to listen to the first people who wrestled with these things, and we find they have things to say that are both startling and familiar. Williams returns us to the vital moment in the history of democracy when it was not at all a sure thing that the experiment would survive. The celebrated Athenian model that would be used as the template for fresh new governments in the eighteenth and nineteenth centuries, including the infant United States of America in 1781, almost perished 2,400 years ago due to its own poor choices. Prof. Williams locates the extraordinarily fragile period after democracy had just been restored to a defeated city, like the streetlights coming back on for the first time after a hurricane. During a narrow window before conquest by the Macedonians, key figures, intent on helping Athens rebuild its shattered heritage, began to re-educate the literate survivors on how to make their voices, their words, and their participation in public life function all over again. And during that critical window, what those educators had to say would, strangely enough, fashion the thought by which the rest of us, down the lengthy corridors of time, would come to measure our own sense of the purposes of education and its vital connection to discourse in the public sphere.

In this book, we meet the Big Three of those early educators: Gorgias, Isocrates, and Plato. Gorgias, the eldest, was the controversial yet consummate professional who taught people how to leverage their moment to the greatest advantage; Isocrates was the classic pragmatist "man behind the curtain" who strove to rally the Athenian elite to seize the day, to Make Athens Great Again, to bring every will into sync with the noble goals of the state. And Plato was the young idealist who felt that neither opportunistic showmanship nor stirring nationalism were capable of resurrecting Athens from the ashes. Permanence abides with Transcendence, and until humans learn to yoke their souls to something higher and truer, they are doomed to repeat the failures of previous generations, he thought.

It was a long time ago. We might well ask whether the effort to dust off these old parchments is worth it. Even reading a scholarly text like this one, we are just as likely to view its chapters on a high-resolution screen infinitely more advanced than the inked animal skins of old. But our technological splendor has not eliminated the need to take care of the common weal. In fact, what technology may very well have done is elevate the sheer level of noise surrounding public discourse, making strategic choices on just how to be heard, even in our own communities, much more critical than they were in the days of sheepskin pages and platforms in the public square. In every generation since the Athenian experiment, warning voices have wailed that the commonwealth is in grave danger. This is because the commonwealth is, as the direct responsibility of the populace, in very truth always in grave danger. And the tools for its proper care and feeding are as simple and straightforward as they were in Plato's time.

What you will find in these pages is that our popular consumerist rhetoric, from the soundbite, to the meme, to the 180-word social media post, to the rant into the online void—all these are replete with echoes of Athens, with Sirens of power, money, and privilege. Today's rhetorical apogee is to go "viral," an ironically destructive adjective. Can a clear, quiet voice still penetrate the noise, break through symbolic walls, and build something new and lasting? Plato suggests that capturing a tiny, distilled essence of *aletheia*, of inspired truth, as in "Like the Cicada," can move mountains, even nations.

J. Matthew Melton, PhD
Decatur, Georgia
September 10, 2023

Prelude

Educating Ourselves to Death

Veniet tempus quo posteri nostri tam aperta nos nescisse
mirabuntur.
[The time will come when our descendents will be amazed
that we were ignorant of things so clear to them.]

—Seneca, *Questiones Naturales* VII

THINK OF THIS BOOK AS *the scenic route*. Its point is to reflect, in our troubled times, on the status of education, the understanding of language, and the nature of religion as they interact. But it spends most of its pages examining how these powerful ideas play off one another 2,400 years ago in one particular city in Greece that was still in the nightmare stages of recovery after losing a horrendous war. That may seem an odd way to begin, but it is not without its reasons, as we will see.

This book has grown out of courses I have regularly taught at my university for two decades. Over the years, I have had students tell me they would love to see the subjects of our discussions appear in a book. Here is that book, in part at least. I have provided no more than the first third of one of those classes, but this is the foundational material upon which all later discussions, through Rome, the Middle Ages, the Enlightenment, Modernism, and the contemporary perspectives, were built.

While it has roots in contemporary scholarship from a variety of disciplines, this book offers few original insights or discoveries. It does argue that some of the present ideas of "theory" inside the humanities traditions within the university are far less textured, rewarding, or capable than they seem at first glance, and it does raise questions about our own ideas of how words and education and religion and reality are related and what we can do with those relationships. Still, the scholarly contributions of this work are largely found in the realm of synthesis. If the process of drawing together ideas from different fields manages to raise questions that various scholars can carry back to their own enclaves and work with, that will be more than satisfying.

But since we live in an age where virtually any expression is judged as promoting some sort of political agenda, I shall be happy to save readers of this sort some trouble by stating here, with as much transparency as I can possibly muster, what it is that *I* think I am doing and why. Witty or insightful readers who discover other projects or motives within the text may have seen things I have missed, or they may be wrong. But here are my motives, as I understand them.

I find the present age unusually perilous. It is my contention that the present family of theories hovering around the humanities within the university life have, by linking themselves to the unchallengeable certainties of subjective experience, in fact made the exact error they sought to avoid in their rejection of Modernism and its mechanistic certainties. And these contemporary ways of thinking, especially about discourse and language, end up totalizing the identity of the self or the group in such a way that every disagreement becomes a potential existential threat. This totalizing step herds discourse away from the possibility of mere disagreement and debate and toward the phenomenological experience of threat, with its accordant justifications for violence. I believe, therefore, that the present scope of our ideas about language—how language works and what it is able to do—needs to be reconsidered. Perhaps even corrected. I will suggest in the coming pages that the most likely place to find that corrective will be in minds that thought about the world and about meaning in profound and powerful ways before the advent of Modernism. On a slightly less apocalyptic note, one attendant difficulty of our present view of language is an almost contradictory tendency to dissipate thought rather than focus it, cataloguing trees to the exclusion of any hint of forestry.

At the university where I teach, for example, we offer a rich array of GE, or General Education, courses to our students. These classes are supposed to be the foundational education that all students receive, no matter what their chosen major, and they are meant to acquaint students with a broad scope of ideas and perspectives. For our students—and we are not unique—options in the GE courses abound. In fact, our GE program is structured in such a way that students have some 34.188 quintillion paths they might follow in their own GE course of study. That is the number 34 (rounding down by more than 188 quadrillion) followed by eighteen zeros. The more precise number of options looks rather like this: 34,188,422,000,000,000,000.

To put that into perspective, if my own university had been admitting a freshman class of 1,000 students every year since the earth formed, and if each of those students had taken a different course of study from every other student, we would have exhausted 0.00000013% of our options for earning a degree. At that rate, we could continue to award degrees to students (who have never had the same set of classes, remember) until the sun goes nova without ever coming close to exhausting our options.

Such a broad spectrum of offerings provides a pragmatically limitless set of choices to the students. This will not seem like much of a problem to many people. For some folks, in fact, the idea that no two students with the same degree have studied the exact same material may even be cause to celebrate, and, frankly, I share in those celebrations to no small degree. If diversity is the sole (or primary) criteria for judging education or behavior, then we have arrived at the happy shores of the best of all possible worlds, it seems, and those who share such assumptions have cause for joy.

If, however, we believe that diversity in course offerings is one of many criteria for judging education, and perhaps not the most important one, we might suggest that—at least on the educational front—we are nearing too much of a good thing. While celebrating our diverse university and the options it offers, I am also sympathetic to this latter view.

I do not believe that diversity of perspective is bad. I do not believe that I am right about everything I hold dear, and certainly I depend on those who disagree with me to straighten me out. Their efforts have not always ended up as they hoped, but then neither have mine when I tried to straighten them out. Such intense conversations (between people who actually respect one another and just happen to actually disagree with one another) are simply part of what makes life fun.

On the other hand, there is some peril for a democratic society that achieves such a critical mass of diversity that it becomes impossible to begin with shared assumptions, common perspectives, and agreed rules of reasoning when discussing a public decision. One need only check the local newsfeed for evidence of the claim. Diversity is poisoned when it morphs into idiosyncrasy. When my own diverse viewpoint has become so idiosyncratic that it both (1) confuses the idea of raspberries and rattlesnakes and (2) closes down my ability to understand arguments that point out my error, then I have a problem. When the word *rational* has become little

3

more than shorthand for *me and my sort*, then everything we mean by a *commonwealth* begins to come apart, and democracy itself has a problem.

This book will not solve that problem. But it will address the idea of how we arrived in the present setting, for better and for worse. It will do this by identifying certain key ideas, terminologies, and themes that were part of education in the Western tradition from its beginning until the Enlightenment, some of which—*justice* comes readily to mind—are attempting to make a comeback. Make no mistake, however: this book is not a call to return to a golden age in a Camelot past. Nor is this book an attempt to return to a single orthodoxy about The West (whatever that means). But it does hold that, whatever The West is, there belongs to Euro-American culture and history something of a coherence and cohesion that has slipped through the cracks lately. And if your own days in university felt (or feel) incomplete, with too many trees and not enough forest (much less any advice on how to tend the flourishing woodlands and meadows of your life), then it is quite possible that this book will allow you to begin the process of filling in some of those gaps in order to see the larger picture in what used to be called a *liberal education*: an education proper to the *liberalis*, that is, to those who are free.

My own education and scholarly work have focused on language, and particularly the way language might be artistically crafted to shape human decisions and attitudes. The old word for this study was *rhetoric*. The word rhetoric is used today mostly as an insult. But in the ages before algorithmic news, omnipresent sales, and sought-out propaganda, rhetoric was a discipline of formal study that focused on how discourse and language shape the material, intellectual, and psychological aspects of human experience. This was considered a noble and worthwhile pursuit, and rhetoric is arguably, second only to music, the oldest discipline to be given systematic study in education. In most of Classical Greece and certainly by the time of the Romans, a command of rhetoric was the core idea of what it meant to be educated.

To understand where we are today, and to review that stance wisely, we need some grasp of how the ideals and goals of being educated have changed over time. We need to be aware of what we have held onto and what we have let go, and why. This book is an invitation to that conversation. Structurally, it would be presumptuous to call it a history of education or a history of rhetoric. I am not a historian. I lay no claim to understanding, with any special insight, the nuances of their methods or the intricacies of their academic debates. This book might be better thought of as a—not *the*, but a—narrative about the beginning of education in the traditions that have defined U.S. and European culture. This is a narrative from an angle that has been so glossed-over and ignored that its absence has, I will argue, distorted our understanding of a number of disciplines, political ideals, and social abilities. The telling of this story in this form may correct some misunderstandings. It may create others. But at least the conversation will be more whole and inclusive.

In short, that conversation suggests that rhetoric, loosely defined as the study of how human language shapes human experience, cannot be understood as thoroughly as it should be without reference to two close companions: education and religion. If these seem an odd grouping to educational, theological, and rhetorical scholars, that is rather my point: most folks in the rhetorical tradition prior to the modern era would not have considered this a strange grouping at all. This volume focuses on the three basic ideals of education, language, and religion that have echoed down to our own days. We will obviously be painting in broad strokes, but it is to be hoped that enough specificity can be employed that we do not overgeneralize to the point of error. Nevertheless, difficult choices about what to put in and what to leave out are required. For example, James Fredal's book on rhetorical artistry champions the spatial, physical, and gendered ideals of Greek culture. This is a welcome addition to the history of rhetorical thought and extends a number of areas for consideration and exploration by scholars.[1] We can borrow from such scholarship, but in the end, this book will grapple mostly with the written texts that come down to us. And even among these, choices will have to be made. These choices will not please everyone, but they have been guided by a simple idea.

The Greek word for "individual" is *idiōtēs*. It takes very little thought to puzzle out the implications of that bit of etymology. An *idiot* was a person alone, a person without much commerce in the accumulated wisdom of their community. They were captivated by their own private and limited affairs. To think without the benefit of an honest and deep understanding

---

[1] *Rhetorical Action in Ancient Athens* (Carbondale: Southern Illinois University Press, 2006). Fredal goes so far as to caution against a review of rhetoric that leans too much upon texts (pp. 7–9). The perspective is worth considering, but the further we move from text the more, not less, we speculate about meaning. Still, gendered space and religious architecture and cultural rites of passage are fit aspects of the study of rhetoric in history, and these should take their place alongside the texts as part of a concert of understanding, certainly.

of our communal past is to embrace the path of the *idiōtēs*. That path is like trying to remove your own appendix based on what you remember from eighth-grade biology class: the enterprise is apt to end poorly. No one person is adequate for the task of living life fully. We need our communities badly, and perhaps especially those communities from our communal past. The past cannot be exiled if the present is to be civilized; memory is the prerequisite of social order.

And if we pause to think about it, it is not even difficult to see why. At the core, our problems are not substantively different from the challenges of the past, despite the distracting veneer of today's technology. We are not the first to grapple with the question of how to unite diverse peoples and views. We are not the first to wonder whether words are moral agents or neutral tools. We are not the first to raise questions about the nature and limits of human sexuality and erotic desire. We are not the first to wonder what our humanity means in the face of new technology. We are not the first to find our citizenry divided against itself. We are not the first to struggle with the relationship between the authority of the state and the authority of the divine. We are not the first humans.

There are two ways to dance with the music of the distant past. The first, and by far the most fun, is to simply bounce about laughing at their blunders and mocking their blind spots. We take pleasure in pointing out the unconscious privilege of Augustine and Quintilian, the mindless embrace of slavery in Cicero, the intricately reasoned misogyny of Aristotle. And all this is true, of course. They were worse than us in so many ways. And pointing out their blind spots is a valuable, if not a particularly challenging, enterprise. By considering their shortcomings, we see what we will become if we forget the lessons we have learned.

But there is a second set of steps in this dance with the past, and these steps are far more difficult to master. This second dance tries to understand, as best we can, not what they failed to see but what they saw: not how they were worse than us, but where they were our equals or, perhaps, even better than us. In this dance, we seek as much as possible to let the past lead so that we come to understand their world in their way. Once we get a hint of how they saw the world, we can stand in their place, to some small measure, and begin to sense their astonishment at our own horrifying blind spots. For it is not only the past that made stupid assumptions about the world. We do too. We just do not know what they are. For us (just like for them), the stupid assumptions are buried under so many layers of sedimentary obviousness that they have become the invisible "of course" that grounds the vision of our age and everyone in it. That is what a blind spot is. The only cure for the cultural idolatries of the present moment is to escape the outlook of our own era in order to try to catch a glimpse of ourselves from a temporally distant outside point of view. And the further outside we go, the more likely we are to hear those in that other era whisper, "Why in the world would they think *that?!*" And suddenly we discover that we do—or, often enough, do not—have real reasons for why we think *that*. In other words, when we learn to think a bit like the past, we may begin to sense not one more of their stupid ideas, but one of ours.

And so, the goal of this text is not so much to critique the minds of the past for their shortcomings as it is to allow those minds to critique us. In this interrogation, let us see if we might overhear them whispering about some of our own assumptions that they would find outlandish. Then we can ask if they might be right. C. S. Lewis once wrote that this challenge to the limits in our own way of thinking is one of the primary benefits of reading books from long ago, and it is this view of Lewis's that I take as my guide here.[2]

We do not have to ignore, like Miniver Cheevy, the difficulties of a past draped in "the grace of iron clothing" in order to learn valuable things from that past.[3] If we are paying attention, some of those lessons will make us uncomfortable about those who came before us. If we are paying very careful attention, some of those lessons will make us uncomfortable about ourselves. And this is likely to be true no matter what our present politics or religious convictions are. But that discomfort is perhaps the best gift the past has to offer those of us living in the hypermediated Global Strip Mall of the present partisan moment.

This second approach to the past is of course much harder than the first and fraught with challenges. It is all too easy to smuggle into Plato what we want Plato to say; he can no longer object. But this present text operates from the scholarly assumption that it is possible to avoid this error to some significant degree and to understand the past on its own terms and in ways that matter, if we are careful. True, we are stuck with overheard conversations, and we cannot ask the speakers to clarify what they meant. But we

---

[2] C. S. Lewis, "On the Reading of Old Books," in *God in the Dock*, ed. Walter Hooper, 200–207 (Grand Rapids, MI: Eerdmans, 1970).

[3] Edwin Arlington Robinson, "Miniver Cheevy," in *Anthology of American Literature, II. Realism to the Present*, 2nd ed., ed. George McMichael (New York: Macmillan, 1974), 977–78.

can listen intensely, compare what they say about one another, and work to undermine the reductive assumption that we understand them and their world better than they did. We can include in our diversity an incomplete but not fictitious voice from Pagan Greece or Feudal France. Not every understanding of the past, in my view, is a smuggled agenda from the present. Nevertheless, when a book like this one is drawing contemporary lessons and parallels to the past, there is a thin line between emphasizing the relevant views and reading presumed outcomes into past views. I have exerted honest labor into the goal of the former, and it is for that very reason that I spend four chapters in careful examination or in close readings of specific texts from the ancient world and one prior chapter laying out the core cultural shifts that preceded those texts I focus on; almost three-quarters of the book is spent in trying to understand the original authors' views and listen to their voices. Only after that exploration—a scenic route through a very different country—does the book shift its focus, in the closing chapters, to contemporary ramifications.

Finally, a word about the intentionally ambiguous title of this book. *Just Words* may, of course, mean merely words, or it might designate words that are *just*. As an attentive reader will have discerned from my remarks thus far, I do not believe, as some theories of communication might suggest, that words are shackled to the corpse of self-expression. If they are, then they are little more than idiosyncratic eruptions of self, gushing into a world and colliding with other gushing selves. But if words are able to rise above and reach beyond self, then and only then do they carry the possibility of being instruments and expressions of justice. The core of justice is to treat the *other* according to what they really are rather than what I have thought them to be or perhaps even what they think themselves to be. There are plenty of souls who underestimate themselves. There are an equal number who overestimate themselves, of course. Justice is at the core of a language that transcends such limited self-estimates.

Until communication can reach beyond self and work in community (past and present), it is merely sound and fury. But not every attempt to reach beyond the self ends in grasping what is best. Sometimes people join the Klan. So, the reach of language must, at some level, in some way, also be able to offer a just critique of the content that we grasp, as well as the mechanisms we use to grasp it. I do not believe that we have, at present, very robust skills for doing this.

As I have mentioned, I find the present age unusually perilous and our present theories of language, religion, and education unusually thin in light of the actual challenges of the present.

This book will not give much succor to those on the right who believe in a gilded past (desecrated by a mushy-headed left) to which we must return. It will not give much encouragement to those on the left who think we were on the correct path before the derailing interference of those knuckle-headed fanatics on the right. It will not serve those who think that by leaving God we have left all possibility of being human. It will not serve those who think that by leaving God we have finally found a way to be human. What it will do, perhaps, is offer some deep context that provides all sides with new ammunition and all sides with a more coherent sense of how we arrived at this bifurcated moment in our endlessly interesting life together. Should dreams, beyond all hope, come true, it might even help a very few of us talk to one another more clearly and treat one another more justly.

Chapter 1

On Rhetorical Hippopotamuses: Education, Religion, Rhetoric

ASSUME WE MEET AT A social gathering and I draw you aside into a quiet, private conversation where I earnestly propose that, between now and five-thirty tomorrow morning, you will meet a hippopotamus selling boiled turnips at a roadside stand. You would likely have no difficulty coming very quickly to believe that my proposal is false. You might, of course—and just as quickly—come to believe a few things about me as well, but that is a different question. What we are interested in is *how* you came to your beliefs. And the short answer is, after hundreds of years of rational inquiry into every amazing aspect of human neurophysiology,[1] with at least twenty-five centuries of psychology behind us, with seven major (and sometimes mutually exclusive) theories of human personality currently in use by scholars and therapists,[2] with university libraries across the world groaning under the weight of countless dissertations in a host of social sciences—well, the short answer is: we do not really know.

---

[1] Rational neurophysiology can arguably trace its roots back to the ancient Egyptians. The earliest known example is the Smith Papyrus, dating from at least 3,500 years ago and perhaps a thousand years before that. This ancient text laid out in purely physical and material terms almost fifty specific diagnoses, treatments, and surgical procedures for dealing with trauma to the head, neck, spine, and chest. See Marc Stiefel, Arlene Shaner, and Steven Schaefer, "The Edwin Smith Papyrus: The Birth of Analytical Thinking in Medicine and Otolaryngology," *The Laryngoscope* 116, no. 2 (2006): 182–88, as well as John Nunn, *Ancient Egyptian Medicine* (Norman: University of Oklahoma Press, 2002). Contemporary neurophysiology certainly begins no later than the early 1600s. For more, see Mary A. B. Brazier, *A History of Neurophysiology in the 17th and 18th Centuries: From Concept to Experiment* (New York: Raven, 1984), as well as her *A History of Neurophysiology in the 19th Century* (New York: Raven, 1988).

[2] In *Personality Theories*, 9th ed. (San Francisco: Cengage Learning, 2013), Barbara Engler names them as Psychoanalytic, Neopsychoanalytic, Behavioral, Biological, Humanistic, Cognitive, and Non-Western theories of personality. Each of these seven is subdivided into an array of competing (and, again, sometimes mutually exclusive) schools of interpretation, prioritization, and application. In the end, there may be dozens (if not hundreds) of viable views of human personality today. A good historical introduction is G. P. Lombardo and R. Foschi, "The Concept of Personality in 19th-Century French and 20th-Century American Psychology," *History of Psychology* 6, no. 2 (2003): 123–42.

11

Obviously, what we think and believe is larger and more intricate than simple psychology, and to beat up primarily on that one particular field does little but offer an introduction to the fact that what we say and believe and do is always a messy jumble with a rather sketchy provenance. We know, for example, that we do not form our beliefs in anything like a mechanically logical way. Your conclusion regarding the turnip-selling hippo seems logical, but Christopher Cherniak pulls back the curtain of mere seeming and shows us, mathematically, that it cannot be *purely* logical. There simply is not enough time for you to work out the formal logical consistency between my suggestion and what you have already come to believe about the world.[3] But it has been a long time since humans tried to pretend that we were all going to be better off if we just worked more like computers and based every decision on a measurable dataset and a mathematical calculation. It has been a while since we tried to anchor the act of being human in, and only in, *knowledge* of the mathematical and scientific sort. That view, which we broadly characterize as the fundamental error of Modernism, has faded. Most of us—not all of us, evidently—still very properly value science and data in our decisions, but we have added things like our own experience and our own unchartable and ever-changing moods and desires into the mix of reasoning and belief.

But moods and desires have their limits, too. If you do not believe you will meet that turnip-selling hippo tonight, such a belief did not emerge from your own personal preferences. You did not form your belief according to what you *wanted* to see. (What sane, good-natured soul would not want to meet a hippo selling boiled turnips at a roadside stand!?) Rather, you formed your actual belief according to what you actually thought would actually happen, independent of your desires.

We live, and every day we place into inherited categories the minutia of our beliefs and conclusions regarding capitalist hippopotamuses and the stunning regularity of eastern sunrises and the fact that we still recognize our spouse every day—and that we prefer Candidate Stultus over Candidate Querulous—and we are not thinking too much about the fact that there are presently soldiers inside bunkers on at least three continents who would, if

---

[3] Christopher Cherniak, *Minimal Rationality* (Cambridge, MA: MIT Press, 1986). His fourth chapter (see especially note 13) lays out the mathematics, which I will not duplicate here. Suffice it to say that if you had been checking consistency with your held beliefs in a formally logical way, and if you had been doing so at impossible speeds for an impossible amount of time, you would not yet be able to reach a conclusion about whether my claim is logically consistent with your other beliefs.

a specific string of letters and numbers showed up on their screens, launch devices that would kill us all. And how do I know what is right or wrong? Is there a God? Or life on other planets? And do we have one of their crashed spaceships or not? And why did Dad die so young? And how much does recycling my water bottle accomplish, really? And why are we still using oil, for crying out loud? Why can't I cheat? Am I gonna die as young as Dad did? And did Queen Victoria and Prince Albert *really* have such a great marriage? Better than mine? Why? Should we have kids? How many? And given the huge number of conspiracies that have shown up in my newsfeed this week, surely at least one or two of them *must* be true. Also, humming-birds. Like how did *that* happen?

We live in a world that is lovely and horrifying and maddening, and it seems rather like most of us experience it as a swirl of barely examined phenomena and passively unverified data that hold our attention for less time than it takes to click "like." We do not seem to understand the mechanical psychology of being human very well. And none of us is purely logical. And all of us believe some things to be true that we very much wish were not true, and vice versa. But if our beliefs are not the conclusion of absolutely rational thought and if they are not simply the outworking of our own desires, then what are they, and where do they come from? Think of three things you believe to be true about politics or religion. How did you settle on those beliefs? How did you choose them? Or make them? Or surrender to them? Or chase them down and capture them?

How do we weigh our options and make decisions and be human? As we explore that question, we will come to learn, perhaps, a bit about our own beliefs and our own way of believing, about education and faith and science and, most of all, about *words* that, through some alchemy, change our thoughts and emotions and relationships into convictions about life and death and God and politics and community and family and patriotism. These are not small matters. These are convictions that many people say they would be willing die for. A few are even bold enough to live for them.

This book will attempt to look at the interactions of three powerful forces in culture that help form and shape our instincts and decisions: religion, education, and rhetoric. The key assumption undergirding this text is that these three are interdependent in ways too often neglected in contemporary teaching and scholarship. Each can be studied independently, never referencing the others. But without a keen awareness of their interdependence, I suspect none of them can be as deeply understood as it should be. Each of these three interactive dimensions of culture requires a bit more introduction.

Education appears to be the easiest of the three to discuss, partly because we have all been educated in some fashion, and partly because our politicians make education a recurring focus of their policies and ideologies, though not their attentions and reflections. But to grasp our concern about education in this text, perhaps it is best to begin with a simple question: *Why does it rain?* The question is hardly difficult; it rains, any elementary school child can explain, because water evaporates from the seas and lakes and streams, and as the water vapor rises, it cools and condenses. As it condenses and becomes heavier, it falls back to earth in raindrops.

That explanation is accurate, but there is a problem. This reply does not exactly answer the question. It does not tell us *why it rains*. It only tells us *how it rains*. But *how* and *why* are two very different questions. If I ask, "Why are you reading this book?" it is no answer at all to reply, "Well, patterns of light and dark on the page are transferred by my optic nerves into my brain where they are decoded into the symbols recognized as letters and words, and these are cognitively reprocessed so that I derive meaning from them." True, of course, but once again it does not answer the question. My inquiry was about *motive*. The reply was all *mechanism*. And with this question about reading a book, we immediately see that, at least in some situations, it is quite ridiculous to provide a *how* answer to a *why* question. Why did we not see that when we were asked about the rain? Why can we so easily submit a *how* answer to a *why* question in that context and not even notice what we have done? The briefest reply is, "Because that is the answer we were taught; that is how we were educated."

But surely evaporation is not the only answer to the question, "Why does it rain?" We might just as easily answer, "It rains because God in his infinite wisdom wills the earth to be fecund and bring forth life for his own glory and for the sustenance of all peoples, and your question arises from the desire, given to you by God, to seek for meaning in all the changes and chances of this life, so that you will be led to Truth." An alternative answer might be, "There is no *why*. Rain is a mindless, meaningless, pointless repetition of material-chemical processes without design or purpose, and your question is as nonsensical as asking, 'How much larger than Nietzsche is ketchup?'" Or this answer might be offered: "It rains because the hearts of citizens are pure; when drought comes, it is because there is impiety in the land, and this impiety has offended the god of rain, and he requires a propitiatory sacrifice to restore purity." Or perhaps, "We don't know why it rains or even if there is a reason, and that is not our concern. Rather, we want to understand the mechanisms of rain so that we may take charge of nature and make nature do what we want." A young person might be taught any of these answers, but each carries with it a certain set of assumptions about what is (and is not) real, what is (and is not) important, and what is (and is not) true about our lives.[4] That is, each answer carries within it a metaphysical lesson as well as a material lesson. These metaphysical lessons are an inescapable part of being educated: moral and religious frames of life are irretrievably embedded within every process of education.[5] This point serves as one of the fundamental assumptions of this book.

One of the conundrums of the modern American model of a nation is that we almost universally support the idea of offering public (that is, state-sponsored) education, but at the same time we want to maintain a wall of separation between religion and the state. This experiment is actually quite new, and whether it is possible to do both remains an open question. Even if we exclude all literature and history and civics, if we do away with economics and business and women's studies, if we remove psychology and philosophy and anthropology, if we simply make our public schools and universities about absolutely nothing but the perfectly neutral field of mathematical processes (never applications!) and material measurements, then we have either said (1) all these other things do not matter or said (2) education cannot deal with anything that might have a sliver of nuance in it. Neither seems a very satisfying—or even

---

[4] The first alternative answer above might be given by a Medieval Benedictine, the second by a contemporary materialist, the third by a Pagan of the Roman Empire, the fourth by an early twentieth century engineer or by a fascist who vaunts efficiency and control over all other ethical matters. To be clear, Aristotle discusses several species of *why* in his *Metaphysics* and *Physics*. These discussions give rise to his four causes, and with him as our guide, we would observe that the elementary school answer, involving evaporation and condensation, is in fact a perfectly legitimate, but a very incomplete, answer, giving us the *efficient* cause of rain.

[5] I do not wish to conflate the distinct categories of *morality* and *religion*. Whatever the relationship between moral and religious beliefs, my only point at present is that education will inevitably involve both, carried forward in its assumptions. Education is moral because it implicitly and explicitly establishes values and hierarchies of value. It is religious because it implicitly and explicitly establishes a pietistic (i.e., ideologically devoted) response to natural phenomena: either it suggests that nature is the set of all things that exist or it allows for (or champions) some reality beyond the limits of natural phenomena and thus serves as a gateway to the supernatural.

defensible—answer, and such reflections push us back on an uncomfortable reality: education instills virtues and metaphysical views. In other words, education is as much about in-forming the soul as it is about information for the mind, as much about interior pilgrimage and enlightenment as it is about exterior data and measurement. And this seems inescapably true. Education is inevitable; education is laden with the values of its culture; cultures change; therefore, education will always be complicated and in flux. One task of the present book will be to examine which aspects of education survive those complicated cultural adaptations and which do not. It is to be hoped that such observations will suggest what is and is not the very core and character of education itself.

Education is always complex and fluid, but for some years now, the contemporary debates have been unusually intense about the content and purpose of education; the role of ideological, moral, and political assumptions and conclusions rooted in various curricula; the value (and threat!) of technology and teachers and professors in the educational process (can't an AI just handle this?); the worth of an education that is not specifically designed to find employment; and the purpose and role of gatekeepers and graders. Questions are raised, in other words, about the scope and value of a liberal arts education: an education designed to teach the skills needed by *libera hominem*, a *free person*. The Classical world, of course, is where the very idea of a "liberal education" was first crafted, and that is where this book begins. We will look at three views of the point and purpose of education as responses to changing ideas of religious and cultural identity in ancient Greece.[6] And at the core of those updates, adaptations, and dynamic shifts in cultural identity, we will find questions about moral behaviors, social values, the nature of language, and the gods. Always the gods. They are inescapably present in the educational process.

But if education is blended with religion among the ancient Greeks, it raises the very real question of what the word *religion* means in such a mélange. Certainly, the Greeks thought of their gods in ways quite unlike anything we, today, would be likely to encounter in a religious setting. For one thing, it is well known that the Greeks had no word that matches our idea of *religion*.[7] They spoke of *eusēbias* and *asēbias*: states of piety and impiety.

---

[6] The dates here are fluid, but this volume will follow the story from about 600 to 350 BC. This is roughly from the time of Thales until the death of Plato.

[7] The English word *religion* is derived from the Latin *religio*, which referenced a duty owed to the gods. The Roman statesman Cicero defined *religio* as "a practice that properly

But before attempting to see their point of view, perhaps we need to clarify our own. The word *religion* is today a loaded term and often a flashpoint for political, cultural, and ideological expressions. Is religion anti-science? Is it a cause of violence in the world? Is it *the* cause of violence? Or is it a reliable path to peace? Is true religion inevitably narrow and fanatical? Or is it primarily a broadening experience that blossoms into tolerance and loving acceptance of others?[8]

Almost certainly religion is, of itself, none of these. Religion seems rather like that publicly neutral system of interaction we call politics. Certainly, politics may, in specific situations, move nations to war and individuals to acts of terrifying violence. At other times, the political process can stifle and refrain such impulses. Much the same could be said for religion as a generic concept. Conflicts emerge when questions of our identity and visceral tribal affiliations are at stake. Wars are fought over "our way of life," and that may involve religion, political parties, wealth, or any of a host of complicated combinations of these and many other things that have been woven into an *us* that can be clearly differentiated from *them*.

And so, *religion*, like *education*, begins to look like a complex idea that cannot be reduced to social simplicities by anyone who wants to reflect honestly and carefully on the nuance and texture of human life, human communities, and human possibilities. But this level of complexity does not make the word *religion* undefinable. At a minimum, we can frame a functional working definition that captures much of what we mean by *religion*. Religion is clearly not a political perspective, though religion may influence politics or even in some cases serve as the political system. Religion is not a statement of a specific set of beliefs, though many religious expressions have creeds that state their beliefs. Religion is not sentiment, though many religious people find their faith is a source of deep emotional experience, both comforting and disturbing. But if religion is not exactly these things, what is it? Leaning on the work of Roger Stump, we may identify three primary aspects of a religious life as religious believers themselves experience and explain it.[9] First, religion is structured as a mixture of both beliefs and practices. As in any social organization, these beliefs and practices explain

---

honors the gods" ("cultus deorum") in *De Natura Deorum*, trans. H. Rackham, Loeb Classical Library 268 (Cambridge, MA: Harvard University Press, 1951), 2.8.

[8] See, e.g., Karen Armstrong, *Fields of Blood: Religion and the History of Violence* (New York: Anchor, 2015).

[9] Roger W. Stump, *The Geography of Religion* (London: Rowman & Littlefield, 2008), 7.

and reinforce one another. They are intimately intertwined. Second, these beliefs and practices are connected to realties that are outside of normal space-time. The central acts and beliefs of religion are tied to something beyond the time and space of ordinary life; they commune with the infinite and eternal. Third, these beliefs and practices relate to some god or gods—a being or beings with attributes and powers beyond mortal people.

Such a working definition is not completely satisfactory, but it captures something of the core of *religion* as experienced by not only a contemporary Hindu in New Deli but also a Catholic Christian in Chicago, a Medieval Viking dedicated to the Norse gods, a follower of Islam in the Ottoman Empire, a Roman Pagan in the Republic, or a Greek citizen at the time of Socrates. And with such a definition, we are ready to look a bit more closely at religion in the political and personal lives of those in the ancient world.

Perhaps the most important thing to recognize about the Classical world, at present, is that the spheres of religion, politics, and personal life were interwoven in ways that most citizens in the West have never experienced today. Religion was a participant in, and more often than not the very foundation of, a *commonwealth*: a core of shared priorities and perspectives that became an *identity*, an *us*. Religion—beliefs and acts relating to the gods and connected to realities outside of normal space-time—was simply an unquestioned dimension of politics. Political life was religious. Much the same could be said for what the Romans would call *familia* and the Greeks referred to as *oikon*.[10] The terms refer to the "household," generally meaning all those living under one roof (grandparents, parents, children, slaves, freedmen) and guided by one person, the owner of the property, and usually the oldest male. The household was recognized as central to the civilized life of both the Romans and the Greeks, but we must be careful not to identify it too closely with modern ideas of *family*. There is overlap, certainly, but nothing like a strict correspondence between our ideas of family and the Greek and Roman vision of a good household.

---

[10] These terms are the sources of our contemporary words *family* and *economy*, respectively. But *familia* and *oikos* reference a somewhat larger idea than one associates with the modern word *family* and a much smaller idea than is associated with the modern word *economy*. Furthermore, the idea of a household varied between Greece and Rome. The Greeks, for example, never seem to have invested the head of the household with the sort of legal status found in Rome, where the *pater* held almost unquestioned rights of life and death over those within the *familia*. Nevertheless, the force and dominance of the *oikos* is clearly demonstrated throughout Greek literature. Think, for example, of how Socrates is appalled and scandalized when he discovers that Euthyphro is filing a suit in the Athenian courts against his own father.

But for the present, we only need to note that this personal sphere, as close as most in the ancient world would come to an idea of private space, was intimately tied to both the state and religious identity. The head of the Roman household had specific religious responsibilities to the local gods (as a citizen) and to the household gods and ancestors (as head of the household). The quality of domestic life depended to a large degree on how piously and properly these religious duties were fulfilled. The head of the household was also responsible for educating the children in how to be a good Greek or Roman citizen, passing on the religious-civic traditions. Again, notice how religion was intimately intermingled with the world of politics—and with the world of private life. And all of these were mixed up in education. And the capstone of education became that third, and in many ways central, theme of this book: *rhetoric*.

Like *education* and *religion*, the word *rhetoric* is a term that is hard to define. Despite the way the word is used today in the popular culture (meaning something like *pointless prattle*), rhetoric is actually an ancient discipline of formal study focused on how discourse and language shape human beliefs and experiences. Central to this understanding of rhetoric is the idea that words, used carefully, have specific relationships to reality, and because of this, words are a primary tool in changing beliefs and shaping convictions. In this role, rhetoric served as the central course of study in education for two thousand years. Among scholars who focus on the study of rhetoric today, there are different emphases and of course hearty debate about the nature and scope of rhetoric.

Rhetoric is, in other words, what academics call a *contested term*, meaning it has many possible definitions and each definition has a different set of assumptions and consequences. The differences between definitions are often quite serious, reflecting divergent, sometimes conflicting, hierarchies of cultural values, scholarly assumptions, ideological perspectives, and personal identities. But if rhetoric is a contested term, the present text does not pretend that all definitions are equal, nor that this book will somehow float magically above the fray without a perspective of its own. This text will employ the following working definition: *Rhetoric is the artistic use of language to shape the heart, the mind, and the will of a human being or some human enterprise.* The word *rhetoric* is also used, confusingly, to describe the *study* of this artistic use of language. Of course, the definition offered here can be challenged on almost any of its terms. What is meant by *artistic? Language? Will? Enterprise?* For that matter, *human?* Rhetoric is a contested term.

Briefly and roughly, for those who are specifically rhetoricians and give scholarly study to the field, I will suggest how I resolve the two main terms within the definition. First, by *artistic use* I mean that the language has been willfully crafted. Behind the utterance, there is a motive directed at human belief or act. An accidental moment of speech (an exclamation uttered by someone who stubs a toe, or a child, unaware they are being observed, singing a nursery rhyme unconsciously) is not, by this definition, rhetorical. It may be psychologically interesting (or not), culturally revealing (or not), personally satisfying (or not), but such actions will not generally be explored as rhetoric *within this book*. This choice will seem unduly limiting and theoretically naïve to many within the field of communication and rhetoric. But the vast majority of rhetoric to be examined here will fit quite comfortably within the *willed* frame of this working definition. Should others find cause to expand the conversation and add to the ancient story, they will hear no objection from me.

Second, the word *language* within this definition has a slightly larger scope than *words*, though not as broad a scope as many contemporary rhetorical scholars would like to see. We might think of *language* as "a set of symbols, spoken or potentially spoken, that seek to result in a sharing of meaning between two or more human beings." Again, many rhetoricians will find this a ridiculously reduced field of exploration, and I quite agree that there is great profit to thinking of action, architecture, space, visual artistry, music, and a dozen other things as rhetorical. I have myself taken that view in my own research in other arenas.[11] But for the most part, we will be looking in this book at the power of words, not violence or weapons or objects, as our boundary of rhetoric, though nothing in the book should be read as suggesting this is the only or even the "best" focus for rhetorical study, generally; the best focus for any study is dependent on what the scholar is investigating. All the same, the emphasis on words here is hardly a frame we are forcing on the past. Most of those in the ancient world understood a fairly narrow definition of *words* as the focus of rhetoric and the source and capital of power, as we will see.

Rhetoric was largely a public and political enterprise, but it was deeply rooted in the cultural education of both the Greeks and the Romans.[12]

---

[11] See, e.g., Meagan Schreiner, Mark A. E. Williams, and S. David Zuckerman, "Inspirations and Limitations: Reason, the Universal Audience and *Inspire* Magazine," *Journal of Communication & Religion* 36, no. 1 (2013): 196–210.

[12] Michael V. Fox has argued that ancient Egypt should rightly be considered part of the earliest theories of rhetoric. See "Ancient Egyptian Rhetoric," *Rhetorica* 1, no. 1 (1983):

Schooling for the Greek youth, almost certainly a boy, fastened upon several threads that were interwoven in their culture. More than a century ago, J. P. Mahaffy glowingly described these as "first of all, such political training as is strange to almost the whole of Europe; secondly, moral training of so high a kind as to rival at times the light of revelation; thirdly, social training to something higher than music and feasting by way of recreation; and fourthly, artistic training which . . . taught the public to understand and to love true and noble ideals."[13]

While effusive in its description, the goals offered up here would likely have pleased most of the educators of Greece at the time of Socrates: political wisdom, moral discernment, social discretion, and noble artistry. Different educators would have different priorities and understandings of each goal, of course, but the scheme Mahaffy lays out is, on the whole, a solid guide, so long as we excuse the gilded idealism. At the capstone of the educational enterprise, at least at Athens, was rhetoric: training in the way words and beliefs can become entwined. Rhetoric's place as the core of education would be virtually unchallenged from Plato until the French Enlightenment in the seventeenth century of the Christian calendar.[14]

Religion informed the cultural identity of every city-state in Greece. That cultural identity was passed along in the education each polis gave to

---

9–22. However, as he himself acknowledges, the texts he examines are mostly tracts of proverbs as well as advice in etiquette and circumspect speech within the courts of the pharaohs. These texts are intriguing, but at no point do they become a systematic and theoretical consideration of the interactions between the power of words, the nature of reality, and the presence of human convictions. Slightly more promising might be the rhetorical traditions of China, which may be read to include a somewhat more self-consciously developed sense of rhetorical action in shaping and reflecting character. That said, even at their best, these texts, like the Egyptian documents, never seem to show interest in a systemic, theoretical approach to the study of language, reality, and conviction. In this regard, the scholar's approach to the Egyptian and Chinese texts must be more like the use made of Homer: a speculative assembling of rhetorical instincts within a given cultural space rather than a disciplined consideration of a specific, socially recognized "art of rhetoric," such as one sees in Plato's *Gorgias* and *Phaedrus* or Aristotle's *Rhetoric*. For more on Egyptian views of eloquence, see also David Hutto, "Ancient Egyptian Rhetoric in the Old and Middle Kingdoms," *Rhetorica* 20, no. 3 (2002): 213–34. For more on Chinese rhetoric, see Xing Lu, *Rhetoric in Ancient China, Fifth to Third Century B.C.E.: A Comparison with Classical Greek Rhetoric* (Columbia: University of South Carolina Press, 1998).

[13] J. P. Mahaffy, *Old Greek Education* (New York: Harper & Brothers, 1882; Folcroft, PA: Folcroft Library Editions, 1977), 3–4 in the Folcroft reprint.

[14] In the Medieval era, theology, not rhetoric, would become the highest focus of academic life, but rhetoric remained, even in these times, a core facet of the educational enterprise and the capstone of the trivium.

its citizens. The crown of education, at least in the stream that would come to define European civilization, was rhetoric. With these three aspects in mind, we are ready to turn a more detailed eye to the way they interacted in ancient Greece. Those interactions became the foundations upon which the unconscious assumptions of the world of Europe and the contemporary Americas were founded.

In Chapter 2 we will examine the Presocratic introduction of *logos*—reason, speech—as an equal partner to *mythos*. *Mythos* was an act of imagistic religious storytelling about heroes and gods, and these stories served as the cistern of meaning and the source of discernment in Greek life. Once this addition of *logos* to the system of meaning-making is understood, we will complicate its sense by looking more closely at how it functioned in three key characters at a crucial moment in that Greek era: the aftermath of the Peloponnesian War between Athens and Sparta.

After that brutal defeat, post-war Athens produced some of the most stunning reflections on language and education that the world has ever seen. The visions hammered out in this era explored the relationship of words to reality, to the human soul, to the divine, to what can and cannot be preserved in cultural upheaval, and to the potential of human intellect.

Chapter 3 will explore Gorgias's sense of the power of language by examining his own writings that have survived. Chapter 4 will look at Isocrates's attempt to create a civic discourse rooted in community vision and identity. Chapter 5 introduces, and Chapter 6 continues, Plato's response to both Gorgias and Isocrates. Plato, in the end, believed that there were specific qualities to reality that made discourse possible, and without these qualities, language was inevitably reduced to a tool of ideological power, severed from all divine and just use. Chapter 7 will draw these themes together in a more contemporary reflection, and Chapter 8 serves as a brief epilogue.

We live in a time when civil discourse is rooted in ideological fire-breathing, arbitrary reality-making, and self-redefinition. The process of meeting another's mind in disagreement *and* joy is in danger of becoming a lost art and a misunderstood sliver of history. It may turn out, perhaps less ironically than we would like to hope, that these voices from the turmoil and traumas of Classical Athens's darkest days are some of the most valuable critics commenting on our current moment.

Chapter 2

Myths, the Word, and Schools:
Religious and Educational Changes

WHEN WE IMAGINE "ANCIENT GREECE," what usually come to mind are the philosophy and amphitheaters and temples of Athens, with the marble Parthenon in the days when Socrates wandered barefoot through the streets begging his neighbors for directions to the home of wisdom and justice. But scholars are always (occasionally with good cause) dividing and subdividing human experience and history. This popular picture of Athens and the Parthenon is what scholars call *Classical* Greece. But Greece existed for centuries before Classical Greece, and scholars call that earlier era *Archaic* Greece.[1] The roots of Greek education, the depths of Greek religion, and the foundations of Greek rhetoric rest there in those more distant, archaic days. And so, to understand how religion, education, and rhetoric interact in the Greece of Socrates and Gorgias, we must first think of that older Greece: a Greece that felt as distant to Plato as Medieval knights feel to us, a Greece of heroes and monsters and myth. But there we hit a roadblock. Greek myth can easily become a source of misunderstanding because we fail to realize its place in the deep past.

Mythology was not for the Greeks a literary endeavor, at least not primarily. These tales were, instead, an aspect of life ordered in relationship to the divine beings and supernatural realities.[2] What we call mythology is a fragmentary remnant of what was, for them, a vibrant, living religion. The Greek word *mythos* meant *story*, and the recitation of these stories was

---

[1] Archaic Greece is roughly dated from 800 to 500 BC. The traditional dates of Classical Greece run from the Ionian revolts against Persia (which led to the Battle of Marathon in 490 BC) to the death of Alexander the Great in 323 BC.

[2] For more, see my "From Here to Eternity: The Scope of Misreading Plato's Religion," in *Communication and the Global Landscape of Faith*, ed. Adrienne E. Hacker Daniels, 13-26 (New York: Lexington, 2016), 13. Of course there are many voices, contemporary and ancient, who explain the myths as coded psychology or an expression of minds too primitive to understand basic natural phenomena, though evidently profound and nuanced enough to compose great literature. Socrates comments on this very idea near the opening of the *Phaedrus*.

part of that structure of belief and practice that made up their religion. The myths, thus, are a defining aspect of Greek religious identity. But Christopher Lyle Johnstone writes, "Learning the myths of one's people constitutes the *most ancient form of education*, the means of passing from one generation to the next the fundamental truths that give meaning to the world."[3] The Greek citizens learned the *mythos* of their religion and the accompanying rituals, and in this way, they were being educated, being *in-formed*. That is, their inner life was given a form, a shape, a frame. This point cannot be overemphasized. Education was never, in their understanding, the gathering of some static thing called *information*. It was not about culling data. From the first records forward, education was a very different enterprise, one focused on the formation of the soul. Their instinctive, unconscious reactions to and explanations of the world were established and honed within the scope of their religion. This religious formation helped explain what they could and could not control in their world. It suggested why there was this difference. It established the relationship each of them had with the sublime first mysteries: Sky, Earth, Desire, Change, Time, Justice.[4] Greek religion explained not only the human relationship to these primal things but also the relationship between humanity and the gods, which was at least as complex.

In Greek religion, the gods did not create the universe; the universe created the gods. The poems and stories of this cosmic genealogy taught the average Greek what the hierarchies of existence were and how to proceed in life without offending the powers that be.[5] Johnstone notes: "What is distinctive about myth is that it locates . . . causes of events in the actions of superhuman beings—powerful, sometimes terrible, usually immortal. . . . Each being has a sphere over which it has dominion, each must be propitiated in its own way."[6] At the most basic and simplistic level, then, education and religion are intertwined aspects of cultural identity within Archaic Greece.

The pragmatics of how education was done are a deeper mystery in this era. We know far less than we would like about the daily life of the

---

[3] Christopher Lyle Johnstone, *Listening to the Logos* (Columbia: University of South Carolina Press, 2009), 17. Emphasis added.

[4] N. G. L. Hammond, *The Classical Age of Greece* (New York: Harper and Rowe, 1975), 37.

[5] Central to all Greek self-understanding were the epics of Homer, Hesiod's writings, the "Homeric Hymns," and later the so called *Gnomics*, who composed easily memorized poems filled with pious proverbs, proven maxims, and sage advice for living.

[6] Johnstone, *Listening*, 16.

average citizen. What we do know of the time suggests a complex web of interrelationships that involved overlapping social circles: military units, the household, local religious duties, hunting clubs, choral groups, and of course the apprenticeships associated with a citizen's job.[7] Most of these facets of daily life had a direct religious dimension. Choruses performed religious acts of ritual or worship, and apprenticeships in skilled trades were generally "reinforced by shared cults."[8] Blacksmiths, for example, were united by their worship of Hephaestus, healers by their devotion to Asclepius and Apollo. Mark Griffith points out that one aspect of the Hippocratic Oath is the creation of solemn pledges of a fraternal bond with other healers.[9] Our best guess is that it was not unusual for a young boy of no particular wealth to receive rudimentary private training in basic (at the most) reading and writing before turning, around puberty, to an apprenticeship in the trade of his father, though certainly no more education than that would be expected.[10]

In addition to these trade groups, however, there were the religious festivals particular to each local deity—honoring Athena in Athens, Poseidon at Corinth, Hera at Argos, Helios at Rhodes, and so forth—and requiring the participation of local associations such as the choruses. There were also larger festivals such as the Olympiads that united virtually all of the Greeks. Furthermore, within each city various associations and rites of passage were celebrated. There were both male and female groups which formed these sorts of civic and religious associations and in which participants were taught both myth and, possibly, music or other topics of educational interest.[11] For example, we have no evidence of any formal education in reading and writing for women, but by the fifth century we have numerous and widespread images of women reading texts. But again, these are bare outlines. We know very little about the structure of these groups and how they wed education, worship, literacy, and citizenship for the average Greek.

---

[7] Mark Griffith, "'Public' and 'Private' in Early Greek Institutions of Education," in *Education in Greek and Roman Antiquity*, ed. Yun Lee Too, 23–84 (Leiden: Brill, 2001), 26.

[8] Griffith, "Public," 30n19.

[9] Griffith, "Public," 31n20.

[10] Griffith, "Public," 68.

[11] See. e.g., Mark W. Padilla, ed., *Rites of Passage in Ancient Greece: Literature, Religion, Society* (Cranbury, NJ: Associated University Presses, 1999). For rites of passage affecting women, see especially 129–80.

We have a slightly more complete picture of the practical education of the aristocratic warrior castes in the Archaic era. Pragmatically, education of the elites focused on both fighting skill and a sort of socio-political savvy that worked by inspiring and persuading others through dynamic speech. This power in speech was tied to one's reputation for *aretē*. The word meant *excellence* and its ideal served as "the quintessence of early Greek aristocratic education."[12] The word might reference skill in battle as well as power in speech and a forceful character, among other things. These skills—martial and rhetorical and virtuous—were learned by physical training, imitation of others, and the memorization and recitation of the culture's poems and myths. The spiritual and character formation of a young man would often take place as the youth served something of a civic apprenticeship to an older citizen-warrior who had proved his worth.[13]

One well known example of such a civic apprenticeship is found in Homer, the "school master of Greece" as Plato would later call him.[14] A few famous lines from Book IX of the *Illiad* capture this blend of militant and persuasive skill within a pious civic apprenticeship. When Phoenix approaches Achilles to offer him gifts and ask him to return to the battle and assist the Greeks in their war on Troy, Achilles refuses to fight again; furthermore, he plans to leave Troy entirely, he announces, and sail home. There, he will live a long, content life, though free from the glory that comes to men of exceptional *aretē*. He offers to take Phoenix to safety with

---

[12] Werner Jaeger, *Paideia*, vol. 1, *Archaic Greece; The Mind of Athens*, trans. Gilbert Highet (Oxford: Oxford University Press, 1973), 5.

[13] These apprenticeships would, over time, expand and contribute significantly to the ideal of the Greek schools. See Henri I. Marrou, *A History of Education in Antiquity*, trans. George Lamb (New York: Mentor Books, 1964), 21–34, as well as Richard Leo Enos, *Greek Rhetoric before Aristotle* (Prospect Heights, IL: Waveland, 1993), 2–22. Obviously, this was a very masculine space and the "young man" and "his" is intentional. There are, however, fragmentary evidences that, once the transition to formal "schools" took place, similar social and educational apprenticeships may have existed between women, Sappho being the most famous female poet and teacher. If Maximus of Tyre is to be trusted on this point, Sappho's was one of several schools for girls operating in her day and competing for students. Assuming Maximus's (very late) report is accurate, these feminine spaces were not only educational and religious but also erotic, just as the masculine spaces often were. See *Oration* 18, cited in Mark Joyal, Iain McDougall, and J. C. Yardley, *Greek and Roman Education: A Sourcebook* (London: Routledge, 2009), 7. Also, see *The Dissertations of Maximus Tyrius*, trans. Thomas Taylor, esp. Dissertations VIII and IX, 81–101 (London: Whittingham, 1804), where similar comparisons between Socrates and Sappho are made. Also, Marrou, *History of Education*, 59–62.

[14] Plato, *Republic* 606e.

him. Phoenix, after a stunned silence, bursts into tears and reproaches the younger Achilles. Phoenix recalls how Achilles was

> a youngster still untrained in the great leveler, war,
> still green at debate where men can make their mark.
> So [your father Peleus] dispatched me, to teach you all these things,
> to make you a man of words and a man of action too.[15]

The passage presents a gold standard of education that would come down into Classical Greece from Archaic Greece: the production of a citizen excellent in speech and excellent in act.[16]

The approach, hinted at here, was one of training young citizens in the behaviors appropriate to their place in society and of showing them what that society was, in a significant way. The *gymnasion* was where the physical training took place, and in some locations it incorporated music to teach rhythm and coordination in military movements.[17] Beyond the *gymnasion*, however, the topics of musical performance and poetry were also taught. Here, examples of *aretē* were sung and praised while those without such excellences were scorned. Banquets, a common aspect of an elite young man's social apprenticeship, were generally accompanied by recitations of the mythic heritage and appeals to excellence: nobility and honor and glory.[18]

These aristocratic elites were not entirely isolated from other citizens. Some of the social associations and clubs discussed above were more or less mandatory, filled by lot, and had no particular requirements for financial or social status. But the education of the aristocratic and wealthy citizen was fundamentally different from the education of the poorer masses.

---

[15] Homer, *Illiad* ix.440–43. I have used Robert Fagles's translation (London: Penguin Books, 1990), 266.

[16] Plato places a similar expression in the mouth of the famous sophist Protagoras, who says he teaches young men to hone their skills "in speech and action"; *Protagoras*, trans. Stanley Lombardo and Karen Bell, in *Plato: Complete Works*, ed. John M. Cooper, (Indianapolis, IN: Hackett, 1997), 319a. Xenophon is praised for his "words and deeds" after one particularly rousing speech to his troops on the certainty of death; *Anabasis*, trans. Carleton Brownson and John Dillery, Loeb Clasical Library 90 (Cambridge, MA: Harvard University Press, 1998), III.1.45. And Aristotle lists "the ability to speak and to act" as one of the goods associated with the subject of rhetoric in his *Art of Rhetoric*, trans. J. H. Freese, Loeb Clasical Library 193 (Cambridge, MA: Harvard University Press, 1975), 1362b.

[17] Griffith, "Public," 53, 74.

[18] Marrou, *History of Education*, 70–72.

We do not know when this method of in-forming the soul through social apprenticeships began. What we do know is that around, very roughly, 600 BC—about 200 years before Socrates was executed—there was already a movement afoot that challenged this old aristocratic pattern on two fronts. The first challenge was a shift in the most fundamental way of looking at the world, and the second was a shift in the fundamental way of educating the young. These transitions, one aspect of which would eventually come to be known as *sophistry*, are central to our story.

The New Seer: *Logos*

First, the new view decentered the mythic and religious perspective as the sole authority for explaining the cosmic order. It relocated the power to interpret the world, at least in part, within *logos*, as distinct from *mythos*.[19] *Mythos* established the community's inherited way of viewing everything, and it gave the inspiration and maxims needed to order life appropriately within the received cultural traditions and religious hierarchies. *Logos* was different.

Logos is a complicated word, incorporating ideas of language, expression, argument, proportion, thought, reasoning, accounting (economic and ethical), explanation, and scope—among some forty other related meanings.[20] We usually use the term *word* to approximate the ideas found in *logos*. *Logos* differed from *mythos* because it allowed human reason and

---

[19] The *mythos* versus *logos* terminology characterizing these two views is taken directly from Johnstone, though the tension between *myth* and *logos*, *reason*, *philosophy* is not an uncommon theme in the literature. See, e.g., Robin Waterfield, *The First Philosophers: The Presocratics and the Sophists* (Oxford: Oxford University Press, 2000), xi; Eric Voegelin, *Order and History*, vol. 2, *The World of the Polis* (Baton Rouge: Louisiana State University Press, 1986), 111–13; and Marcel Detienne, *The Masters of Truth in Archaic Greece*, trans. Janet Lloyd (New York: Zone, 1996), where this tension is the central focus of the whole text. While the explanations about this transitional period in Greek culture are many, Johnstone's account focuses on language use and the intellectual abstraction involved in this shift, and his consideration is finely nuanced. It should be compared, however, with Detienne's powerful work.

[20] H. G. Liddell, R. Scott, and Sir Henry Jones, *Greek-English Lexicon* (Oxford: Clarendon Press, 1996). The scope of the term, from prosaic to ethical to mystical, can be seen in well-known texts from the Christian tradition. Matthew 18:23 (RSV) records the parable of the king who "wished to settle accounts with his slaves." The very practical word *accounts* is *logos*. Hebrews 13:17 (RSV) discusses leaders who "will give an account" of their choices, and again the word is *logos*, this time heavy with ethical implications. Compare this with the mystical opening of the Gospel of John, where we are told, "In the beginning was the *logos* and the *logos* was with God and the *logos* was God."

reflection to participate in the way people explored the questions of where things came from, what was worthy of honor, and why things happened. *Mythos* established the truth of these questions through the authoritative, divinely inspired pronouncements of the seer, the poet, and the warrior-king.[21] *Logos*, however, did not merely repeat the proclamation of theological authorities and the stories of the gods; it asked questions about the nature of the divine. Generally, these were questions about whether the gods were really as much like people (scheming and treacherous and filled with sexual passions) as the myths seemed to suggest. There were questions about *cosmology*: the order of the world around them. *Logos* asked where order came from and what things were made of and whether the events of nature might happen without the direct actions of the gods.

These types of questions—about the nature of events, the nature of material actions, and the nature of the gods—often seem to overlap in the fragments of writing that have survived from the Archaic era. This intermingling suggests that some of these so-called Presocratic thinkers employed reason as an addition to, not necessarily a replacement of, the mythical-religious inheritance of their culture. Others, of course, clearly rejected the gods outright. Johnstone observes that for the Presocratics, "it is clear that the quest for divine knowledge has led the human mind away from the supernatural and deeply into the natural."[22] Many thinkers of the time argued that "large portions of the tradition [should] be rejected as untrue, grotesque, exaggerated, and by implication, immoral."[23] But the Presocratics must not be read as monovocal. Certainly, some of them understood themselves to be honing, not replacing, the religious perspective. "There is no sense in cutting off Cosmology from the previous Mythology . . . with any legislative finality," as Robert Scoon notes,[24] though it is still common today to find remarks that characterize the Presocratics as those who "rejected traditional mythological

---

[21] Detienne, *Masters*, 15–17.

[22] Johnstone, *Listening*, 53.

[23] Thomas Cole, *The Origins of Rhetoric in Ancient Greece* (Baltimore: Johns Hopkins University Press, 1995), 55.

[24] Robert Scoon, *Greek Philosophy before Plato* (Princeton: Princeton University Press, 1928), 19–20. See, e.g., Thales's remarks on the divine, such as, "The most ancient of beings is god, for he is unborn" in André Laks and Glenn W. Most, eds. and trans., *Early Greek Philosophy, Volume II: Beginnings and Early Ionian Thinkers, Part I*, Loeb Classical Library 525 (Cambridge, MA: Harvard University Press, 2016), P17c, 224–25; or his most famous quote, "everything is full of gods," as reported by Aristotle, *On the Soul*, trans. W. S. Hett, Loeb Classical Library 288 (Cambridge, MA: Harvard University Press, 1957), 411a.

explanations . . . in favor of more rational explanations."[25] This is true enough, but the reality was far more nuanced.

The struggle to understand the quality of matter and the source of causes in the natural world led the Presocratics to seek out what they thought of as a "divine principle of being."[26] But this abstract divine principle of being hardly looked like the concrete gods of *mythos*, and so there were naturally tensions. But these were hardly secular scientists. Robin Waterfield captures their view well:

> [T]he Presocratics differ from the preceding world-view and from fully fledged scientism. They differ from their predecessors not so much in the kinds of questions they asked (above all, "What is the nature of reality?"), but in the kinds of answers they gave—in not adhering to the traditional framework, in assigning the functions of the gods to natural phenomena, in using what we can recognize as logic to reason things through coherently . . . They differ from hard-line scientism in lacking scientific method altogether, and in lacking some scientific attitudes, in being too visionary. They were interested in constructing elegant systems, not verifiable systems.[27]

Those tensions would be present in Greek culture for centuries. Though the *logos* approach would grow in favor and influence, the transition from a sort of *sola mythos* to a willingness to incorporate *logos* was neither simple nor quick. And exactly why this change began in the first place is also uncertain. There are, however, a variety of hypotheses that can be quickly reviewed.

Jean-Pierre Vernant locates a decisive inspiration for change within the new political demands of the emerging *poleis*, or city-states. These appeared around 750 BC, at the latest, and Vernant sees them as a significant break with all past political organizations.[28] Of course, the *polis* must not be thought of as synonymous with democracy. The early *poleis* were often run by a *tyrranos*, or absolute ruler; more often, they were oligarchies.

---

[25] See, e.g., Luke Mastin, "Pre-socratics," *The Basics of Philosophy*, June 1, 2023, https://www.coursehero.com/file/107569056/359588813-Philosophy-Basicsdocx/.

[26] Johnstone, *Listening*, 53.

[27] Robin Waterfield, *The First Philosophers: The Presocratics and the Sophists* (Oxford: Oxford University Press, 2000), xxiv.

[28] Jean-Pierre Vernant, *The Origins of Greek Thought* (Ithaca, NY: Cornell University Press, 1996), 49–68.

Democracy does not appear anywhere until 500 BC when it takes shape in Athens. Even before democracy, however, there was an intimacy within the structure of the *polis* which allowed for a public awareness of decision making, particularly in the oligarchies. Vernant notes that a core frame of the political life within the *polis* "was the full exposure given to the most important aspects" of the community.[29] But public awareness of decision-making (spread over the years that Athens moved toward democratic participation in decision-making) ignited a taste for discussion about decisions and an attendant need to ask questions and seek clarification. This taste for discourse and inquiry, no doubt, helped encourage the Presocratics' focus on *logos*. Allowing discourse and inquiry into the political life invited its extension into religious life as well because the structure of the polis presumed a shared religious community.

Anthony Snodgrass follows Vernant's lead, focusing on the formation of new political systems as the epicenter of changing attitudes and opportunities that would close the Archaic era and lead to the cultural triumphs of Classical Greece. But he also pointedly reminds us of the interwoven quality of their political and religious culture: "Every Greek polis was, among other things, a religious association; its citizens accepted a community of cult with a patron deity presiding over each state."[30] Religious identity was part of the very cement of the emerging political structures, and so the new way of thinking about the world always carried the risk of appearing dangerously unpatriotic. Like Vernant, Snodgrass suggests the tumultuous eighth century as the pivotal moment that allowed the slow emergence of this new, challenging, way of addressing life's questions.[31]

Henri Marrou believes the real inspirations emerged later, probably in the century that ends in 550 BC after the *poleis* became more confident in their political self-definitions and education became increasingly independent of military training. This independence allowed for a less regimented and more speculative view of the world, and so it became a place where

---

[29] Vernant, *Origins of Greek Thought*, 51.

[30] Anthony Snodgrass, *Archaic Greece: The Age of Experiment* (Berkeley: University of California Press, 1980), 33. Snodgrass offers an extended argument for his position in the first three chapters of his book, citing not only politics but also changes in metallurgy, agriculture, artistry, and religion as contributors to the new views. He favors the political as the primary cause, with other aspects as outgrowths of that political change, but he is not dogmatic on this point and acknowledges that cause and effect are difficult to untangle and that the era is an especially complex one. See, e.g., 160–63.

[31] Snodgrass, *Archaic*, 32.

reasoned reflections could find a way to begin contributing to new political and religious structures; change in the educational model became inevitable.[32]

Detienne recognizes seeds of this break as far back as the early warrior-councils which had built a space where speech could be held in common among all those who had qualified as soldiers.[33] But the crucial, conscious insight came when poetry was recognized as not just an inspired utterance, given by the divine muses, but as an art that could be crafted and reworked by a human author.[34] This, combined with the expansion of the military councils to include an ever-wider group who was authorized to speak, became the flower of that ancient seed.[35]

Johnstone, on the other hand, sees a kaleidoscope of cultural and religious contributions to the transition, which he explains as far more philosophical and complex. He will only commit to a slow shift in perspective during the four hundred years (or so) between Homer and Socrates, though he acknowledges some specific periods of more rapid change.[36]

Whatever the pace of change or the date and origin of the immediate causes, what we know can be summed this way: around roughly 600 BC, a movement was present and growing in Ionia, the eastern reaches of Greek culture along the Mediterranean coast of what is today Turkey. This movement began to review the *mythos* of religious life and ask penetrating questions about it, subjecting it to tests of *logos*: reflection, reason, explanation. What does it mean to be divine? Are the gods really petty and subject to jealousy and passion, like human beings? Or must the divine be higher and better than human passion? What is the extent and reach of the divine? Must the gods—or the quality of divinity, or God—supersede the changes and chances that are part of nature? How is the divine related to material nature? Is each and every event in nature the act of a god, or is there some

---

[32] Marrou, *History of Education*, 63–75.

[33] Detienne, *Masters*, 89–106.

[34] Detienne, *Masters*, 108–9. This tension between craft and inspiration was, in the end, hardly settled as tidily as Detienne suggests, and it remained a core tension in Platonic theology, as we will see.

[35] The Hoplite Reforms gave those in the infantry a voice in the war councils equal to the older, more aristocratic families, who were usually in the cavalry. These reforms grew at about the same time the *poleis* were solidifying. See Aristotle's *Politics*, trans. H. Rackham, Loeb Classical Library 264 (Cambridge, MA: Harvard University Press, 1932), IV.13, 1297b, 15–25 as well as remarks in Detienne, *Masters*, 89–90.

[36] Johnstone, *Listening*, Chs. 1–3, but see especially pp. 3–5 for a succinct presentation of his view. Also see note 19 above.

principle within matter itself that makes things happen, perhaps without the direct intervention of the divine? If so, does it matter whether the gods exist? Do the gods exist? Is there anything outside of material and time and chance? What are things made of, in their most elemental form? Why do they stay together? Why do they fall apart?

These were challenging questions. Arguably, they still are. Not one of them can be definitively answered, which is revealing. Human intellect, brought to bear on the realm of the supernatural and theological, will find that it has its own set of limitations. But those limitations were, of course, not immediately obvious to that group of thinkers who first set out to *reason* about the *gods*, to bring *logos* into a position to explore *mythos*. The problems with this approach would only begin to emerge in the century or so after this transition began, and they would culminate in the most vibrant debates we are acquainted with in the Classical era. The evangelicalism of Socrates, the zealotry of Plato, the patriotism of Isocrates, the sophisticated knowing of Gorgias: all these names and all their ideas were, in the Classical era, locked into a struggle over what it meant to be pious, to educate the young, and to speak so as to shape the heart and mind and will of another. "Everywhere in Greece . . . attention was now focused on the principal question: *What type of education leads to aretē?*"[37] These struggles would, before all was said and done, cost Socrates his life, make Plato into a mystic, drive Aristotle into exile, and bring the armies of Alexander the Great to the Indus Valley.

These changes in world view, however, were not accomplished without a corresponding change in educational procedures, and that brings us to the second aspect of this important transition.

Schools: Expanding Minds

The model of education based on the aristocratic social apprenticeships of the Archaic period begins to shift within this new movement we have been examining, and this is particularly true as education expands. Once more, we know far less than we would like, but the transitions appear clear enough in broad outline. From 650 to 550 there was a decreased emphasis upon direct military drill within a number of *poleis*, and particularly Athens. Soldiers were still training and the aristocracy, especially, remained a source of leadership among military men. But the educational methods

---

[37] Jaeger, *Paideia*, 1:286. Emphasis in the original.

within the *gymnasia* had escaped military maneuvers as their only focus.[38] Physical health, beauty, and *aretē* within the scripted fields of sport were increasingly the goals. Outside the *gymnasia*, the study of music, astronomy, and poetry also championed the excellence of an ordered beauty, and *aretē* itself became an ideal of *kalokagathia*—a merger of beauty and goodness on all levels and "a concept which was now consciously taken to include a genuine intellectual and spiritual culture."[39]

The world's first democracy began in Athens around the year 500 BC, and these new political structures unquestionably broadened the sense that becoming a citizen of "noble words and noble acts" was a worthwhile pursuit, even for some of those not born into the aristocracy. Times appear to have been good for many, and those who found they could afford education discovered that, sometimes, it improved their ability to make their way in the new system. The democratic way of organizing social life made fresh demands on citizens, requiring them to sharpen their ability to address others within formal settings, such as the assemblies. Here, a man (always a *man*) would need to navigate the narrows of showing proper respect to some other citizen (perhaps someone older, perhaps someone he might need as an ally on another day) while also making a clear case that his own advice was better than theirs. Skill in discourse became an increasingly powerful tool for obtaining and securing a citizen's position. Naturally, people with means increasingly sought after those skills.

This influence of democracy should not be pushed too far; the democratic Athens that was making the transition from the Archaic to the Classical world was hardly a meritocracy of boundless opportunity and social mobility. The aristocracy resisted change, of course, in a number of ways. "The nobles inevitably felt that *aretē* should be maintained and transmitted by means different from those used by the . . . peasants or the citizens of the *polis*," and they believed the common citizenry actually lacked "any special means to perform that function" of excellence.[40] The aristocrats championed an argument that would be debated for centuries, essentially claiming that any form of advanced schooling was wasted on the lower classes and

---

[38] Marrou, *History of Education*, 64.

[39] Jaeger, *Paideia*, 1:286.

[40] Jaeger, *Paideia*, 1:286.

that education properly fell only to those of inherent worth, that is, those of noble blood who could (often) trace their lineage to one of the gods.[41]

Equally important in the democratic reforms was the emergence of a structured legal system.[42] Around the year 650 BC, laws began to be written down and specific punishments prescribed. Accompanying this development was, naturally, the introduction of a court system to review cases and make judgments. Eventually, large juries of several hundred (the smallest possible jury at Athens was 201, in order to complicate any attempts at bribery) would be assembled. Accusers and accused would present their cases directly to the jury. There were no lawyers or legal representatives of any sort; each citizen had to stand and make their own case in their own words within a predetermined time limit. The jury would hear these two speeches and then vote immediately, without deliberation or discussion. This system did not appear in full force in the year 650, of course, but over a century, it took shape and, with various adaptations, spread throughout much of the Greek world. By 500 BC, Athens had a public assembly where political debate took place and a vibrant legal system where citizens spoke before their peers to defend themselves or accuse another. It cannot be coincidence that these political institutions began to take shape at the same time we see the first formal schools emerging between 550 and 500 BC, but whether one was helping to cause the other is lost to us, and the question is probably a chicken and egg inquiry.[43] Education, the assemblies, and the courts all simply grew up together, each nurturing the others, in all probability.

Though the decades from 499 to 479 were dominated by a sporadic war with Persia, the new schools continued to spread.[44] By 400 BC, formal

---

[41] Protagoras pointedly observed that education required a person of a specific nature, in addition to training. See the fragments of Protagoras's work in *Early Greek Philosophy, Vol. VIII: Sophists, Part I*, ed. and trans. André Laks and Glenn W. Most, Loeb Classical Library 531 (Cambridge, MA: Harvard University Press, 2016), 80DK, D11, 42–43. The implication was always that those without aristocratic blood had no need to be inner-formed; their souls were simply not worth it. They were the *hoi polloi*, the masses, whereas those with the right nature for education were the *aristocrats*—those few with the potential for *aretē*. Those few had souls of a different sort: more divine, more noble. When their souls were polished with the proper formation, they shone bright as gold. But the attempt to polish mud is wasted.

[42] See Detienne, *Masters*, 104–5, for a background and precursor to this movement.

[43] Griffith, "Public," 66, but see 61–73 for a more rounded commentary.

[44] In 499, the culturally Greek region of Ionia, where many of the Presocratics had begun their intellectual journey, broke into open rebellion against their Persian rulers. Athens quickly supported the rebellion. There was war for six years, but Darius the Great of

schools were found in virtually every significant Greek city, and they had settled upon a fairly predictable pedagogy that started with reading and writing and then moved to music, astronomy, poetry, and athletic training.[45] This is still, recall, a rudimentary education, but there are indications that it was relatively widespread, even in 500 BC. The ancient historian Herodotus, in the first reference we have to a formal school, tells us about a season of bad omens. A plague struck down ninety-eight young men (out of 100) who were part of a chorus. This reference is followed immediately with a further example that seems to imply a parallel between the chorus association and what comes next: the roof at a school collapsed and killed 119 of the 120 students inside.[46] Herodotus's wording implies that these were students learning to read and write. Whether they were separated into groups with various tutors or were simply in a single "lecture hall" is not clear, but we are able to date the incidents quite precisely: 496 BC. These omens took place on Chios, an important Greek island just off the coast of Ionia. Important, but not central, and that is telling. If the Greeks of Chios were schooling 120 children to read and write inside one building during a period of war and social unrest, what might the situation have been like in Athens or Sparta, the two primary cultural centers on the mainland of Greece? We do not know.

We do know enough to try to head off a couple of misunderstandings here. It must not be assumed that these facilities were somehow "public schools" in any contemporary sense, where every (male) youth attended for free. Parents paid teachers for the lessons, and those who could not pay did

---

Persia defeated the Greek Ionians in 493. In 490, Darius landed a major force at Marathon on the Greek mainland, intending to destroy Athens in retaliation for their support of the Ionians and then to subjugate all of Greece. Sparta, allied with Athens, was in the middle of a solemn religious observance and could not send troops in a timely fashion. Athens, along with a few hundred soldiers from a nearby city, fielded an army and, in perhaps the most famous battle of the ancient world, defeated the invading forces at Marathon, though badly outnumbered. This led to a lull in the conflict, but the war was renewed in a second invasion. This culminated in another Persian defeat after the battles of Thermopylae, Salamis Strait, and Plataea in 479 BC.

[45] Griffith, "Public," 67.

[46] Herodotus, *Histories*, trans. Robin Waterfield (Oxford: Oxford University Press, 2008), 6.27.1–2. See the discussion in Joyal, McDougall, and Yardley, *Greek and Roman Education*, 13–14. Griffith, "Public," 68, points to another story involving an Olympic champion who, in 492 BC, went mad and killed sixty children who were inside a school on a small and insignificant island called Astypalaia.

not, presumably, attend.[47] Nor were lessons compulsory for anyone of any social status. There is no indication that the *poleis* viewed this sort of formal education of the basic citizen as necessary, much less a community responsibility. Nor should we think of these new schools as somehow replacing the earlier system of social apprenticeships among the aristocrats, as we have noted. Nor do we have any indication that these schools replaced vocational apprenticeships. Rather, the schools appear to have emerged as one more overlapping club or association within the Greek *poleis*. Combined with the new institutions of democratic policy debates and formal courts in Athens, however, these new schools laid the groundwork for an adaptation of, especially, the social apprenticeships that had earlier been the hallmark of the aristocratic elite. Young men of the upper classes began to seek out what we would call advanced or higher education that came after the elementary forms of the schools. And for this new education, a new sort of teacher appeared on the scene.

Sound and Fury Signifying Superior Sophists

Sometime between 500 and 450 BC, a new set of instructors began to address the interests and concerns of the elite young males. These teachers became known as *sophists*, purveyors of the wise and cultured life. They often travelled from one city to another, staying for a season in Athens, or Thebes, or Corinth before moving on to their next location. This created a bit of a stir.[48] Since they were not generally citizens of the *polis* where they were teaching, they always carried about them a vague air of suspicion on the one hand and exoticism on the other, and this likely added to their appeal. Aristocratic sons smelled a chance for nights on the town in the company of edgy celebrities and days in the square filled with battles of wit to impress their peers and crushes. Aristocratic fathers sensed a way to provide the family with a further distinction from the masses as democracy took hold, as well as a way to better secure the future of the family name

---

[47] Griffith, "Public," 67.

[48] Plato's *Timaeus*, trans. R. G. Bury, Loeb Classical Library 234 (Cambridge, MA: Harvard University Press, 1929), 19e, provides one example of criticism based on the sophists' itinerate lifestyle. Another may be discerned in Isocrates's *Antidosis*, in *Isocrates, Vol. II*, trans. George Norlin, Loeb Classical Library 229 (Cambridge, MA: Harvard University Press, 1992), 155–56, which suggests at least some of the sophists stayed in one town long enough to build a following, but left before they had stayed long enough to be legally responsible for paying taxes.

through their sons' political successes. But the reputation of the sophist was always suspect, not least because they charged—exorbitantly, by many accounts—for their services of turning rich young men with a family name into sophisticated young men with a political future. Evidently, no payment ever changed hands between Phoenix and Achilles's father.

But beyond the price of this sort of education, there were also concerns about its content, about whether it partook, perhaps too much, of *logos* rather than the old proven ways of *mythos*. Wealthy aristocrats tend toward a conservative view of things, since one of the things such a view conserves is their own aristocratic wealth. So, while the new sophistic education was clearly an asset for an up-and-coming young man of wit and savvy social instincts that were waiting to be honed, it also carried a tension, at least at first, of being aligned with newer and dangerously different ideas.

Smooth Operator: Becoming a Man of Word and of Action

Some of the more famous sophists possessed an almost cult-like follow-ing. We have evidence that Protagoras was one of the very first (if not the first) of these sophists. A number of authors identify him as the source of a variety of advances in teaching about discourse. He is credited with, among other things, being the first to require his students to argue both for and then against a claim, to recognize specific moods of speech (request, statement, command, and so forth) that have different uses in argument, to compose grammatical principles in order to teach clarity of speech, and to formulate specific types or templates for arguments. He was a committed agnostic, but seems to have considered deep familiarity with the poets to be the chief source of education.[49] Assuming Plato has given us more or less

---

[49] See Paul Woodruff, "Why did Protagoras use Poetry in Education?" in *Plato's Protagoras: Essays on the Confrontation of Philosophy and Sophistry*, ed. Olof Petterson and Vigdis Songe-Møller, 213–27 (New York: Springer, 2017). Recall that the poets were rooted in the religious, mythic tradition. For specifics on Protagoras's various contributions, see Laks and Most, *Early Greek Philosophy, Vol. VIII* D10, D17–23, D27–29, D31, especially. On the cult status of some of the sophists, note Plato's description of the way Protagoras walked around the portico with his followers in *Protagoras* 314e–315b. There may have been some dramatic hyperbole involved in the image, but the scene is remarkably believable and lifelike.

accurate information, Protagoras probably opened his career around 470 BC and taught for over forty years.[50]

He shows up in Plato's *Protagoras* as a charming, poised gentleman and the account he gives of his job is revelatory.[51] In this dialogue, Socrates has just greeted the older Protagoras in order to introduce him to Hippocrates, who was interested in becoming his student. Socrates then suggests the three of them might discuss this matter in private or in front of the followers who were already present, gathered around Protagoras, whichever setting the sophist found more comfortable. He replies:

> Your discretion on my behalf is appropriate, Socrates. Caution is in order for a foreigner who goes into the great cities and tries to persuade the best of the young men in them to abandon their associations with others, relatives and acquaintances, young and old alike, and to associate with him instead on the grounds that they will be improved by their association. Jealousy, hostility, and intrigue on a large scale are aroused by such activity. Now, I maintain that the sophist's art is an ancient one, but that the men who practiced it in ancient times, fearing the odium attached to it, disguised it, masking it sometimes as poetry, as Homer and Hesiod and Simonides did, or as mystery religions and prophecy, witness Orpheus and Musaeus, and occasionally, I've noticed, even as athletics. . . . Your own Agathocles, a great sophist, used music as a front, as did . . . many others.[52]

Notice, first of all, how Protagoras acknowledges the suspicions of citizens toward the traveling professors of sophistication. But notice also how he moves seamlessly from this remark to placing his own teaching within the frame of inner-forming that was the mark of the traditional aristocratic social apprenticeships and associations. His claim is that the sophistic education is simply a natural outgrowth of the old ways; indeed, it is simply the old ways come out in the open. He is doing what Homer and the poets did, what the prophecy and mystery religions work toward, what music and athletic training strive for and hint at: he is in-forming his students' lives,

---

[50] Plato, *Meno*, trans. G. M. A. Grube, in *Plato: Complete Works*, ed. John M. Cooper (Indianapolis, IN: Hackett, 1997), 91e.

[51] See Plato, *Protagoras* 316d–317c.

[52] Plato, *Protagoras* 316c–317a. The Greek word translated *jealousy* here is the plural of *phthonos*, a complicated word that forms a crucial part of Plato's critique of rhetoric and is a defining sign for discerning meaning and significance, as we will see.

shaping their souls. Sophistry draws all these together and positions itself as the most essential purveyor of *aretē*, excellence. This is echoed more specifically only a few lines later:

> Young man, this is what you will get if you study with me: the very day you start, you will go home a better man, and the same thing will happen the day after. Every day, day after day, you will get better and better.... What I teach is sound deliberation, both in domestic matters—how best to manage one's household, and in public affairs—how to realize one's maximum potential for success in political debate and action.[53]

To this, Socrates remarks, "You appear to be talking about the art of citizenship, and to be promising to make men good citizens," and Protagoras replies, "This is exactly what I claim."[54] Socrates, being Socrates, will not allow that answer to stand without a thorough interrogation, but what follows in the dialogue is less relevant to our immediate topic. The snippets of conversation above give us a general window into the quality of soul the sophists understood themselves to be crafting.[55] Given that sophistic education was so expensive, "what did they communicate to their students that was felt to be worth so much?"[56] The answer is not in the bits and pieces cited above (music, athletics, poetry, religious devotion), but in the synthesis of the whole. The sophist offered a certain interwoven, embroidered quality of life that approached a cultural ideal. Sophists viewed themselves as creating young men excellent in speech and excellent in act who would thus carry forward the Homeric vision of harmonious *aretē*. That is what they sought to accomplish. How they sought to accomplish this formation of the soul is a different question.

Clearly one aspect of this schooling would be, as Protagoras notes, "sound deliberation" in private and public matters. In other words, discourse and debate were part of this training. Andrew Ford reminds us that

---

[53] Plato, *Protagoras* 318a–b, 318e–319a.

[54] Plato, *Protagoras* 319a.

[55] Plato, of course, is an enemy of this sort of sophistic education, and it is his portrayal quoted here. But the description of a sophistic education offered here is a fairly neutral one and remains consistent with other sources from the ancient world. As we shall see, his portrayal of sophistry in the *Gorgias* is a bit more strained.

[56] Andrew Ford, "Sophists Without Rhetoric: The Arts of Speech in Fifth-Century Athens," in *Education in Greek and Roman Antiquity*, ed. Yun Lee Too, 85–109 (Leiden: Brill, 2001), 87.

we must not reduce sophistry to the issues of public speaking and debate.[57] James Fredal echoes and broadens these sentiments, noting that we must expand simple questions to include more complex inquiries such as "what other expressive and interpretive skills were learned, taught, and practiced, by whom and toward what end?"[58] Both pieces of advice are good to hold in mind: there was more teaching going on than just the top-tier sophists (as we will see), and there was more to the top-tier sophists' teaching than just public speaking, of course. Sophists were trying to produce a specific type of soul: an urbane and knowing sort of character who got things done, and this involved skills beyond public speaking. But there are two sides of this coin. First, we must contextualize a sophist's training in public speech within their broader educational goals, certainly. But, second, we must also recognize that speech was an important—and in many cases, certainly, the primary—aspect of sophistic education. These were young men being prepared to operate skillfully and powerfully in a dangerous public square where failure of a championed political cause could lead to appearances in court, loss of property, even exile. Skill in discourse mattered, and its importance increased yearly as enemies were made and alliances formed and restructured. Given rhetoric as one of the anchors in our present text, we will obviously focus on that aspect of the sophistic education that was rooted in language and what that revealed about their religious and moral universe, while always keeping in mind the broader educational goals.

Philostratus, writing around AD 235, set down his *Lives of the Sophists* in which he reviews a number of sophistic teachers and their contributions. Of interest to us is his introduction, where he divides the very early sophists into two groups, the first generation and the second generation, and he contrasts their teaching methods. The differences between their methods are suggestive. He tells us that the first generation of sophists (Protagoras may have been the first, but Gorgias of Leontini was the crown jewel of this group) approached general themes and ideas and they "discoursed on courage . . . justice, on the heroes and gods, and how the universe has been fashioned into its present shape." The second generation (Aeschines is identified as the touchstone here) took a different tack. They were more likely to apply their discourse to specific settings and to observe set rules: the "followers of Aeschines handled their themes according to the rules

---

[57] Ford, "Sophists," 86–88.

[58] James Fredal, *Rhetorical Action in Ancient Athens: Persuasive Artistry from Solon to Demosthenes* (Carbondale: Southern Illinois University Press, 2006), 2.

of art, while the followers of Gorgias handled theirs as they pleased."[59] In other words, the first generation of sophists seemed to have had less script and fewer rules on how to accomplish their tasks in speech. By the second generation, those rules were taking a more definite, prescriptive, form.

This view reflects, to some degree, what Aristotle explains in his own remarks within *Sophistic Refutations*. He closes that essay by noting that the approach of Gorgias and others like him was to provide a series of set speeches for the students to memorize. Often the sophistic master would also deliver such set pieces. Discussions followed and the teacher would entertain questions and offer explanations to the students. Within these set pieces there were carefully structured templates (what came to be called *topoi* in Greek and *loci* in Latin; *commonplaces* we often say in English) that could be adapted to various situations. The students internalized these speeches and their templates (such as comparisons of likely and unlikely events or motives, exploring probable consequences and causes, examining past reputations of the accused and accuser, and so forth). Once internalized, students could quickly shuffle and rearrange these templates so as to form a new presentation and then "fill in the blanks" of the templates with specifics relevant to the topic of the moment.[60] This skill allowed them to throw together a persuasive case quickly—to throw together almost any persuasive case quickly. And that, we shall see, became a haunting problem. In fact, Aristotle notes (with qualified, but clear, disdain) that these standard discourses would require students to speak first on one side and then on the opposite side of their stated themes: they would argue that justice was to be preferred in all cases, then turn the tables and construct arguments that justice was to be preferred only in some cases. Or that good and evil were absolute opposites, and then that good and evil were actually the

---

[59] Philostratus, *Lives of the Sophists*, in Philostratus, Eunapius, *Lives of the Sophists. Eunapius: Lives of the Philosophers and Sophists*, ed. and trans. Wilmer C. Wright, Loeb Classical Library 134 (Cambridge, MA: Harvard University Press, 1968) 481. The last remark quoted "as they pleased" is a bit confusing. The Greek references a *technē kata to doxan* but it is unclear how one might have an art "rooted in opinion" or ordered "according to preference" (see Ch. 6 of the present volume). "Doing whatever you wish" is hardly a matter of technical artistry. Probably, this phrase is meant to reference the practice of the student's intuition and instinct so as to be able to speak in an extemporaneous or impromptu fashion on any topic that presented itself, a skill Gorgias was renowned for and one Philostratus praises Gorgias for in *Lives*, 482, the very next section of his work.

[60] We will examine this process in greater depth in the next chapter.

same thing viewed from different perspectives. Aristotle considered this a shallow approach where learning was hasty and undisciplined.[61]

Training of this sort would obviously sharpen wit in talented students and teach them to think on their feet: to draft quick and forceful replies in an ongoing, dynamic, heated political debate. And that seems to have been the point, at least to a large degree.

But in all this, we have been tracking only the sort of training that would help establish a reputation for taste, sophistication, wit, and urbanity for a young aristocrat and then, thus equipped, prepare him for political life in the debates of the assemblies. There was, however, another side of public life in Athenian democracy, and that was life in the legal courts, for the Greeks generally and the Athenians particularly were notoriously sue-happy. And learning to speak in the law courts took a very different track than the training that prepared one for the assembly.

Guilty as Charged: Speech in the Law Courts

If the assemblies remained largely the domain of the sophisticated aristocrats, the law courts were far more egalitarian. Almost anyone could end up standing in front of a jury with their property or life at risk. And that meant teaching someone to give a decent speech in the courts could not, routinely, involve large sums of money paid to a sophist: most citizens simply did not have those resources. For the average person, other means of preparation had to be sought out. George Kennedy notes, "Men who could afford a liberal education for public life attached themselves to a sophist, practiced his commonplaces, and learned almost incidentally the techniques of [legal] oratory."[62] But those who could not afford such an education were not able to pick up legal oratory by osmosis. They needed more specific instruction, and this came in a variety of price ranges.

Greek law, recall, required each citizen to present his own case to the jury in a single speech. There were no options for cross examination, though certain statements taken under oaths (or torture) could be read to the court as part of the speech. One option for preparing a speech, and probably a relatively expensive one, was to hire a speech writer. The job was

---

[61] See Aristotle, *On Sophistical Refutations*, trans. E. S. Forster, Loeb Classical Library 400 (Cambridge, MA: Harvard University Press, 1978), 183b–84b.

[62] George Kennedy, *The Art of Persuasion in Greece* (Princeton: Princeton University Press, 1963), 57.

reviled by most. David Depew refers to the speech writers as ambulance chasers.[63] True enough, perhaps, but that of course does not change the fact that an ambulance-chaser might do quite well, financially. Lysias, for example, was one famous speech writer, and we have a large number of his compositions. His clientele tended to be, while not aristocrats, rather well-off business or agricultural men of the town, suggesting something of the cost of his wares.[64] He was originally a well-educated, wealthy arms dealer, but after a series of reversals in fortune, he seems to have settled into the speech-writing trade a bit later in life.[65] The written texts provided by the speech writer would be taken and memorized. There may or may not have been coaching in issues like vocal delivery and gestures. On the appointed day, the citizen would show up in court and present the speech, then await the jury's vote, which, remember, happened immediately after the trial speeches and without deliberation.

But if a speech writer was still too costly, a citizen of more modest means might be able to hire something of a speech coach who would come for a brief session or two to teach a few pointers about ordering ideas and what each part of a speech should accomplish.[66] Less expensive than a speech writer, such training sessions could still be costly, and certainly too costly for some. And if so, there was always what was sometimes called a *technē*.[67]

A *technē* was, in this context, essentially a pamphlet or small handbook that explained how to give a speech. These were the rough equivalent of putting "how to give a speech" into an internet search engine. The handbooks focused on the various parts of the speech, with comments on what each

---

[63] David Depew, "The Inscription of Isocrates into Aristotle's Practical Philosophy," in *Isocrates and Civic Education*, ed. Takis Poulakos and David Depew, 157–85 (Austin: University of Texas Press, 2004), 160.

[64] Kennedy, *Art*, 57.

[65] Lysias saw something of the golden age of Athens, and its downfall in the Peloponnesian Wars with its rival Sparta. His brother was rounded up by the oligarchs and executed in the brief but tyrannical Rule of Thirty at the end of the wars when Athenian democracy collapsed. Lysias managed to escape and fled the city, barely avoiding his brother's fate. In exile, he was a constant supporter of the democrats. One brief overview of Lysias's life, noting the tumultuous political drama of which he was a part, can be found in the Loeb translation of his works by W. R. M. Lamb, *Lysias*, Loeb Classical Library 244 (Cambridge, MA: Harvard University Press, 1988), ix–xxvi.

[66] Kennedy, *Art*, 58.

[67] The word meant an "art" or "skill" in something. In this case, an "art of speaking."

part was supposed to do and suggestions on how to do it.[68] The texts were probably little more than minimalist instructions on assembling a speech, and their perspective and organizational systems were clearly targeting those headed into the law courts. The emphasis was on pragmatics. There were no highfalutin ethical debates about the emotional manipulation of the audience by, for example, parading your weeping children across the stage, a highly recommended and frequently used tactic, evidently.[69] Stakes were high and winning was what mattered. The handbooks were generally disparaged by the better educated, but these handbooks remained popular and were consistently updated with new and better tactics. The handbooks are often referred to by ancient authors, but none have survived intact.[70]

Corax and Tisias are the famous names here. According to the sources, they took up this business of coaching clients and writing handbooks in Syracuse around 467 BC. The overthrow of a tyrant created a series of land disputes that brought a large number of common and less educated folks into court to defend or reclaim their ancestral properties. Obviously, these clients were eager to learn how to plead their cases most effectively but were without means to pay much. Corax and Tisias seem to have found a solution by serving as temporary coaches and selling handbooks. Many early sources consider the duo to be the founders of the discipline of rhetoric, the first to give systematic study to using language effectively in order to achieve specific goals. Our sources are often inconsistent and, if truth be known, we cannot tell what is fact and what is fiction in the stories we have of the duo,[71] but at the least, we get a sense of rhetoric emerging among the

---

[68] Kennedy, *Art*, 32–33. Contemporary public speaking teaches the parts as introduction, body, and conclusion. Greeks organized their most basic speeches in four fundamental parts: the *prooimion, diēgēsis, pistis, epilogos*—or prologue, narration, evidence, conclusion. The prologue, like an introduction, was supposed to lay out the theme and capture the goodwill and interest of the audience. The narration provided an account of the events to be considered, as the speaker understood them. Evidence was then championed to support the speaker's claims and interpretation of the events. The conclusion reinforced the evidence and rallied the audience with an emotional appeal for support.

[69] See, e.g., Aristophanes, *Wasps*, trans. Jeffrey Henderson, Loeb Classical Library 488 (Cambridge, MA: Harvard University Press, 1998), 560–72.

[70] For an overview of the handbook tradition, see George A. Kennedy, *Aristotle, On Rhetoric: A Theory of Civic Discourse*, 2nd ed. (Oxford: Oxford University Press, 2006), 293–306.

[71] See Kennedy, *Art*, 58–61. One story is revealing. According to the tenth century Byzantine encyclopedia *Suidae Lexicon* (Oxford: Oxford University Press, 1834), *k*171, Tisias, who was being sued for refusing to pay his fees to his sophistic teacher Corax, argued something like this to the jury: "You cannot ask me to pay my teacher Corax,

low and the high simultaneously, so it is probably fair enough to think of Protagoras being the first in a line of aristocratic sophists who focused on political life and saw themselves as continuing the high mission of soul-formation and the crafting of elite leaders, as seen in the ancient world of Homer. Set against this, and at roughly the same time, we can equally accept Corax and Tisias as the foundational merchants of a more populist sophistry centered in the law courts.

And with this division, we are reminded that education at this moment in Greece had several types of teachers, even after the basic schools. But at the top of the tier was the aristocratic sophist. And the chief aristocratic sophist was Gorgias of Leontini.

---

because if Corax has succeeded in teaching me how to persuade others, then you will be persuaded by my words and side with me, and I will not have to pay. But if I don't persuade you to side with me, then clearly Corax has not done his work well, and I should not have to pay." The jury was repulsed by the young man's sophistry, and they almost rioted. The story is likely apocryphal, but it sheds light on how the sophists were viewed by many: purveyors not of sophisticated wisdom, but of pointless paradoxes. The tale in the *Suidae* is recounting one possible origin for the maxim "rotten crows give rotten eggs." *Corax* is the Greek word for *crow*. Presumably, after this legal kerfuffle, Corax complimented his student's wit, and the two sophists, now reconciled, started a lucrative partnership holding seminars and writing introductory textbooks on public speaking.

Chapter 3

Gorgias of Leontini:
Words—Charting a Course Through
Change and Defending Nothing

When Plato opens his dialogue *Gorgias*, Socrates is on his way into the house of Callicles (after a somewhat testy greeting at the doorway) to visit the agéd sophist Gorgias. Socrates urges his own companion Chaerephon to pose a question to Gorgias. "What should I ask?" Chaerephon wants to know. Socrates replies, "Ask him *what he is*."[1] The question is an excellent place to begin. Gorgias might be the rhetorical equivalent of a cinematic superhero: a rich, cool, sophisticated person of calculated self-preservation who still manages to get the job done, all while leaving the audience feeling great. Or he might be some sort of gateway drug to a professorial postmodern "hysterical cum Dionysian schizo"[2] state that will save language by the "overlapping of many fibres,"[3] or, as Derrida might say, many *fib-res*, many deceiving-things that unmake it up. Maybe. Who could know, really? Or perhaps Gorgias is the ancient Greek precursor to the modern strip mall of identity where (rather like Yuval Harari suggests)[4] we completely remake ourselves in our own *l'image du jour* by painting over all the windows of the past and letting be what will be, guided only by the calculus that stuffs immensities like *duty* and *the gods* into the demitasse of a "small and cramped eternity" of

---

[1] Plato, *"Gorgias": A New Translation*, trans. Robin Waterfield (Oxford: Oxford University Press, 2008), 447c–d, emphasis added. Socrates poses the same question to the sophist Protagoras as well in Plato's *Protagoras*, trans. Stanley Lombardo and Karen Bell, in *Plato: Complete Works*, ed. John M. Cooper (Indianapolis, IN: Hackett, 1997), 311b.

[2] Victor Vitanza, *Negation, Subjectivity, and the History of Rhetoric* (Albany: SUNY Press, 1997), 124.

[3] Vitanza, *Negation*, 17. Vitanza is actually quoting Wittgenstein here.

[4] Yuval Harari, "Homo Deus: A Brief History of Tomorrow with Yuval Harari," University of California Television (UCTV), 24 April 2017, video, 57:11, https://www.youtube.com/watch?v =4ChHc5jhZxs, minutes 8–10:30, especially. The point of Harari's presentation is actually that sources of power are slipping out of the hands of human beings, but his introductory remarks show his celebration of reinvention and self-determination as a laudable goal since one's own thoughts and feelings constitute the foundational basis of authority and identity. Note 21:00–21:40.

pleasure.[5] Or he may be the savvy, slight-of-voice politician undercutting violence and tyranny by dissipating the power of tyrants and annexing it into the gardens of Emperor Logos, as Nathan Crick suggests.[6] Or perhaps he is simply The Lord of the Influencers, delivering silken self-evident maxims and savvy straight-forward insights to those not quite fortunate enough to be him? Maybe Gorgias is all of these and more besides. But whatever else he might be, he is an educator: a sophist instructing aristocratic young men how to navigate the rip currents of Greek politics so that his students might maximize their ability to act without being acted upon.

In Plato's fictional discourse, when pressed by Socrates, Gorgias says he teaches the art of *rhetoric.*[7] Two of Gorgias's original rhetorical works have survived, and we have two independent outlines of another argument he made, in addition to a series of snippets we can garner from later authors who are quoting or paraphrasing him from texts we have lost. Gorgias's works have a unique style: flamboyant, strikingly symmetric, and filled with jingle-jangle phrases having a tingle-tangle rhythm. One has the impression they would commit to memory as easily as "I think that I shall never see/A poem as lovely as a tree/A tree whose hungry mouth is pressed/Against the earth's sweet flowing breast," a poem that children of my generation were forced to memorize in fourth grade and have been unable to forget since.[8]

---

[5] G. K. Chesterton, *Orthodoxy* (Garden City, NY: Image, 1959), 20.

[6] Nathan Crick, *Rhetoric and Power* (Columbia: University of South Carolina Press, 2018), Ch. 5.

[7] Plato, *Gorgias* 449a. The first time we ever see the word *rhetoric* appear in any text is here within this fictional conversation. We do not know whether Plato the author is coining a new word and putting it into fictional Gorgias's mouth or whether Plato is adapting some self-reference that the historical Gorgias made about his teaching, or perhaps directly quoting historical Gorgias, or even taking a term that was around (though not used by historical Gorgias) and applying it to fictional Gorgias as a way of stereotyping him. Scholars, like the sophists of old, have put forth convincing arguments on all sides of the question. When *rhetoric* first appeared as a named art is important, but it won't be resolved in these pages. See Andrew Ford, "Sophists Without Rhetoric: The Arts of Speech in Fifth-Century Athens," in *Education in Greek and Roman Antiquity*, ed. Yun Lee Too, 85–109 (Leiden: Brill, 2001), 86–87, and Thomas Cole, *The Origins of Rhetoric in Ancient Greece* (Baltimore: John Hopkins University Press, 1995), 2, 98–99. For our purposes, it is sufficient to note that, by any reasonable understanding of rhetoric as a discipline of studying the production of effective speech, Gorgias fits the definition, whether he called himself a teacher of rhetoric or not.

[8] "Trees" by Joyce Kilmer was a standard in American anthologies of poetry in the previous century. See Joyce Kilmer, "Trees," *Poetry Foundation*, Accessed October 4, 2022, https://www.poetryfoundation.org/poetrymagazine/poems/12744/trees.

In addition to his own impressive words, we have a caricature of Gorgias offered in Plato's writings and some direct criticism from Aristotle. Both men disagreed with Gorgias's philosophical and educational outlooks, so we must use their remarks cautiously as we try to understand who Gorgias was and what he taught. Here, we will give primacy to Gorgias's own writing; his own words, as few as they are, show something substantive of his methods, perspectives, and priorities.

Gorgias's interwoven vision of education, metaphysics, and rhetoric is clearly shaped by the approaches found in the Presocratic debates. These questions explore the relationship between words and the world, between *logos* and *kosmos*. Do words reveal an unchanging order that is already present in the world, or do they create an order of our own making? Do they lead to knowledge or illusion? Do they touch the infinite and eternal things, or do they insulate us from them? Do they do none of these things, or do they do all of these things—and if all, how do you tell which is which in any given moment? How do you sift knowledge from illusion, news from propaganda, mediated truth from mediated lies? Gorgias addresses these questions—or at least these themes are present, both directly and indirectly—in his three extant works, and these works reveal something of the sophist's view on how the world is ordered and ornamented.

Probably Innocent: "Defense of Palamedes"

In mythology, Palamedes was the messenger sent to bring Odysseus to Agamemnon as the Greeks set sail to make war on Troy. Odysseus, not wanting to go, pretended to be mad. Arguably, this was a very sensible thing to do, but Palamedes outwitted Odysseus and revealed the ruse. Odysseus nursed a grudge against Palamedes for this and later murdered him, or had him murdered, according to the myths. In one story, Odysseus hides gold in Palamedes's tent and forges a letter from the Trojans that makes it seem like Palamedes was planning to betray Greece. This is the story Gorgias is following.

In *Defense of Palamedes*, Gorgias lays out a fictional scene where Odysseus has accused his enemy of treason and Palamedes is on trial for his life, pleading his case.[9] The speech opens with Palamedes briefly calling into question the motives of his accuser Odysseus and attempting to lower audience

---

[9] Crick, *Rhetoric and Power*, 94, notes that not only is the speech itself an imaginary composition but the very courtroom setting in which it is delivered would not have been

expectations about his own performance.[10] These are the standard tasks of an introduction in Greek legal oratory. He specifically notes one intriguing theme when he observes in passing, "I know clearly that my accuser has accused me without clearly knowing" what really happened.[11] This is a point he will return to in greater depth. For now, it is enough to note how this opening is designed to weaken Odysseus's charge and to remind an audience that the accusation they have heard must not be treated as a foregone conclusion. If it were an established fact, there would be no need for a trial. And so, it falls to Palamedes to discuss whether this thing (which has not been proven) is *likely* to have happened—or not. Palamedes will argue, of course, that the treason he is charged with is profoundly improbable.

The speech encapsulates a host of possible strategies for objecting to almost any accusation. Palamedes begins by claiming the act he is accused of is unlikely to have taken place at all. He then lays out three arguments for this, some of them subdivided into further aspects. Once he finishes discussing how unlikely the act itself is, he takes up his second set of arguments. Here he focuses on how unlikely it would be for him to have a motive to perform such an act, even if he could. This time, six arguments about motives are put forward (also with various subdivisions), all showing how unlikely it would be for Palamedes to have any motive to betray Greece.[12] The section closes by reemphasizing the obvious conclusions: that it is highly unlikely Palamedes would have had the chance to betray Greece even if he had wanted to, and it is even less likely that he would have wanted to.[13]

Palamedes then takes up the unreliable motives of his accuser.[14] In this section, he returns to the theme of incomplete knowledge. These intriguing remarks are close to the core of at least some assumptions within Gorgias's educational plan. Palamedes points out that *certainty* is quite rare

---

an aspect of Greek war culture at the time of Homer. This speech is, in every aspect, a cultural fiction.

[10] Gorgias, *Defense of Palamedes*, in *Early Greek Philosophy, Vol. VIII: Sophists, Part I*, ed. and trans. André Laks and Glenn W. Most, Loeb Classical Library 531 (Cambridge, MA: Harvard University Press, 2016), D25.3–5. Brief segments of Gorgias are sometimes difficult to quote with clarity, so I have taken the liberty of making minor adjustments to the translation in some places.

[11] Gorgias, *Palamedes* D25.5.

[12] Gorgias, *Palamedes* D25.13–21.

[13] Gorgias, *Palamedes* D25.21.

[14] Gorgias, *Palamedes* D25.22–27. This is followed by a discussion of Palamedes's own character (D25.28–34) before concluding with an appeal to the judges (D25.35–37).

in the world, and we are reduced, thus, to reliance on mere *beliefs, opinions.*
Palamedes addresses his accuser directly, saying that since Odysseus has no
actual *knowledge* to base his accusation on, the accusation must be based
on mere *opinion.* "Have you, most audacious of all humans, found the au-
dacity to accuse me of a capital crime by trusting in opinion (that most
untrustworthy of things!) without knowledge of the truth?"[15] But what,
exactly, does Gorgias mean by "knowledge of the truth"?

The Greek word for truth, *alētheia*, is, like its English counterpart, am-
bivalent. On one hand, the word had deep philosophical and religious—even
mystical—undercurrents which implied that the soul was able to commune
with the nature of the divine beings, and thus encounter infinite and eternal realities beyond nature, outside of time and space. On the other hand,
it might just as easily mean something as prosaic as "knowledge of what-is-
so," as in, "It is true that Julian is terrified of clowns." In this latter context,
truth means only what is accurate and real rather than inaccurate and false.[16]
On the surface, Palamedes's remark seems to fit comfortably in this second
frame: he is merely saying that Odysseus has no "actual knowledge of what
really happened." But with Gorgias, there is almost always more going on
than what appears on the surface of his discourse, as we shall see.

But with either meaning, Gorgias's theme, that human decisions happen in the absence of absolute certainty, is central: we make decisions with
only a partial understanding of what is true. We do this both in our most
mundane affairs and in our most far-reaching metaphysical and religious
beliefs. Our actions are rooted in "the most untrustworthy of things"—our
opinions, our beliefs. The word is *doxa* in Greek.

We have three take-home points from this examination of Gorgias's
speech. First, Gorgias frames two significant transitions in the speech by

---

[15] Gorgias, *Palamedes* D25.24.

[16] Bruce McComiskey overstates the case when he unequivocally claims "that the term
alētheia did not develop its philosophical sense of The Truth until Plato. In most Presocratic and sophistic usages, *alētheia* simply refers to sincerity of speech." McComiskey,
Gorgias and the New Sophistic Rhetoric (Carbondale: Southern Illinois University Press,
2002), 38. While such a use certainly existed in popular discourse, the term *alētheia*
is central to philosophical-theological questions of unchanging eternal realities as set
against the world of unpredictable temporal appearances. In other words, *alētheia* is
absolutely interwoven with the difficulties of philosophical-theological speech prior to
Plato. See, e.g., Marcel Detienne, *The Masters of Truth in Archaic Greece*, trans. Janet
Lloyd (New York: Zone, 1996), 35–52, and Karl Reinhardt, "The Relation Between the
Two Parts of Parmenides' Poem," in *The Pre-Socratics: A Collection of Critical Essays*,
ed. Alexander P. D. Mourelatos (Princeton: Princeton University Press, 1993), 300–301.

pointing out that the core of human choice is ruled by an absence of absolute knowledge or understanding. Only direct experience of something provides a reliable guide to what is true about it. "One should not trust in those who have an opinion (*doxa*), but in those who have knowledge, and one should also not consider *doxa* to be more trustworthy than *alētheia*, but on the contrary *alētheia* to be more [trustworthy] than *doxa*."[17] Knowledge of what is true about something stands against *doxa*, untrustworthy opinion. But the implication is that such knowledge is limited to your own experience. Palamedes truly knows what happened (because he experienced it), but Odysseus is stuck with, at best, only a vague opinion of what might have happened; Odysseus has no full knowledge or experience of the events. The legal logic here is straightforward: the burden of proof is on Odysseus, and it is a significant burden. Without evidence that makes Odysseus's opinionated accusation overwhelmingly likely, the smart money is on those with direct experience, those with real knowledge of the events (Palamedes) rather than those with fickle opinions and uninformed beliefs about vague possibilities (Odysseus). But the broader implication is more serious.

If *alētheia* and knowledge are tied to direct experience, and if we admit that direct experience is actually quite limited, then it follows that virtually every act and every reason for acting can be traced to something unreliable and easily altered: *doxa*, rooted in our incomplete understanding. In the first generation of sophists, then, in the most famous sophist of that generation, tensions between knowledge, truth, and belief are on prominent display within Gorgias's educational program, and those tensions are present in all theological claims and most natural claims as well. This is crucial. How words navigate the treacherous currents between our partial understandings and our confident conclusions will be one of the defining debates of the following century, and its terms will echo down the entire history of education and religion in the European tradition.

Second, we see another, related, preoccupation within this speech that will play a central part in the coming century of debate about words and gods and education. Gorgias consistently focuses on the issue of probability, on what is likely. Within the speech, his arguments are all, without exception, designed to persuade an audience that Palamedes is not likely to have done the act he is accused of. The lesson here is that words reach their highest possible achievement when they arrive at a *probability*. Palamedes probably didn't do it, but we cannot know for sure. The *probable* conclusion

---

[17] Gorgias, *Palamedes* D25.247.

is the goal of discourse. There is no room for *alētheia*. Language is always hedging its bets about what is true, and words are used to debate probabilities, not observable certainties. Nobody argues about whether water boils at 100 degrees Centigrade at sea level. We argue about things where the truth of the claim is, reasonably, up for grabs. But for Gorgias, that is almost everything.

Between the lines of these first two points, we should not neglect another emphasis: the communal context of rhetoric. Gorgias clearly sees rhetoric as a community event, rooted in assumptions shared by the community and thus flowing, in some degree, from that community. He is no existentialist, cut off and isolated in his unknowing. Rather, he is eager to root his uncertainties in a context of larger vision and a community to which rhetoric offers direction, and with which it cooperates in its course of action.

Third, and finally, we see in this discourse the methods of Gorgias on display. The speech presents nine primary arguments tightly arranged in staccato order with virtually no hint of smooth transitions between them, followed by a series of similarly ordered ways to attack the character of an accuser or the consistency of an accusation, followed by ways to strengthen the reputation of someone accused. This is obviously not intended to be an actual speech given in an actual court. It is designed to provide a series of templates that can be quickly shuffled and filled in at the opportune moment with the appropriate material to move an agenda ahead or to undermine someone else's proposal.[18] Thomas Cole sums up the point succinctly. Gorgias "provides appropriate grounds for dismissing such cases in almost any situation. . . . And this is, one suspects, precisely Gorgias's intention. There is to be no case to which some of his arguments would *not* apply."[19]

So, *Palamedes* shows us the method of Gorgias, and the assumptions behind that method are clear: knowledge is rare, and language is about possibilities and probabilities more than certainties. But this is not Gorgias's only showpiece. He sets himself a much larger challenge—and provides different insights into his thoughts and methods—in his attempt to praise Helen of Troy.

---

[18] This outline is consistent with Gorgias's important treatment of *kairos*, a seizing of the moment. See Thomas Cole, *The Origins of Rhetoric in Ancient Greece* (Baltimore: Johns Hopkins University Press, 1995), 151. Gorgias seems to believe, as Cole points out, that a teacher cannot teach a student to see and grasp that moment of opportunity, *kairos*. What the teacher can do is provide tools to use within that moment once it has been intuitively recognized.

[19] Thomas Cole, *Origins*, 76. Emphasis in original.

Innocence Abroad: "Encomium on Helen"

The *Encomium on Helen* is stylistically more flamboyant than *Defense of Palamedes*, but there are also striking differences in content.[20] First, while *Palamedes* puts forward a variety of general arguments that were easily adaptable to various situations, *Helen* puts forward only four arguments, none of which could be considered broadly adaptable in the real world. In fact, as John Poulakos points out, only one of them has any reasonable merit at all.[21] *Helen* has another goal. This speech considers the power and possibilities of language far more obviously and directly than *Palamedes* does.

In Greek mythology, Helen was a demigoddess, child of Zeus and Leda, and she was, naturally, the most beautiful woman ever to live. She was kidnapped by Theseus when she was still a child of twelve, but then rescued by her brothers Castor and Pollux in a later skirmish. More conflict was brewing, so the suitors all gathered together to make their case to Helen herself. On the advice of Odysseus, all competitors swore an oath to protect and defend Helen from future abduction once she chose her husband. Menelaus, king of Sparta, won her favor by speaking sweetly while avoiding overwrought flattery. Helen married him while still a young lady. Shortly after this, Paris, a young Prince from Troy, was invited to visit Sparta.[22] When he saw Helen, he decided—as young heroes generally do in the presence of beautiful women—that he could not live without her. When Menelaus was unexpectedly called away to attend a funeral, Helen remained behind, overseeing the entertainment of the guests. A few nights later, Paris slipped away unannounced in the middle of the night, sailing back to Troy; Helen was with him. Menelaus and his brother Agamemnon summoned all the Greek heroes to fulfill their oaths by taking Helen back from Troy and returning her to Sparta. This began the ten years of the Trojan War.

---

[20] Gorgias, *Encomium on Helen*, in Laks and Most, *Early Greek Philosophy, Vol. VIII.* Laks and Most strive for a literal translation, which results in a sometimes stiff English syntax. George Kennedy provides a smoother translation in *The Older Sophists*, ed. Rosamond Kent Sprague (Indianapolis, IN: Hackett, 2001), 50–54. Kennedy's translation is reprinted (but lacking the Classical reference numbers) in Patricia Bizzell and Bruce Herzberg, eds., *The Rhetorical Tradition*, 2nd ed. (Boston: Bedford/St. Martin's, 2001), 44–46. A translation that attempts to follow Gorgias's stylistic flourishes can be found in John Dillon and Tania Gergel, *The Early Sophists* (New York: Penguin Classics, 2003), 43–97.

[21] John Poulakos, "Gorgias's *Encomium to Helen* and the Defense of Rhetoric," *Rhetorica* 1, no. 2 (1983): 3.

[22] Paris is also known as "Alexander," and this is the name Gorgias uses in his speech.

Gorgias, according to the title of his speech, sets out to praise Helen, to make his audience warmly disposed toward her despite her unfortunate baggage of having caused a decade of (literally epic) war that killed most of the best of the Greeks. Praising her under these cultural conditions was no small challenge, of course, but success would be an impressive way to show one's oratorical skills, and it could serve as a form of advertisement if one were looking for students.

On the other hand, the last sentence of the speech includes the phrase, "I wished to write a speech [*logos*] that would be an encomium for Helen and an amusement for me."[23] This is the line that launched a thousand scholarly debates. The word *amusement* here is the Greek *paignion* which means *plaything* or *game*, and it raises the question of just how seriously one should take this brief speech. Poulakos suggests one rendering of the last line is "You've been had!" and that is hardly a persuasive close for an advertisement—unless you are advertising just how persuasive you can be, in which case it might be the perfect ending.[24] So is the speech a witty commercial, an elaborate joke, or something else? The answer is nothing if not ambiguous, and that itself may be an echo of a point we have already seen played by Gorgias: speech (*logos*) never gets you to certainty. We cannot be certain about how seriously we should take this speech, but given that the speech itself talks about the power of speech, it is *probably* true that the irony is a self-conscious part of the game.[25] Gorgias takes the power of *logos* as the primary theme of his speech (*logos*), and he places the speech within an ambiguous frame that undercuts certainty—which is exactly the circumstance words (*logoi!*) always operate under. Words edge toward *likely*, but they never touch *certainly*. Probably, our best view is to consider

---

[23] Gorgias, *Helen*, 21. The closing phrase is typical of Gorgias's style: . . . *men egkōmion, emon de paignion.*

[24] John Poulakos, "Gorgias's *Encomium*," 3.

[25] We must not turn Gorgias into a postmodern ironist, to state the obvious, but Gorgias certainly found champions among scholars at the end of the last century who were working within a postmodern and ironic frame. And while he does not fit perfectly into that camp, there are important overlaps. Susan Jarratt's *Rereading the Sophists: Classical Rhetoric Refigured* (Carbondale: Southern Illinois University Press, 1991) is one example of this sort of embrace. She sets out to "forward the cause of politically progressive composition pedagogy," 117, by reinterpreting classical rhetoric, and she leans heavily on Gorgias and the sophists. John Poulakos, "Gorgias's *Encomium*," is an alternative view; his reading seeks to read the work within its historic context as much as possible. McComiskey provides an overview and attempts a synthesis of the two approaches in his *Gorgias*.

the speech a statement about language, but one that does not present conclusions of an extended and thorough argument. Rather, the piece parades itself forward as an image of the spectacle of language. An audience who surrenders to the spectacle becomes unmoored from familiar definitions and is set adrift upon an open-ended linguistic sea. These are words about words, and among their themes are questions about the ethical dimensions of language and the source of power within any words, including the ones we use to discuss the power and ethics of words.

The speech proceeds with an intriguing introduction followed by a series of considerations about why Helen might have been on that boat when Paris left in the middle of the night. Gorgias argues that, however she got there, it probably was not her fault. She probably did not do anything unjust, but endured injustice. And so, "would it not be plausible," he asks, "for her to be pitied rather than defamed?"[26]

In short order, here are the four possibilities for Helen's departure as Gorgias lays them out. First, the event may have been willed by the gods, in which case you can hardly hold Helen responsible: she was simply a tool used by others.[27] Second, it may have been a simple act of physical violence and force: Paris may have kidnapped and raped her, in which case, once again, she is obviously not at fault, and she requires pity not slander. Helen had no way to resist brute violence.[28] Third, she may have been swept away

---

[26] Gorgias, *Helen*, 7. Note Gorgias's emphasis upon plausibility.

[27] Gorgias, *Helen*, 6.

[28] Gorgias, *Helen*, 7. Crick points out, in *Rhetoric and Power*, 82, that this view represents a forceful denunciation of violence against women, hardly common for its time and therefore all the more praiseworthy. The point is a welcome emphasis—one of several in his insightful text. That said, Crick may overreach in his passing implication that this might have been a generalizable conclusion in which Gorgias "wishes to even more definitively condemn violence as a means to an end, *particularly* when it comes to relationships between men and women," 82, emphasis added. I certainly agree that Gorgias offers a particular and rare (and therefore especially laudable) condemnation of violence against women, but if the implication here is that Gorgias might have generalized this view to *other* contexts, I find no evidence for that. The fragments of his "Funeral Oration" certainly praise the Greek war heroes unambiguously and with no hint of a pacifist's undercurrent. Gorgias may have thought violence was an unfortunate, but a sometimes necessary and therefore acceptable means to some ends, or not; we simply do not know. Perhaps he would surprise us and take a more general view that rejected violence, but it seems at least as likely that his thought reflected the broader development of Greek theory on the status of peace and war. That peace (*eirēnē*) was preferred is obvious. But the theory of *eirēnē* became, in Greek thought, ironically tied to militant conquest and the implementation of peace and order under imperial force. For more, see Kurt A. Raaflaub,

by words. This possibility introduces the longest and most complex part of the speech, and the discussion about words occupies almost as much of the discourse as the other three reasons combined.[29] After the discussion of words, Gorgias takes up the fourth possibility: that Helen herself was swept away by passionate desire and love, an echo of the first point, since love is, of course, one of the gods. But also, in a peculiar way, this is an extension of the third point, on words. The echo here of both human words and divine acts is probably not accidental. Love is discussed as an overwhelming passion that seizes the soul. Such a description mirrors rather precisely the language Gorgias uses to describe the way words seduce the soul. Gorgias is subtly subverting the divine act to the power of speech. Remember that Peitho was the goddess of both persuasion and seduction, and she was an attendant to Aphrodite, goddess of love. The two shared a common sanctuary on the Acropolis in Athens. Gorgias probably meant his discussion on persuasive words and overpowering passions to go together and shed light on each other (and raise questions about each other).[30]

This structure provides two very clear reasons why Helen could not be held responsible for her actions: first, if she were the tool of the gods or, second, if she suffered the violence of Paris's superior physical strength. But the last two reasons to excuse Helen (occupying most of the speech, by far) do not seem like very good reasons at all. It is hard to see how Helen is alleviated of her responsibility in starting the war if she chose to break her vows and leave her husband after getting smooth-talked, or if she left because of her own erotic urges toward Paris. Both "he talked me into it" and "he was too sexy to resist" sound like answers that would not exactly hold up in a war tribunal. Once again, something besides the obvious is going on in this speech, and so we must consider the deeper details we can garner from Gorgias's gifted discussion of discourse.[31]

"Conceptualizing and Theorizing Peace in Ancient Greece," *Transactions of the American Philological Association* 139, no. 2 (2009): 225–50, especially 234–36.

[29] Gorgias, *Helen*, 8–15. Just over 460 words in the Greek text are devoted to the explicit discussion of *logos* and its power. By contrast, some 490 words are divided between the other three possible reasons for Helen's departure (divine fate, human force, and the overwhelming passions of love).

[30] If we consider as one extended point (a) the discourse on persuasion sweeping the soul away through enchantment and (b) the discussion of love sweeping the soul away in passion, then this theme of enchanting the soul by passionate discourse occupies more than three-fourths of the body of this speech.

[31] If one wishes to take seriously the identification of the demigoddess Helen with the divine power of human speech, one is led to a forceful consideration of the substantive

One place to begin a closer examination is the introduction. The first sentence might be rendered, "The *kosmos*[32] for a city is bold courage,[33] for a body it is beauty, for a soul it is wisdom, for an action it is excellence [*aretē*], and for a speech [*logos*] it is truth [*alētheia*], while the opposites of these yield the absence of such ornament."[34] This opening ties together two essential concerns within the speech. Truth, *alētheia*, we are told, orders *logos* properly, beautifies it, and honors it. When speech is not aligned with *alētheia*, it is disordered, disproportionate, without decorum.[35]

We must pause and reemphasize a point made in our discussion of *Palamedes*. The word *truth*, *alētheia*, is ambiguous. Here, that ambiguity is intentionally framed to frustrate any careful listener. On the surface level of *alētheia* (as an unphilosophical term meaning mere accuracy, a complete grasp of what-is-so), the meaning of this opening line is clear enough: words have more punch when we fully understand what-is-so about a given situation. The better a speaker understands a specific situation, the better the speech can be made to fit that situation. This is all fair enough; lesser talents than Gorgias would have sufficed to discover it.[36] But Gorgias has already warned us that grasping even this much *alētheia* is difficult: as difficult as bringing maturity into politics, or winning a Nobel Prize in physics, or planting wisdom deep in the soul, or having perfect abs. These are fine ideals, to be sure. But we will have to work through most of our life without having achieved these ideals, just as we will have to use words and choose

---

irony taking place beneath the flashy appearance of this discourse. That irony runs deeper than merely attempting to pardon rhetoric for its perceived faults. See Michael Fournier, "Gorgias on Magic," *Magic, Ritual, & Witchcraft* 8, no. 2 (2013): 119–31.

[32] Order, ornamentation, honor.

[33] Literally, *manliness*.

[34] The first word of this first sentence of the speech is *kosmos*, and the last word of this first sentence is *akosmia*, a negation of *kosmos*. Thus, the first sentence opens with *order* or *ornament* and closes with *disorder* or *unornamented*, which suggests what Gorgias thinks is held in the balance here. It is hardly the only tension present. Interestingly, the very last word of the whole speech is *paignion*, plaything. To open the speech with *kosmos* and close it with *plaything*, *amusement* seems an unlikely coincidence for someone with Gorgias's craft.

[35] See Daniel Boyarin, "The Scandal of Sophism," *Common Knowledge* 13, nos. 2–3 (2007): 326. Gorgias seems to be challenging Parmenides's claim that *kosmos* is a deceptive, merely decorative, aspect of *logos* and is divorced from *alētheia*.

[36] I am paraphrasing C. S. Lewis's critical review of Alexander King and Marin Ketley, *The Control of Language: A Critical Approach to Reading and Writing* (London: Longmans, Green, and Co., 1939). See Lewis's *The Abolition of Man* (New York: Macmillan, 1955), 19.

beliefs without full knowledge of what-is-so. This insight will become crucial when Gorgias begins to address the power of *logos* more directly. But there is a hint of a still larger problem.

Being fully informed about what-is-so in any situation is tough, and that begs a deeper question if one wishes to read *alētheia* more deeply. Unquestionably, if one achieved the religious and philosophical perfection of Truth itself—*Alētheia* with a capital A—then certainly one's speech could be cosmically ordered: bold, beautiful, wise, virtuous. It would perfectly embrace every quality suggested in the opening sentence. But seriously, Gorgias implies: how likely is that? If it is impossible to obtain a full and complete idea of *alētheia* as mere accuracy, mere understanding of the situation, how much less likely is it to be able to obtain *Alētheia* as philosophical and religious Truth? The clear implication for anyone bold enough to wonder: far, far less likely. But Gorgias has already warned us that without *alētheia*, we will be forced back on flawed *doxa*. With that awareness, the opening of this playful speech becomes anything but frivolous. However casually or deeply one reads *alētheia* in this first sentence, it is clearly not an encouraging place to begin. For anyone acquainted with Gorgias's broader perspectives, there is an obvious suggestion that words will never reach as far as *alētheia*, and they will have to look elsewhere for their power and employment.

But there is at least one other intriguing aspect of his introduction. Just before launching into the brief presentation of his first point, Gorgias notes that Helen's beauty (equal to the gods, he says) drew together many "men who had great ambitions about great matters, some of whom possessed abundant wealth, others renown for their ancient nobility, others the vigor of their innate strength, and still others the power of acquired wisdom. They all came, driven by the love that desires victory and by an invincible desire for honor."[37] Certainly this is a technically accurate account of Helen's early life, but it also reads suspiciously like a very precise description of what sophists claimed to be doing in their educational programs. Poulakos says this description of Helen suggests her character should be understood as a stand-in for rhetoric throughout the speech, and each argument made for Helen's innocence is, he maintains, a reply to a particular criticism about the sophists' educational offerings, or an explanation of their teachings.[38]

---

[37] Gorgias, *Helen*, 4.

[38] Poulakos, "Gorgias's *Encomium*," 5–6.

For example, in Gorgias's first point we see a reply to a charge often leveled against sophists: the rhetoric they taught was an apprenticeship in deception, and it gave people power to mislead others; rhetoric was always making the stronger case look weaker and vice versa.[39] But in Gorgias's first point, we have an obvious reply to this charge: rhetoric cannot be held responsible for the evil things that come from the way it is used by others. Rhetoric is just a tool employed by others, and the moral responsibility rests with those who use the tool, not the tool itself, just like Helen was a tool, used by the gods to accomplish their will. If the outcome was terrible, do not blame Helen; blame those who used her.[40] As with most of Gorgias, this passage is filled with tensions beneath its frivolously balanced phrases. And one of those tensions is religious.

Most simply, Gorgias has suggested that Helen is not to be blamed for her part in starting the Trojan war if she were only the tool of the gods, used by them to work out their irresistible will. At a glance, this alleviates Helen of any responsibility. But for anyone looking twice (or applying the principle more broadly to, say, rhetoric), it also suggests that human beings bear direct responsibility for the way they use their own tools, including *logos*. People are responsible for the way they use their words. Bruce McComiskey observes that this move on Gorgias's part brings the force of persuasion "into the realm of human control."[41]

This is a fairly significant theological inversion. People had always called upon and cooperated with the divine in order to accomplish their tasks. But Gorgias implies that those who speak are responsible for the persuasion (*peitho*) that takes place. If so, the divine goddess Peitho has been diminished and made a servant of human arts. This is another important "departure from the epic [i.e., *mythic*] impulse to deify mysterious forces."[42] And the step aligns Gorgias comfortably within the tradition of the Presocratics. Before those thinkers, natural events such as drought or volcanic eruptions had been understood as the direct action of divine powers beyond human control. The Presocratics, recall, had eventually come to explore the possibility that there was a principle within nature itself that

---

[39] See Poulakos, "Gorgias's *Encomium*," 5, 7.

[40] Poulakos, "Gorgias's *Encomium*," 8–10.

[41] McComiskey, *Gorgias*, 39.

[42] McComiskey, *Gorgias*, 39. I think McComiskey, in the broader discussion of these passages, clearly overinterprets Gorgias's role here. The sophist was one of many signs pointing toward this broader and ongoing transition from *mythos* to *logos*, though no doubt his teaching contributed to that transition. See Ch. 1 of the present work.

might be responsible for organizing and causing such events, independent of direct divine action. In other words, might it be that nature itself was just built in such a way that stuff happened, without a god who directly caused that stuff? With Gorgias, we see this question has begun to turn inward; a similar question was now forming about not just the acts of nature but about human nature, about the soul itself.

Under *mythos*, those who had the right quality or nature had their bodies shaped and formed by physical training. Likewise, they had their souls polished and formed by divine osmosis through pious ritual and cultural association with the higher things (including other men with these higher quality souls) that moved them toward *aretē*. The soul of the young man was to be exposed and brought into the presence of these higher things and thus polished, shaped, sculpted under the influence of the divine, mysterious, formative powers that acted on the exceptional quality of soul possessed by the aristocratic sort of man.

But under the sophists, shaping these high-quality souls began to look like it was a task within the reach of practical human arts rather than mystical divine acts. At least in regard to the goddess Peitho, a soul with the right nature and right skill in words might become its own master. These are excitingly subversive (and simultaneously flattering) suggestions to put before an audience of ambitious young men. But at the same time, *Helen* offers definite cautions.

When Gorgias turns directly to *logos* in his third main point, we confront the central part of the speech, both literally and figuratively.[43] This third point in *Helen* can be summarized this way: if Helen fell victim to speech, she can be excused because speech is such an intoxicating power, perhaps stronger than brute force, stronger than drugs that alter the mind and body. Its power is in the way words stir the passions and deeply move us, as we all know from our own experience. To support this, Gorgias provides two examples of deeply moving *logos* with which his audiences would be intimately familiar. Both passages are "brief and obscure," as Fournier notes.[44] First, there is the recitation of poetry that makes the soul feel deeply. The soul does not actually experience the events portrayed in the poetic story, but it does find its emotions awakened and directed by the power of the poetic presentation. Note carefully that the words here are not attached to a factual reality, but they move the

---

[43] Gorgias, *Helen*, 8–14.

[44] Fournier, "Gorgias," 123.

soul on their own. This independent power of words is what should be kept in mind when Gorgias moves to his second example, persuasion as a kind of religious magic. Here, he is still more blunt.

Incantation—religious chant, invoking the gods or other spiritual powers—also works in a similar way to move the souls of those who listen.[45] But here Gorgias bluntly states that this happens through a kind of deception (*apatē*). The word is risqué, if not exactly scandalous.[46] For a generation, this sort of *apatē* had been associated with the craft of artists who painted or sculpted.[47] Their images, copied from nature, stirred the soul through a sort of deception that imitated the real world. Poets—servants of the Muses, and sometimes possessed by the gods—made similar claims about their words. Gorgias had already hinted at the idea that words could be actors in the same way the gods could; he did so when he allowed Peitho, goddess of seduction and persuasion, to become a power that responded to human skill. The soul is thus persuaded by *apatē*, by deception, a very human ability.[48] *Logos* is, like paint brushes or chisels, merely a tool to craft something of the artist's own making: namely, to craft an emotional response in another.[49]

Gorgias then explains that to really understand how the soul is persuaded, it is necessary to look at three things. First, examine the speech of astrologers, who "abolishing and establishing one opinion instead of another, have made things that are unbelievable and unclear appear to the eyes of opinion."[50] Astrologers always needed to be ready to update their prognostications or their interpretation of omens as the situation developed, with each view superseding the previous one. Adaptability and

---

[45] We easily forget how much of Pagan religion involved the casting of spells and counter-spells, magical incantation, and the invocation of charms, curses, and the like. See Gregory Vlastos, *Socrates: Ironist and Moral Philosopher* (Ithaca, NY: Cornell University Press, 1991), 176–77.

[46] Fournier, "Gorgias," 123–24. See especially note 20.

[47] Detienne, *Masters*, 107–9.

[48] Gorgias describes the statues of men and gods as "a pleasurable sickness of the eyes" in *Helen*, 18, and certainly would have considered his own speech "a pleasurable sickness of the ears."

[49] Detienne, *Masters*, 109, notes that when sculptors began signing their work, this indicated the beginning of a break with the purely religious production of cult statues. The human was consciously inserting the self into the religious moment, acting as a person with his own autonomous agency: a human medium, standing in the middle, between the divine and the image and the response of the pious worshippers.

[50] Gorgias, *Helen*, 13.

contingency reigned. What mattered was the ability to make things seem believable by adapting to ever-changing circumstances. That is one of the essential persuasive powers of *logos*.

Second, Gorgias asks us to notice the speech contests where orations move the audience with artistry even though the orations are fictional: like paintings and sculptures, these speeches traffic in illusion and *apatē*, not *alētheia*. Contestants would deliver orations hoping for a wreath of glory. Gorgias had seen his share of such contests and knew well that success went to those orations that were "written with artistry, not spoken with *alētheia*."[51] Neither carefully researched historical precision nor hard-won philosophical *Alētheia* were what scored points; rather, leaving a powerful impression did. Large crowds gathered to hear these rhetorical displays; the speaker needed to delight and move those crowds because their applause would be key in the judges' minds. Artistry in composition and delivery was what mattered. A presentation that was impressive and delightful (not necessarily accurate or spiritually true) was another essential element in the power of *logos*.

Third, Gorgias says we must look at the way philosophers argue, moving quickly between thoughts in such a way that beliefs (*doxa*) are easily undermined.[52] Here "swiftness of thought" could be seen making "an opinion (*doxa*) easily changed."[53] The skill championed here was being quick-witted and light on your feet so that you kept the edge in debate.

Thus, the powers of *logos* are found in an easy adaptability, an impressive presentation that responds to a given audience, and a quick wit. But what exactly does the exercise of these powers obtain for the rhetor? In the closing sentence of the speech, Gorgias intriguingly states that one of the goals of this presentation was to undermine the ignorance of *doxa*.[54] Besides that closing sentence, Gorgias uses the term *doxa* nine times in this speech; all of those occurrences appear in his discussion on the power of words.

---

[51] Gorgias, *Helen*, 13.

[52] Gorgias, *Helen*, 13.

[53] Gorgias, *Helen*, 13.

[54] Gorgias, *Helen*, 21. In context he certainly means the audience's ignorant *doxa* regarding Helen. It is hard, however, not to suspect that he was suggesting something else in the phrase, given the distribution of that term within the text.

Doxa, remember, is "that most untrustworthy of things," a belief rooted in less than full knowledge of the specific situation.[55] And yet that is all we have: belief built from the bits and pieces of life we happen to know. We lack full memory of things past, understanding of things present, and foreknowledge of things to come.[56] Lacking what we need for full understanding, "most men on most subjects take opinion (*doxa*) as counsellor to their soul." The result is not encouraging: "*doxa*, being slippery and insecure, casts those employing it into slippery and insecure successes."[57] *Doxa* is all any person has to work with, and *doxa* is not very stable. But it is possible to ameliorate that weakness by wielding the autonomous power of *logos*. The citizen-rhetor who is easily adaptable, pleasantly impressive, and quick-witted can chart a course through the shifting currents of the city's *doxa*. Such a rhetor will be "able to manage public affairs and in so doing to benefit his friends and harm his enemies and to be careful that no harm comes to himself."[58] This is how Gorgias abolishes the perils of ignorant opinion.

In other words, the world is a perilous place filled with shifting and subtle threats and opportunities, dangerous temporary alliances, and slippery successes. Every perspective is founded on ignorance. However, with the skills offered here, it is possible to build a wall of words around the self in order to get what one wants more often than others. Rhetoric is a fortress built around your preferred interests. This appearance of self-interest, however, might be softened by, ironically, Plato's portrayal of Gorgias in his dialogue. There we see a Gorgias who senses how the dangers and vicissitudes of life threaten not just the individual but also the community, and who implies that rhetors, rooted in their community, must speak to the interests of the city and give advice with those interests in mind. This is exactly Gorgias's argument in Plato, though of course Plato will have some questions about that perspective.

---

[55] Gorgias, *Palamedes*, 24.

[56] Gorgias, *Helen*, 11.

[57] Gorgias, *Helen*, 11.

[58] Plato, *Meno*, trans. G. M. A. Grube, in *Plato: Complete Works*, ed. John M. Cooper (Indianapolis, IN: Hackett, 1997), 71e, 872. In the preceding passages, Meno states that he shares Gorgias's views on matters such as the definition of virtue. Socrates then suggests the two "leave Gorgias out of it" since Gorgias was not with them, and he asks Meno to give his own definition of *aretē*, excellence, virtue. Meno responds with the quote above. Though technically Gorgias's point of view has been bracketed, that move is an obvious *paraleipsis*: Plato is almost certainly forwarding this practical self-interest as a summation of Gorgias's perspective. Granted, it is a summation provided by one of Gorgias's arch enemies, but that said, it is also consistent with what we see in Gorgias's own texts.

With these points, we begin to have a sense of what is going on in Gorgias's writings, at least as they have come down to us. If *Palamedes* reveals how Gorgias applied his ideas about teaching persuasion, then *Helen* is a veiled and somewhat ironic suggestion of what some of those ideas were. The emphases are on contingency, adaptability, and impressive delivery, coupled with situational and audience awareness. With these, words can build their own authoritative truths in defense of one's own immediate interests. Certainly, these might be the interests of the community as well. And those words wield a power "higher than any divine or human law."[59] Most certainly, rhetoric could never be nailed down as a principled, established, servant of a higher good. Of course not. It functioned without knowing what *Alētheia* was. Rhetoric adapted moment by moment to the circumstances as they changed, doing what was most expedient to make one's position seem secure, forceful, and acceptable. Rhetoric defended one from the inherent perils of any belief by keeping options open, keeping others impressed, and keeping one's wits focused.

Palamedes and *Helen* emphasize similar issues of how incomplete our understanding is and how our beliefs are rooted in exactly that incomplete understanding. "Gorgias reveals," Cole summarizes, "a very vivid sense of the state of ignorance and uncertainty that is habitual for the human psyche, the resulting tendency for the psyche to be guided by mere opinion, and the way virtually anything one sees or hears can cause the abandoning of one opinion for another."[60] In *On Nonbeing, On Nature,* Gorgias provides something of a capstone to this emphasis, and we will need to examine that argument briefly.

Much Ado About Nothing: "On Nonbeing, or On Nature"

Gorgias presents three specific arguments in this work. First, he says, nothing exists. Second, if something did exist, it could not be known. Finally, even if something did exist and was known, it could not be communicated.[61]

---

[59] Ekaterina V. Haskins, *Logos and Power in Isocrates and Aristotle* (Columbia: University of South Carolina Press, 2004), 110.

[60] Cole, *Origins*, 146.

[61] Gorgias's original text entitled *On Nonbeing, or On Nature* has not been preserved, but we have two ancient sources that have provided consistent summaries of it, and we have a high measure of confidence about its overall content. The summaries are found in

The first argument seems a bit extreme, but if we think about the overall piece and contextualize it within the Presocratic debate about the nature of reality, it becomes a bit less shocking.[62] Gorgias's basic argument might be summarized this way: there is no "Essential Being of anything." He is (perhaps) not denying the material existence of trees or rocks. Susan Jarratt, with at least as much charity as the text allows, states that Gorgias certainly believes "what we see has its own nature, not chosen by us."[63] Perhaps he does. Perhaps not. But *justice*, for example, is not like trees and rocks; *justice* is not some reality that exists apart from choices human beings make in specific situations. *Justice* will be whatever is negotiated between competing interests and found acceptable by both sides in the community—or imposed on one side by the other. *Justice* has no existence apart from those negotiations; it is simply the outcome of a verbal process. It has no true being, no absolute essence, no ultimate definition beyond our rhetorical negotiations. Neither does *good*. Nor *wrong*. These cannot be thought of as having some fixed quality or *essence* independent of our interactions and negotiations with one another. They are simply titles given to the end conditions that emerge within some human exchanges. In short, there is no supernatural or metaphysical reality backing up such judgment calls. This seems to be the point of Gorgias's first claim, and its emphasis on contingency and adaptability fit comfortably with what we have in Gorgias's other writings. As evidence for this claim, he notes that if there were a kind of infinite and eternal quality to *justice* or *good*, these infinite realities

---

Sextus Empiricus and Pseudo-Aristotle. See the texts and translations in Laks and Most, *Early Greek Philosophy, Vol. VIII*, 218–43. As with the *Helen*, there was once debate about whether the text was philosophical or, given its apparently radical claims, was intended as a joke, but "there is nothing humorous about the treatise and no indication that it was ever intended to be so," as G. B. Kerferd observes in his article "Gorgias on Nature or That Which is Not," *Phronesis* 1, no. 1 (1955): 3. Today, the treatise is generally regarded as a serious reflection, situated comfortably within the Presocratic tradition on the nature of reality.

[62] Pseudo-Aristotle specifically makes this connection in the opening of the summary, parts 1–16. See Laks and Most, *Early Greek Philosophy, Vol. VIII*, 218–25.

[63] Jarratt, *Rereading*, 55. But, as I have suggested, Jarrett might be, in the end, overreaching. Gorgias's text itself does not transparently sidestep such radical skepticism, and that skepticism would not, in the end, be inconsistent with anything else in the argument. It may be that he does not think material existence should be granted any greater intellectual indulgence than justice or goodness. Maybe nothing is real.

could not appear inside nature because nature is finite and one cannot fit an infinite quality into a finite space.[64]

This leads to Gorgias's second argument, which is equally pointed and echoes his recurring skepticism about our ability to see the world as it is: if anything does have any sort of essence, you cannot know it. He notes that the human mind can focus on things that fit into the category of *Nothing*, or *Nonbeing*. Imagine, if you will, a fire-breathing butterfly or a fish playing the trombone. You can do this. But these things do not exist, and if you can think of these things which are in the category of Nonbeing, clearly thought is not anchored to any sort of Universal Being or *Alētheia*; thought is capable of fixating on what is false, on what is unreal, on Nonbeing. And if so, you must conclude that you cannot trust your thoughts to reveal what would be true about any realm of Ultimate Being, which would, almost by definition, be beyond the reach of your physical senses. Thus, even if *Justice* (capital J) did exist as some real thing, in a realm of Ultimate *Alētheia*, your mind could never know what is really true about it because your mind is a place where false and true live together and your understanding is always partial and limited by your immediate physical experiences, as Gorgias has repeatedly emphasized.

Finally, and most intriguingly, Gorgias believes that even if *justice* were real and had some sort of Ultimate Being, and even if you did come to know this ultimate justice, you could never communicate it to another. This is because what we communicate is *logos, words*. And of course, the word *justice* is not justice. In the end, our words are all we offer in communication, but even if our words were referencing some Ultimate Reality that actually exists (which, probably, they are not), our words are not that Ultimate Reality that actually exists; they are only words about that reality. Words do not reveal the Real. For Gorgias, *logos* is a *medium*, a thing that stands between our experiences and anyone else.[65]

---

[64] To understand this spatial argument, it must be remembered that the Greeks imagined the material cosmos to be a sphere—a very large sphere, admittedly, but still a finite space. And finite spaces, it was argued, cannot contain infinite realities. See Sextus Empiricus's remarks from *Against the Logicians*, trans. R. G. Bury, Loeb Classical Library 291 (Cambridge, MA: Harvard University Press, 1989), sec. 1.69, where he is summarizing Gorgias, as well as his remarks on infinite regression in *Outlines of Pyrrhonism*, trans. R. G. Bury, Loeb Classical Library 273 (Cambridge, MA: Harvard University Press, 1933), sec. 1.166.

[65] At least. It is possible that *logos* stands between us and our understanding of our own personal experiences, as well.

On Nonbeing carries the subtitle *On Nature.* The ultimate nature of things is that things have no Ultimate Nature, no Eternal Essence, and even if they did, how would we know? And if we cannot know, why would it matter? We are back to living in a world of *doxa* founded on truncated understanding and limited experience, and our best response is a sort of rhetorical *apatē*, a deception that turns the uncertainty of *doxa* back on itself. It does this by wielding rhetorical skill that allows us to craft an ever-adapting road through the world of change and chance so that we may act as we wish and not be acted upon without our permission.

Looking over *On Nonbeing*, we have no reason to assume Gorgias did not accept this as an accurate and serious description of the *kosmos* he lived in. But even if he sometimes doubted his own skepticism, it is not clear this would have made much of a difference in the way he taught. Maybe preparing young aristocratic elites for the bitter realities of hard-knock politics simply meant that contingent convictions and self-interested pragmatism would necessarily dominate the course of study. But beyond the circumstances of his teaching, when we look carefully at the overall stand Gorgias has taken, it still raises some commanding questions.

Under Gorgias's view, words are powerful, of course, but their power lies in the fact that they are the tools we use to carve out our own preferred views of life. Their power does not lie in their ability to access any deeper reality or to reveal any Being or *Alētheia* that rests beyond the natural world in the supernatural realm. Words have no access to anything transcendent.

This position has obvious implications for religion. Even if there are supernatural realities, Gorgias argues, we cannot encounter them in any meaningful way. That is, meaning—*logos*, reason, language—is severed from the divine. We cannot find meaning in the gods. Any encounter with the divine (assuming there even is a divine world) cannot be reasonable but would have to be viciously private and subjectively emotive since *logos—reason, language, words*—cannot access Being. This tension between words, reasoning, and reality will haunt rhetoric, power, and religion in the coming centuries.

Beyond the theological issues, however, Gorgias's position also presents some ethical tensions, as we have suggested. These are fairly clear when we return to the consideration of *justice* as the name of a conclusion that emerges from a negotiated transaction. Under these assumptions, the only logical deduction is that our own ideas of justice are merely a passing fad of recent negotiations, neither better nor worse than those that have come before us or those that will come after us. Tomorrow, we (or others with more power) can renegotiate and arrive at different conclusions. Slavery will, perhaps, become good again. When that happens, we cannot object that the outcome is, in some way, *wrong*.[66]

We ourselves, of course, happen to think slavery and sexual assault are unjust. But by calling them *unjust* we can only mean that, within the community most of us inhabit, we have presently drawn the conclusion that such things are undesirable. If another few years pass, if power shifts into other hands, if different ideas of justice win political or cultural debates, then slavery or sexual assault or the public torture of religious, political, or ethnic groups might very well fit the new definition of what is *just*. And there is no moral or logical objection we can raise to the new definition; we can only say that we ourselves, personally, happen to prefer a different outcome. The only possible meaning of the word *good* or *just* in Gorgias's approach is that we *like*, we *want* that outcome. When we say a thing is *unjust* or *bad*, our words only mean that we, personally, do not like it. In the end, it is hard to see how this equivocation (where *good* means *I like, want*) would not pragmatically reduce all claims of civic, religious, and moral duties to a niche of extremely private transactions and a set of tribalized preferences among like-minded souls.

Standing before the worst moments of Modernism (the slave trade, the Trail of Tears, fascism, the Gulag), one has no way to say, simply, "this is unjust" and actually mean anything besides "this is not to *my* taste, but of course others might like it just fine." Given the sad course of human action in the last few centuries, that seems a rather tepid reply, as if lynching fell into the same category as whether one likes James Cameron movies.

One reading of Plato's *Gorgias* implies that these views were, perhaps, not Gorgias's specific perspectives, but rather the logical outcome of applying Gorgias's pedagogy. We, fittingly perhaps, cannot know with certainty whether Plato's portrait is accurate, but it seems probable that Gorgias is a man whose ultimate goal is to develop savvy characters who weave a network of words in order to provide the greatest possible leeway to act while maintaining the least possible window for being acted upon. His sense of that skill

---

[66] Gorgias here merely reflects the fairly common sophistic views. Thrasymachus defines justice as "whatever is considered advantageous by the stronger." Callicles says, "Might makes right." Critias, anticipating Nietzsche by two millennia, argues that religion is a fiction invented by weaker souls to control stronger people. A discussion of the sources and implications of these sophistic views can be found in N. G. L. Hammond, *A History of Greece to 322 BC*, 3rd ed. (Oxford: Oxford University Press, 1986), 420–36.

was probably a blend, perhaps never clearly defined, of the communal as well as the personal. His world of *caveat auditor* is a place of knowing, powerful people playing a high-stakes game for the limited resources that create material security for the state as well as for specific citizens.

Regardless of whether he was accurately describing Gorgias's motives or philosophically implying that Gorgias's educational approach would inevitably lead to moral chaos, Plato was the enemy of such a view. He was hardly the only dissenting voice, however. Some of Gorgias's own students and associates may have found his arguments too amorphous and amoral, perhaps. One of those former students, Isocrates, would go on to more or less invent what we today think of as a liberal arts education, and, like Plato, he would labor to sever rhetoric from the consequences of Gorgias's vision of education. Isocrates championed a vision of rhetoric that radically minimized the personal aspects of rhetorical power. For Isocrates, rhetoric was always and almost exclusively a public commodity.

Chapter 4

Isocrates: Words as the Wall of the State

GORGIAS AND OTHER SOPHISTS MAY have viewed words as a luxury commodity, unbound by any ultimate reality but unquestionably marketable. They may have had no view of morality or divinity beyond a sort of calculated self-interest. But theirs was not the only view in town. The Greek educator Isocrates certainly had a higher goal and a richer sense of sacred destiny for *logos*.

Education in Interesting Times

Isocrates lived in interesting times, in the worst possible sense of the phrase. He was born to a wealthy family who made flutes. His first years passed under the glow of what is called The Athenian Golden Age. The Parthenon had been completed only a few years earlier. Artistry, craftsmanship, and politics were at a zenith in the city. The famous statesman Pericles ruled over a wealthy and expanding Athenian power base and regional empire. But Isocrates is unlikely to have held many warm memories of those glowing days. When he was about five, tensions with Sparta broke into open conflict and the Peloponnesian War began.[1] And then, things got worse.

A plague hit Athens, killing perhaps a third of the people within the city walls—many of them refugees who had fled to the city from the outlying countryside during a Spartan invasion of the area. Thucydides, an eyewitness and survivor of the plague, describes horrifying scenes as bodies piled up in the streets and temple courts, entire households perished, and social order within the city frayed almost to the breaking

---

[1] This war between the Athenian and Spartan empires began in the summer of 431 BC. Thucydides provides an eye-witness account of the conflict. For contemporary histories of the period, see J. B. Bury, *A History of Greece to the Death of Alexander* (New York: St. Martin's, 1967), 390–513; N. G. L. Hammond, *A History of Greece to 322 BC*, 3rd ed. (Oxford: Oxford University Press, 1986), 345–436; also Peter Krentz, *The Thirty at Athens* (Ithaca, NY: Cornell University Press, 1982).

point.[2] Pericles died in the plague. In the years of war that followed, his leadership was missed. Athens won some victories, but also took some painful losses. After a decade of fighting, with Sparta and Athens in a rough stalemate, a treaty known as the Peace of Nicias was negotiated in 421 BC. Isocrates would have been about fifteen years old when the treaty was signed. In the years of relative peace that followed, his parents provided him the best education money could buy, and the young Isocrates may (or may not) have become a student of Gorgias. Whatever the particulars, his education served him well, and there is little doubt about Gorgias's influence in Isocrates's work.[3]

The peace treaty with Sparta was supposed to expire after fifty years. It made it to seven. In 413 BC, the war resumed in earnest and would continue for yet another decade. This time, Athens suffered even greater losses. In 404 BC, after several crushing defeats, some of which may have involved treason, the civic order in Athens collapsed entirely and the polis surrendered. And once again, things got worse. Sparta installed a brutal oligarchic council known as The Thirty, and they promptly began rounding up and executing anyone who had either democratic sympathies or a great deal of wealth that could be confiscated for the use of the members of the ruling council. The Thirty were shortly overthrown, but not before another one in five Athenians had been executed and their land confiscated.

Given the cruelty, suffering, and unstable social environment he had grown up in, it takes no advanced training in psychology to understand how Isocrates and several of his contemporaries—Plato comes easily to mind—might have turned their attention to larger questions about the purpose and meaning of life. Both thinkers, but especially Isocrates, are rooted in an unshakable sense of the uncertain and tenuous nature of the world, and both of them are occupied with questions about what constitutes a trustworthy foundation for one's life, a reliable model for understanding the conflicted panoply of human horror and beauty.

---

[2] Thucydides describes the plague in II.47–54 of his *History of the Peloponnesian War*, trans. C. F. Smith, Loeb Classical Library 108 (Cambridge, MA: Harvard University Press, 1919).

[3] Whether a formal student or not—and contemporary scholarship is divided on the idea—some substantive connection between the two appears consistently across a good variety of our ancient sources. See, e.g., Yun Lee Too, *The Rhetoric of Identity in Isocrates: Text, Power, Pedagogy* (Cambridge, UK: Cambridge University Press, 2009), 235–39. Too dedicates a full appendix to the question of Isocrates's relation to Gorgias. Whatever the formal connection might be, Gorgias is both an influence and a foil for Isocrates.

There is, of course, a certain peril in spending your life wondering what the purpose of life is. There is, of course, an equal peril in not spending your life that way. Evidently, life is just perilous. But if we posed the questions, "What is the purpose of life? What gives life meaning and makes it secure and worthwhile?" to a representative sample of Gorgias's students, there is every indication that many of them would have replied, "Power, wealth, prestige, pleasure. These are the goals of the sophisticated man of the world, who knows what's what. If you know how to speak and spin, this will increase access to power, prestige, and wealth. These are the things that allow one to act as one will without being acted upon against one's will." The core mechanism of that world view is, of course, sophistic rhetoric: the smooth spin of words to influence others' perceptions in order to obtain your desires without overpaying for your pleasures.

Whatever else Isocrates took from Gorgias, he rejected this privatized moral frame and chose to situate rhetoric within a larger vista. Isocrates offers a vision—it is far too vague to call it a plan—of a united imperialistic Greece. His rhetoric was an attempt to inspire confidence in this vision of unity and purpose. This Panhellenic federation would restore the moral, intellectual, and military vibrancy of the scattered and feuding *poleis*. Once united, they would invade and conquer Persia, the long-standing enemy of Greece. How he developed this dream and how he called for its implementation would sharpen the definition of rhetoric and help change the course of education down through at least the early twentieth century of Europe and the Americas.

As Athens collapsed, near the end of the Peloponnesian war, Isocrates fled the city and remained abroad for two years. When he returned, after the overthrow of The Thirty, the family had lost its wealth and Isocrates had to find a job and earn his own way as Athens, also, tried to rebuild some of its glory.

It was during these years that Isocrates seems to have become a speech writer, but he believed this work was beneath his dignity, by all accounts, and denied any involvement with that occupation in his later years—despite robust evidence to the contrary. In the end, he found his own path in the world of education, and he marked that world with his own unique vision and style.

Isocrates never directly entered into the maelstrom of politics. His voice would not project well, an essential skill for any orator before the days of microphones and amplifiers, and he seems to have suffered some measure of anxiety as well. Whether he would have wanted to be a politician—and the words *politician* and *politics* must be read quite cautiously in this context— remains unclear, but his vocal shortcomings kept him from actively participating in the rounds of political office.[4] They did not, however, prevent him from working well with smaller groups, and his general perspective, honed as a teacher, became one of the cornerstones of education for generations of Greek, Roman, and, later, Renaissance and Enlightenment statesmen. The sophists had been mobile educators, moving from place to place in order (at least in part, it seems) to refresh their clientele, avoid paying taxes, and keep their political options open. In a clear challenge to these motives and perspectives, Isocrates established a new model: he built a permanent, stationary school of higher education in Athens in 391 BC focused on his theories of statecraft. Now in his mid-forties, he published a series of written speeches across Greece and, rather than travel to his students, students came to Athens to study with him.[5] Of course, he drew heavily from the local population as well. Twenty-one written speeches from all across his long career as a teacher have survived. Nine private letters have also survived, and together these give us a fairly consistent image of his ideas, though there are certainly gaps.

Isocrates understood himself to be retooling the old educational tradition of polishing the high quality (that is, aristocratic) soul so that its character shone more brightly, producing a man of excellent speech and wise action.[6] In ancient times, Isocrates notes, the greatest and most famous

---

[4] See Too, *The Rhetoric of Identity*, 29–35. Too rightly complicates the terminology, citing a number of scholars and lines of reason that would urge us to proceed with caution when we think of *politicians* or *politics* in the ancient world. It is a mistake to "backread" our own vision into Isocrates's idea of politics. His view is one which incorporates the aesthetic, communal, and mytho-poetic under the idea of *the political*. This complication should be held in mind throughout the present chapter, and as often as stylistically reasonable, this chapter will refer to *statecraft* in reference to Isocrates's views.

[5] The importance of this transition—from speaking to writing—in Isocrates is a central focus of Too, *The Rhetoric of Identity*, and is also an important aspect in Ekaterina V. Haskins, *Logos and Power in Isocrates and Aristotle* (Columbia: University of South Carolina Press, 2004), 110, and Nathan Crick, *Rhetoric and Power* (Columbia: University of South Carolina Press, 2018), Ch. 5.

[6] Kathleen Welch suggests, rather, that Isocrates believed almost any person could be educated, and, despite his misogyny, racism, and imperialism, serves as a proto-post-modern thinker who subverts cultural norms and broadens categories of aptitude. See her *Electric Rhetoric* (London, UK: MIT Press, 1999), 29–98, especially 50–55. The bulk of scholars, however, continue to see Isocrates as a conservative cultural elitist rather than an instructor intent on subversion of normative constructions. See Michael Leff,

orators were exactly those who brought the greatest good to the city. He sought to duplicate this gift of good to the state: "Those who give most study to the art of words are the best of the statesmen," he observes.[7] And with that as his frame, he set out to teach *logos* so that his students might be among "the best of the statesmen."

By Isocrates's lights, education had slipped a little too close to showmanship and entertainment and a little too far from the archaic past's glorious goal of *aretē* in speech and act. It was time to swing the pendulum back toward that higher glory, but Isocrates sets out to do so while remaining keenly aware of the specifically current challenges and circumstances. His school was neither a nostalgic caricature nor a simplistic continuation of a past tradition. As James Collins notes, "Isocrates attempts to cast the net widely enough to ensnare many conceptions of education and cultivation . . . from the most traditional to the latest sophistic trend."[8] This synthesis of past and present education proved a stunning success in producing stellar students of a specific type, and his graduates are a virtual who's who of famous Greek statesmen and orators in this era.

More than is Dreamt of in your Philosophy, Isocrates

Isocrates's students did not study to understand the workings of the mind nor to unpack the nuances of abstractions. That was not Isocrates's interest. He repeatedly heaps scorn on those who waste their time focusing on abstract ideas rather than on concrete policies. Like Gorgias, Isocrates values practical outcomes; abstract ruminations are, if interesting at all, a distant second. Like Gorgias, Isocrates embraces contingent understanding and limited perspective for every citizen: nobody can know The Truth, and pursuit of The Truth is a squandering of ability. Like Gorgias, Isocrates does

---

"Isocrates, Tradition, and the Rhetorical Version of Civic Education," in *Isocrates and Civic Education*, ed. David Depew and Takis Poulakos, 235–54 (Austin: University of Texas Press, 2004), 236–37.

[7] Isocrates, *Antidosis*, in Norlin, *Isocrates*, 2:231. Throughout, I lean on the text and translations of Isocrates in the readily accessible Loeb Classical Library's three volumes of his work; George Norlin, trans., *Isocrates*, vols. 1–2, Loeb Classical Library 209, 229 (Cambridge, MA: Harvard University Press, 1961, 1992, respectively), and La Rue Van Hook, trans., *Isocrates*, vol. 3, Loeb Classical Library 373 (Cambridge, MA: Harvard University Press, 1945). Welch offers some justified criticism of Norlin's limited handling of the word *logos* in the first volume. See her *Electric Rhetoric*, 45–46.

[8] James Collins, *Exhortations to Philosophy* (Oxford: Oxford University Press, 2015), 175.

not believe that nobility in speech and act can be taught to just anyone. Those who have inherited high-quality souls, however, can be nurtured, inspired, trained, and directed in how to seize the proper moment and make the proper rhetorical moves within a specific situation.[9]

Unlike Gorgias, however, Isocrates is less infatuated with the title of *sophist*, which was beginning to wear thin in his day as the reputations of the sophists came under increasing criticism.[10] Isocrates distances himself from that set of teachers and, while he does not completely reject the title of *sophist*, he announces that he is, in fact, a *philosopher*. What Isocrates means by this term requires some consideration.

In *To Demonicus*, Isocrates identifies himself as one who directs and corrects students of philosophy, and he notes that his philosophical education takes students beyond mere training in oratory. Rather, his philosophy would counsel them in the way to establish their reputations as persons of sound character. Indeed, his education decidedly improves the moral conduct of the student, he says, and such improvement is "the most vital part of philosophy."[11] The statement is a full-throated repudiation of the self-interested rhetoric that seems to have been associated with Gorgias's teaching. Education as a scheme of moral improvement remained a consistent emphasis throughout Isocrates's career. But such a scheme of moral improvement must not be thought of as some individualistic journey toward a better self. For Isocrates, the term *philosophy* embraced the whole scope of formation, the moral formation of the person and, by extension, statecraft.[12] This moral formation of his students, in other words, is con-

---

[9] This ability to discern and seize such fulcrum moments was the heart of *kairos* in Classical rhetoric. See Charles Marsh, "Millenia of Discord: The Controversial Educational Program of Isocrates," *Theory and Research in Education* 8, no. 3 (2010): 289–303, and especially Phillip Sipiora and James S. Baumlin, *Rhetoric and Kairos: Essays in History, Theory, and Praxis* (Albany: SUNY Press, 2002). For Isocrates, this discernment and seizing of the opportune moment was done by certain elite, gifted souls so they could more powerfully shape policy and public sentiment through their character and wisdom. *Kairos* was for Isocrates, as it was for Gorgias, one of the absolutely essential qualities of rhetorical practice. See *Against the Sophists*, in Norlin, *Isocrates*, 2:13. On the need for inherent talent wedded with self-discipline and quality formation, see, e.g., *Against the Sophists*, 14–18; *Antidosis*, 199–201, 207–14.

[10] Isocrates's own *Against the Sophists* lays out a host of what must have been fairly standard criticisms about the group.

[11] Isocrates, *To Demonicus*, in Norlin, *Isocrates*, 1:3–5. Similar points are made in his *Panathenaicus*, in Norlin, *Isocrates*, 2:87, and *Antidosis*, 270, 284.

[12] See Collins, *Exhortations to Philosophy*, 175.

substantial with an even larger project: the bettering of the polis. The logic, on the face of it, seems irrefutable. Since the art of statecraft is essentially people making common cause with one another, it follows that people with better moral character (moral character always includes *practical wisdom* for Isocrates) make better citizens and that these better citizens will make a better commonwealth, one with richer ethical reserves, greater moral capital, deeper aesthetic expressions, and the most insightful practical policies.

If, as Ekaterina Haskins drily observes, "Gorgias does not advocate linguistic temperance,"[13] it is also true, as George Norlin notes, that "Isocrates took from Gorgias a [rhetorical] style which was extremely artificial and made it artistic."[14] What Isocrates accomplished by subduing Gorgias's style he also attempted with Gorgias's worldview by anchoring a critique of rhetoric to the larger good of the state. Eloquence was not, in Isocrates's mind, a skill to obtain private wealth, personal pleasure, and individual power. Eloquence was set the much higher task of building the commonwealth of the polis, the physical security of the community, and the moral authority of the best citizens. All this was to be done through the development of sound public policy while simultaneously contributing to that development. Elevated from service to an individual so that it might be the servant of the community, rhetoric—the heart of aristocratic education—found itself laboring under a specifically Isocratic form of pragmatic *noblesse oblige*. Isocratic philosophy was not about the contemplation of truth, beauty, and goodness, and it was uninterested in puzzling out the relationship between language and reality. Furthermore, it saw even less point—absolutely no point—in questioning what *reality* meant. (That was obvious: reality was whatever set of political conditions was pressing in upon the polis and demanding action.) Philosophic rhetoric could be distinguished from sophistic performance by its concern with practical policy outcomes for the community members and the polis as a whole. These outcomes emerged from the insightful discourse of the educated morally mature elites. Education in true philosophy consisted of "those studies which will enable us to govern wisely both our own households and the commonwealth—which should be the objects of our toil, of our study, and of our every act," Isocrates notes.[15]

---

[13] Haskins, *Logos and Power in Isocrates and Aristotle*, 110.

[14] Norlin, *Isocrates*, 1:xvi.

[15] Isocrates, *Antidosis*, 285. The reference to both households and the commonwealth echo Protagoras's description of his wares in Plato's *Protagoras* 318a–b, as we saw above.

In Isocrates's mind, philosophy was education in noble living. It embraced the rhetorical and the social (which, in Greece, always included the religious), and these contributed to—and coalesced in—the formation of the pragmatic, elite, civic soul: a decent aristocratic citizen who was properly pious (in the Pagan sense of the word), savvy, patriotic, and culturally well-rounded. As Kathleen Welch observes, *philosophia*, in Isocrates's view, is the type of reflection that moves someone toward sound practical judgments made about both personal and, crucially, public matters.[16] In short, Isocrates saw training in *logos* as the key process for polishing a noble soul, but he also saw *logos* anchored to something larger than self-interest: it was linked to the whole community. With its unifying religious cults, with its normative assumptions about how things should be, with its interwoven networks of barter, public offices, courts, trade apprenticeships, and social clubs, with its shared sufferings and celebrations, the community of the polis ranked above the personal, private interests of any one citizen, and the *common*wealth was always to be preferred to private profit.

The study of rhetoric made for better nobles. Better nobles made better decisions. Better decisions made for a better polis. Rhetoric was the primary tool of statecraft, and the communion found in the state was the highest good.[17]

Wisdom as the Practice of Practical Pragmatics

But if the good of the state, rooted in wise choices, is the trademark of Isocrates's vision, that vision necessitates a certain practical definition of what it means to be wise. Here, too, Isocrates is remarkably consistent across his long career. In the letter addressed to Polycrates and known by the title *Busiris*, Isocrates praises a mythical king of Egypt named Busiris for his *phronēsis*, that is, his *prudence* or *practical wisdom*.[18] The oration within the letter, almost certainly one of his earliest writings after establishing his school, is a show piece lauding the Egyptian king in a way that highlights Isocrates's championed qualities of leadership. Isocrates himself considered the piece of little worth, but the letter is notable for, if nothing else, the

---

[16] Welch, *Electric Rhetoric*, 38. See also Norlin, *Isocrates*, 1:xiii.

[17] For a larger discussion of Isocrates's vision "to harmonize individual and collective purposes," see John Poulakos, "Early Changes in Rhetorical Practice and Understanding," *Revue de critique et de theorie litteraire* 8 (1989): 312.

[18] Isocrates, *Busiris*, in Van Hook, *Isocrates*, 3:21.

way it frames Busiris's wisdom.[19] The king's prudence is identified with his policies that, for all practical purposes, establish checks and balances on the privileges of specific groups so that each is led to contribute more deeply to the community as part of its own self-interest.

Priests, for example, were ensured an affluent lifestyle by their payments deducted from the sacrifices. But this wealth did not lead them into idleness and decadence because Busiris rigorously enforced the demands of ritual purity. Ritual purity kept the priests from overindulgence, but it also enhanced their reputation for piety and demonstrated their zeal for the divine rituals; this helped make the people ready to offer the sacrifices, thus ensuring the priests' comfortable lifestyle. By enforcing the ritual purity laws, Busiris supports the priests' wealth while simultaneously keeping them from excess and linking their own successes to the larger community.

In a similar way, older men were wisely entrusted with important elements of decision-making in Busiris's reign while younger men, under Busiris's encouragement and wise guidance, gave themselves to those studies that were (notably) useful but also "conducive to the highest attainment of virtue."[20] Encouraged to postpone pleasures, live virtuously, and embrace hard studies, these students were later rewarded with the prestige of being in charge of important matters.

Because of such balances, according to Isocrates's rather idealistic presentation, the Egyptian priests excelled in medical knowledge and the people of Egypt were the healthiest and longest-lived on earth. The praise here is quick and formulaic, but clear enough to show what Isocrates, near the beginning of his career as an educator, considered to be the backbone of wisdom: prudent policy leading to stability, social interdependence, and community benefits. We also see that prudence must be grounded not only in pragmatic reflection but also in virtue, since vice and self-interest would inevitably erode the community's social order. In fact, the very next section of the oration praises Busiris for inspiring in the Egyptians an enhanced piety and devout worship of the gods. Such piety made the people reflect on the gods' knowledge of their secret actions. A fear of divine retribution, while not exactly congruent with real life, leads the common soul to more virtuous living; encouraging fear of divine retribution is another mark of the king's wisdom, according to Isocrates.[21]

---

[19] For his dismissal of the piece, see his introductory remarks in *Busiris*, 9.

[20] Isocrates, *Busiris*, 23.

[21] Isocrates, *Busiris*, 24–27. See also 30–33.

About thirty years later, in the *Antidosis*, Isocrates reemphasized both his practical definition of wisdom and its important connection to virtue, asserting that only those with the "powers to arrive generally at the best course" of action could be considered to possess *phronēsis*. Those who offered such sound advice were real philosophers, and real philosophy was whatever studies led to practical policy proposals. Those who toyed with abstractions like the *Good* or the *Truth* lacked wisdom and could not be considered genuine philosophers.[22] Isocrates's teachings were "more profitable" for the polis than instruction from teachers who engaged in disputations about the sort of "virtue and wisdom which is ignored by the rest of the world and disputed among themselves."[23] Set against such lofty and impractical academic endeavors is Isocrates's sort of practical excellence, recognized by everyone. He also emphasizes, in the bluntest terms, the need for moral excellence, asserting that "virtue and justice" were the ends upon which all his writing focused and toward which all his writing urged the reader.[24] It is worth noting his somewhat peculiar stance of championing the pragmatic move toward justice and moral good while demeaning those who investigate the source and nature of justice and moral goodness. Isocrates himself never rectified that tension; he never seemed to think such reconciliation necessary.

After an additional fifteen years, Isocrates's position is still unaltered. In the *Panathenaicus*, written in the year before his death, he once more equates the wisest of the city with those who focus on statecraft and give the best counsel in policy questions, and he also notes that these were the citizens who had "lived the noblest lives."[25] Prudent policy and a quality character were the crown jewels of education. A wise life was one consistent with the *nomos*, that is, a life shaped by and conforming to the customs and laws of the city.[26] It is worth hearing the summary in Isocrates's own words, frequently quoted:

---

[22] Isocrates, *Antidosis*, 271.

[23] Isocrates, *Antidosis*, 84. The barb is almost certainly aimed at Plato and his portrayal of Socrates.

[24] Isocrates, *Antidosis*, 67. Norlin translates Isocrates's verb here—*sunteinousin*—with the understated, "All my writings *tend toward* virtue and justice." The term could easily be read as strikingly more adamant than that: *strive for* or *urge upon one*.

[25] Isocrates, *Panathenaicus*, 143.

[26] See Susan Jarratt's *Rereading the Sophists: Classical Rhetoric Refigured* (Carbondale: Southern Illinois University Press, 1991), 41–49 for one précis on the development of the complicated term *nomos*.

Whom, then, do I call educated, since I exclude the arts and sciences and specialties?[27] First, those who manage well the circumstances which they encounter day by day, and who possess a judgement which is accurate in meeting occasions as they arise and rarely [miss] the expedient course of action; next, those who are decent and honourable in their intercourse with all with whom they associate, tolerating easily and good-naturedly what is unpleasant or offensive in others and being themselves as agreeable and reasonable to their associates as it is possible to be; furthermore, those who hold their pleasures always under control and are not unduly overcome by their misfortunes, bearing up under them bravely and in a manner worthy of our common nature; finally, and most important of all, those who are not spoiled by successes and do not desert their true selves and become arrogant, but hold their ground steadfastly as intelligent men, not rejoicing in the good things which have come to them through chance rather than in those which through their own nature and intelligence are theirs from their birth. Those who have a character which is in accord, not with one of these things, but with all of them—these, I contend, are wise and complete men, possessed of all the virtues.[28]

A citizen is wise who consistently exercises good judgment in all circumstances, who is properly sociable and sophisticated (not ostentatious and showy) in his interactions, who conducts his affairs with self-control and without making a scene, and who is given to clear-headed perspectives about his own talents, as well. That is, of course, a tall order. But at the end of his career, Isocrates has shown himself strikingly consistent in his view that moral improvement is the core of rhetorical education and that rhetorical education is the source of community greatness.

Wanted: Gods, Part-time Only, Flexible Hours

Religion in ancient Greece was, recall, an intimate and inescapable aspect of community life, interwoven in the cults, clubs, and careers of every citizen of

---

[27] Isocrates thinks of astronomy, geometry, and so forth as fine things to occupy young minds and keep them from idle trouble, but not, in the end, of much value in terms of being good and prudent.

[28] Isocrates, *Panathenaicus*, 30–32.

every polis. But in the expansion of scholarly texts on Isocrates in the last half century or so (generally setting Isocrates's views in a more nuanced light), his religious perspectives are notable for their general absence. Isocrates approaches the gods, however much they permeated social order, with a notably adaptable mindset, and in this he reflects the early sophist Protagoras, who seems to have valued *mythos* and the public rituals as a vibrant cultural adhesive, but who was notably agnostic toward the gods themselves, and he was emotionally indifferent toward the divine as a whole, it seems. Isocrates's religious views, which Norlin describes as "rationalism in religion combined with acquiescence in the forms of worship," occasionally read like a clear anticipation of Marx, with the obvious exception that Isocrates seems to have robustly approved of what Marx robustly condemns: the idea that simple people are kept in line by believing the divine powers will quite efficiently reward and punish them for their deeds.[29] And if such views are "made to appear more certain than they prove to be" in our lived experiences, this is, as we have seen, an acceptable social illusion for Isocrates, since it ensures that our lives in community are civilized and "not altogether like wild beasts."[30] And, as an added bonus, such religious views (particularly when encoded into law) develop in the masses a habit of obedience that is necessary for an ordered common life.[31] Religion civilizes; it coheres the polis.[32] This reality is the only religious truth that falls within Isocrates's concern. Like rhetoric, religion is a servant to the state's power, assisting in the creation of the cooperative community—and that cooperative community is the highest goal toward which a human life may aspire.[33]

In addition to inspiring virtue and obedience in the masses, religion has other things to offer. Religion also provides a source of social authority

---

[29] Norlin, *Isocrates*, 1:xviii.

[30] Isocrates, *Busiris*, 24–25.

[31] Isocrates, *Busiris*, 24–27.

[32] Religion is not the only mortar in social cohesion, of course. See Takis Poulakos, *Speaking for the Polis: Isocrates' Rhetorical Education* (Columbia: University of South Carolina, 1997), especially Ch. 2, where Poulakos is arguing that rhetoric is what coheres the state in Isocrates. But rhetoric as a cohesive element is always rhetoric *about something*. It never acts in isolation as an abstract principle. For an alternative view of the Isocratic need for social cohesion, see James Muir, *The Legacy of Isocrates and a Platonic Alternative* (New York: Routledge, 2020), especially Ch. 2. Religion may not be the only aspect of social cohesion, but it is clearly one of the most powerful.

[33] The perspectives and tensions are hardly foreign to the present. See Ryan Gillespie, "Religion and the Postsecular Public Sphere," *Quarterly Journal of Speech* 102, no. 2 (2016): 194–207 for a contemporary review of these themes in some pertinent literature.

for the aristocratic leader. In *Busiris*, Isocrates claims that Pythagoras visited the Egyptian king and that while in Egypt he became "a student of their religion, and was the first to bring the Greeks all philosophy."[34] Philosophy and religion work together. They are, notably, co-teachers in the formation of the soul. But remember that philosophy for Isocrates is about pragmatic governance. Isocrates immediately follows this comment about the kinship of philosophy and religion with an observation that emphasizes his own practical view of philosophy, even in a religious context. Pythagoras, inspired by the religious devotion of the Egyptians, "seriously interested himself in sacrifices and ceremonial purity." But, with an unexplained insight into Pythagoras's real motives, Isocrates informs us that this was done because Pythagoras "believed that even if he should gain thereby no greater reward from the gods, among men, at any rate, his reputation would be greatly enhanced." And, as Isocrates pointedly notes, "that indeed happened to him."[35] Keeping the religious rites is simply a mark of civic wisdom because it enhances one's credibility with the citizens of the polis.

"Do honour to the divine power at all times but especially on occasions of public worship," Isocrates counsels Demonicus, and even more bluntly, "for thus you will have the reputation both of sacrificing to the gods and of being true to the customs."[36] Religious observance as practical advice to a political leader is hardly a surprising recommendation coming

---

[34] Isocrates, *Busiris*, 28.

[35] Isocrates, *Busiris*, 28–29. Pythagoras is thought to have founded a secretive ascetic and mystical community in southern Italy late in the sixth century BC, which seems somewhat incongruent with Isocrates's assessment of his motives. But it is also intriguing that while certainly admired, Pythagoras was also frequently mocked, like Socrates, so Isocrates's comment in *Busiris* is somewhat puzzling, given that it suggests unambiguous admiration. While *Busiris* is hardly known for its nuance, there is another possible explanation for this glossing over of Pythagoras's complex reputation. Perhaps Isocrates is specifically targeting a younger Plato, slyly suggesting that Plato has been taken in by more radical Pythagoreans. The real Pythagoras, Isocrates may be implying, was someone whose view of the divine was more natural and less mystical than what Plato thought it was. Reframing, and thus taming, the mystical so that it becomes natural is hardly an uncommon act in religious history. This admittedly speculative interpretation, however, stretches the chronology of Plato and Isocrates's rivalry a bit, though not incredulously. See William Benoit, "Isocrates and Plato on Rhetoric and Rhetorical Education," *Rhetoric Society Quarterly* 21, no. 1 (1991): 60–71.

[36] Isocrates, *To Demonicus*, 13. Norlin translates the last phrase, *kai tois nomois emmenein*, as "abiding by the laws," but given the religious context, *customs* or even *traditions* seems the better rendition of *tois nomois*, though established law, ancient custom, and religious rites are intimately intertwined in Greece.

from Isocrates. Nor is this view some isolated and idiosyncratic sliver of ancient Greek statecraft. No doubt any number of presidents and prime ministers from the last few centuries have attended Christian churches across Europe and America for exactly the reasons Isocrates recommends. The pragmatism of the old Greek schoolmaster reaches even unto the heavens.

Given his remarks, it is safe to say that Isocrates's view of religion as a whole is markedly uninspired and shows none of the passions found in, for example, Plato's portrayals of Socrates, whose life and discourses are permeated by pointed prayers, intense invocations, and deeply personal concerns about his interactions with and responsibilities toward the divine realm. For Plato, such responsibility outranked adherence to the community, as we shall see. But Isocrates saw religious preoccupation as an inversion of priorities. What built the state was good; what did not build the state was not good. And Plato and Socrates were, according to Isocrates, extremists, philosophically and religiously.

The closest, in fact, that Isocrates comes to anything like a heartfelt engagement with religious perspectives is, notably, found in a stunning passage from the *Panegyricus*. This oration was written at what may have been the very nadir of political life in Greece, about twenty-five years after the end of the Peloponnesian War. Sparta, the victor, had proved so much a tyrant in success that the hometown of the heroic Leonidas had squandered all goodwill among the Greek states, and a recent treaty had actually made the hated king of Persia—so long resisted by Greek warriors at Ionia, at Marathon, at Thermopylae (where Leonidas fell), at Salamis, at Plataea—the official and final enforcer of several disputes between Greek poleis, effectively establishing Sparta as a proxy ruler backed by Persian military power.[37] Against this backdrop, Isocrates pleads passionately for a return to an older order where Athens would unite and lead the Greek

---

[37] The Peace of Antalcidas, or The King's Peace, as the treaty was known, was negotiated more than a century after the Ionian uprisings which had led, eventually, to the Battle of Marathon. The Persians planned to avenge their defeat at Marathon with the full-scale invasion of Greece a decade later. This invasion led to the famous battles at Thermopylae, Salamis, and Plataea. The first, though technically a loss for Greece, birthed a tale of Greek courage and heroism that rallied the whole of Greece and is repeated to this day. The latter two were thorough defeats for the Persians. Salamis decimated the invading Persian navy; Plataea destroyed what was left of the invading Persian army. What the Persians lost militarily in these battles, however, they gained diplomatically some ninety years later, many Greeks believed, through the Peace of Antalcidas, which was negotiated largely by Sparta to help keep order in the Greek states that were increasingly resisting Spartan rule after the Peloponnesian War.

states against the Persians. In making his case, he waxes (somewhat, and yet even here, very pragmatically) pious.

Near the beginning of the piece, Isocrates is justifying Athenian leadership over a federation of all the Greek poleis partly on the grounds that "two gifts, the greatest in the world" were given to all the Greeks by Athens.[38] The first was agriculture, "which enabled us to rise above the life of the beasts." The second was "the holy rite which inspires in those who partake of it sweeter hopes regarding both the end of life and all eternity." The allusion here is to the Eleusinian Mysteries, a religious cult that is, second only to the Oracle at Delphi perhaps, the most famous religious ritual in all of Greece, at least by name.[39] Its actual rites were kept in solemn secrecy by the initiates. What we know is that the cult focused on the agricultural myth of the seasons of fruitfulness and celebrated Persephone's return to the earth (in spring) to bring a fecund season of growth. Like the gift of agriculture, the Eleusinian Mysteries were, according to Isocrates, shared with the whole of Greece by Athens, since Athens was so "beloved of the gods but also so devoted to mankind" that the polis served the whole of Greece. Athens is the exemplar of those who choose the greater good.

What is notable is that Isocrates opens this discussion by observing that, although the story "has taken the form of a myth, yet it deserves to be told again." Indeed, though the story is ancient, this in and of itself makes it "worthy of our trust."[40] The clear point is that the claim—*Athens civilized Greece*—is supported in part by the cultural cohesion that results from its telling, and the long history of Greece proves its cohesive power. The various Greek poleis regularly gave Athens a sacrifice of their first-fruits in thanksgiving for the gift of agriculture received from the Athenians, thus binding the whole of Greece together (under Athenian leadership, naturally). These ancient customs were further supported by oracles from Delphi. And in closing this line of appeal, Isocrates hits upon a sudden strikingly optional formulation: "Whom, then, must we think the most likely either

---

[38] For the relevant passages here, see Isocrates, *Panegyricus*, in Norlin, *Isocrates*, 1:28–33.

[39] For one foundational work on the topic, see George Emmanuel Mylonas, *Eleusis and the Eleusinian Mysteries* (Princeton: Princeton University Press, 1961).

[40] Isocrates, *Panagyricus*, 30. Norlin translates *pista* as "worthy of our *faith*." But despite the religious context—or perhaps because of that context—the word *faith* becomes somewhat misleading here. *Pistos* means *trustworthy, worth confidence*. It is the adjectival form of *pistis*, which will come, in the later Christian texts, to be translated as *faith, confidence, conviction*. In our own day, *faith* is most frequently a religious term, but in Isocrates's time the word had no specifically religious flavor.

to have received this better life as a gift from the gods or to have hit upon it through their own search?"[41] Maybe it was the gods. Maybe it was the Athenians themselves.

The whole tradition, including the powerful mythic tale, is worthy of trust and confidence (*pista*). But suddenly, and in a passing phrase, we discover that you can quite easily and completely reject the religious aspect of the tale and still keep what is important about it.[42] That Athens was the first to master the art of agriculture in Greece, and that Athens had taught the other Greeks this skill is confirmed by ancient tradition. (Well, and oracle too, if you wish.) But the gods are not the important thing here. Embrace that part of the *mythos* if you wish, but even if you do not, the ancient traditions which cohere vast, distant regions of Greece still point to Athens as the giver of agriculture, and these traditions, ancient in nature, prove that this trust in Athens was well placed; such trust has built, for generations, a coherent culture. And that is worthy of leadership. But what if (perhaps especially if) these great civilizing feats of farming skills and Eleusinian religious mysteries were not exactly divine but simply worked out by the efforts of those mortals in Athens? Well, that, too would surely indicate that the Athenians were, of all the Greeks, the ones "endowed with the greatest capacity for the arts" and that "no one could find a reward great enough to match the magnitude" of a polis capable of such feats.[43]

Of course, alternatively, maybe these gifts really were given to Athenians by the gods, in which case Athens is clearly seen to be, of all the Greeks "the most devoted in the worship of the gods" and exactly the same conclusion must be drawn: no reward would be sufficient for what the Athenian devotion to the gods has won for greater Greece.[44] Leadership belonged to Athens by right; whether that right was divine or human mattered little.

This passage, arguably the most intensely religious moment in all of Isocrates's writings, presents the divine as a means to an end. There is nothing in these words to suggest the faintest wisp of intimacy, or even intellectual engagement, with the divine, even if we—at something of a stretch—accept his comments on eternal life as a sincere expression of his own views. Those remarks pale in the context of this passage. And more so

---

[41] Isocrates, *Panegyricus*, 32.

[42] This sounds suspiciously similar to the attitude Plato will excoriate in *Phaedrus* 229c–230a.

[43] Isocrates, *Panegyricus*, 33.

[44] Isocrates, *Panegyricus*, 33.

when this passage is seen in the context of Isocrates's broader views. The religious, in Isocrates, is simply a robust but practical tool in the building and ordering of community life.

But if religion is a domesticated creature kept in a small cage within Isocrates's menagerie, there is parallel creature whose power is being expanded.

Wanted: Rhetoricians, Full-time, With Benefits

As we have seen in texts above, Isocrates broadened the study of rhetoric to include the whole of reasoned, considered life. The idea of rhetoric "is both the outward and the inward thought: it is not merely the form of expression, but reason, feeling, and imagination as well."[45] To study how language worked was to braid the moral, the aesthetic, and the state into a network of sense-making and purpose, all with a very different scope and focal point than what is found in the narrower view of the sophists. In this way, Isocrates laid the foundation for what would come to be considered for centuries a liberal arts education: the informing of the soul by acquaintance with the best of high culture and the best of deep human reflection. And if the idea of "deep reflection" came over time to embrace fewer practical considerations than Isocrates would have liked, that was frequently a circumstantial adaptation to later views about statecraft and spiritual sensitivities.[46] But under the ideal of rhetorical education, Isocrates gathers a refreshing and, even in the twenty-first century, a recognizable view of human agency, uniting both the personal and the political in a single frame of a nuanced, reflective internalization of core ideals about ethics, power, influence, perspective, and performance.

---

[45] Norlin, *Isocrates*, 1:xxiii.

[46] Under the Imperial vision of Rome or Byzantium or under the feudal organization of western Europe in the Mediaeval era, the pragmatics of political debate were naturally curtailed, given the absence of legislative forums. Curtailed, yes, but perhaps rhetoric was somewhat less dramatically curtailed than we often assume. Imperial Rome, Byzantium, and Medieval Europe lacked the technologies to become a modern police state, and local day-to-day affairs were often left with local political bodies who had quite some leeway, albeit with some Imperial boundaries, of course. And even these limitations will, pragmatically, almost evaporate in the late Imperial era when Christian definitions (that will reframe the entire Roman identity) become entrenched in everything from literary debates to Imperial edicts to café shouting matches to team rivalries in chariot races.

Education was about infusing the student's soul with cultural values, ethical sensitivity, and aesthetic vision. All of these were assumed to lead to wiser choices, the performance of a better, more noble life. Isocrates's definition of a *better life* was, however, left undefined—probably under the assumption that *better life* simply meant the cultural milieu of the *Zeitgeist*.[47] While Isocrates expands the view of rhetorical education, he did not argue about the definition of terms like *justice* or *goodness* or *the good life*. He was willing to leave such definitions to be worked out by the elite members of the community in each given situation; these educated elites would discern the most relevant circumstances and recommend the most prudent actions.[48] But discern *relevance* and recommend *actions* according to what end, what purpose? Clearly not their own self-interest because education had formed within them a heightened morality, had given them a broader perspective, had made them *better men* (always: *men*) who sought the greater good. Individual interests would obviously not guide their recommendations. The interest of the state would. In Isocrates, as James Muir notes, "the normative intentions of education are deduced from an external and lexically prior political doctrine."[49] And this suits everyone, naturally enough, who embraces this "prior political doctrine." But, with the perspective of the last few centuries—perhaps with a perspective reaching no further than the last few decades—attentive readers could be forgiven for feeling a bit uneasy about this prescription for improving their lives through education. Sometimes community consensus fails to inspire confidence. There is a thin line between community consensus, a mob, and the propagandized *doxosophos* of either unregulated corporate monopolies or a totalitarian dream-state.[50]

In the end, the Isocratic view emerges as somewhat naïve. No doubt the full scheme is robustly appealing either when living in a thoroughly homogenous culture with a well-established tradition of conformity or when people *like us* are writing the texts that defined *the good* in that "prior political doctrine." But the appeal of such a scheme becomes far more tenuous

---

[47] This is one of Aristotle's chief criticisms of Isocrates, and one of the things he sets out to remedy.

[48] See Michael Leff's discussion on certain contemporary attitudes toward Isocrates in "Isocrates, Tradition," 236–37.

[49] Muir, *The Legacy of Isocrates*, 56.

[50] The Greek *doxosophos* implied an individual with pseudo-wise convictions that were popular, insubstantial, and unreflective, but expressed in resonant sloganeering. The term is used deridingly by Plato in, e.g., *Phaedrus* 275b and *Philebus* 49a–d. In both of these examples, the term is likely intended as a criticism of Isocrates.

when there is an absence of powerful homogenic cultural consensus or when *Other People* with very *other* ideas get their hands on the power to define what *justice* means within our community today.

There are far too many, far too recent, far too easily available examples of communities, corporations, and political parties arriving at horrifying definitions of what is *just* or *good* to suggest much contemporary confidence in such an Isocratic model. Isocrates, believing that some souls—aristocratic souls—were simply made of better stuff than the rest of us, seems to have thought these better souls would be somewhat unlikely to make many serious moral mistakes, if taught properly. But a closer examination of Isocrates's pedagogy reveals that *taught properly* means schooled in conforming to the homogenous traditions and customs of an idealized political order, a pedagogical principle that does nothing to comfort our concerns and might do much to enflame them.

In a certain Isocratic irony, Isocrates has been read through rather heterogeneous contemporary lenses. David Depew and Takis Poulakos note two different approaches to Isocrates that are symptomatic of contemporary perspectives on his work. Victor Vitanza, they observe, interprets Isocrates's writing as a narrowing of vision leading to "the paradigmatic gesture of all imperialistic impulses" that is finally and perhaps most fully "actualized in Nazi Germany."[51] By way of contrast, Kathleen Welch interprets Isocrates's writings as a broadening vision that is "a paradigmatic critique of formalistic education and an anticipatory gesture toward post-Marxist notions of critical pedagogy."[52] But, pragmatically, what Vitanza and Welch offer, in the end, are not mutually exclusive critiques. The tribalisms of post-Marxist pedagogy can certainly lend themselves rather tidily to exactly that paradigmatic arc of vague absolutism that ends in the divinization of ideology and the banal practicalities of totalitarianism—just like in fascism. And if Vitanza draws a more direct line, Welch's Isocrates should concern us no less, given our history of watching whole groups acquiesce with disturbing speed and comfort to enforced orthodoxies of cruelty, periodic lynching, and genocide, both well-planned and spasmodic.

[51] David Depew and Takis Poulakos, *Isocrates and Civic Education* (Austin: University of Texas Press, 2004), 4. They are summarizing Chapter 3 of Vitanza's *Negation, Subjectivity, and the History of Rhetoric* (Albany: SUNY Press, 1996). In that chapter, Vitanza also cites the American ideal of Manifest Destiny, leading to the Trail of Tears and a legion of other atrocities, along with the rise of the Third Reich, as examples of Isocratean rhetorical performance.

[52] Depew and Poulakos, *Isocrates and Civic Education*, 4.

In other words, leaving the definition of a *good life* or *justice* to be worked out by community standards seems rather arbitrary, morally, as if the NAACP and the Ku Klux Klan of the 1920s were equally viable social options—which, arguably, they were. But something in the gut suggests they were certainly not equally *good* social options.

Both community standards and ideology are, in other words, ambiguous and not very helpful when one community has decided upon standards of behavior that are blatantly immoral. In order to fend off the moral ambiguity present in community standards, one may reply that some moral positions are, in fact, inherently more worthy of being taught in our educational system: the Klan is morally *wrong*, for example, and their repugnant views have no acceptable place in our pedagogy. But this looks suspiciously like the endorsement of a universal moral norm indifferent to community consensus and superior to it. But such universal moral hierarchies are to post-Marxist critical theory what Mentos are to Diet Coca-Cola.[53] In the end, it is only possible to argue that immoral actions sanctioned by a community are, actually, *immoral* (as opposed to being merely *undesirable under the rubrics of my preferred community standards*) by either stepping outside of critical theory in order to fix upon some source or standard of moral judgment that rises above community consensus or by covertly smuggling some absolutist norm into one's critical theory. Either there are normative moral positions that are independent from and impervious to community conclusions or the accusation that some community's actions are immoral (even though they are politically legitimate) is nothing more than propaganda.[54] *Lynching is autonomously wrong, regardless of its legal status*; if this is not a true statement, then all reasons to stop lynchings are

---

[53] Though Horkheimer argues that Critical Theory must be normative, the debate over how this recommendation is to be understood and applied by contemporary Critical Theory is not settled, and both Marxist pedagogy and Critical Theory in general can lend themselves to an unmaking of norms, per se. See Max Horkheimer, "Traditional and Critical Theory," in *Critical Theory: Selected Essays*, trans. Matthew J. O'Connell (New York: Continuum, 1973); Amy Allen, *The End of Progress* (New York: Columbia University Press, 2017); and Peter McLaren and Nathalia Eugenia Jaramillo, "Not Neo-Marxist, Not Post-Marxist, Not Marxian, Not Autonomist Marxism: Reflections on a Revolutionary (Marxist) Critical Pedagogy," *Cultural Studies ⟷ Critical Methodologies* 10 (2010): 251–62.

[54] Plato will, of course, forward a form of this solution, presenting moral frames as fundamentally and robustly ontological, existing independently of anyone's speech or thought. This leaves him with the problem of how human beings might explore such (literally, supernatural) realities, but it does offer one solution to Isocrates's dilemma here.

merely propagandistic power plays by some anti-lynching faction with no more *moral* standing than those they seek to undermine.

Alternatively, one might try to sidestep such a conclusion about the necessity of external moral standards by appealing to a better internal moral standard. Perhaps one can avoid both the ironic error of critical theory's absolutism and the march toward nationalistic imperialism by assuming that, of course, *The New Group* will naturally be better stewards of real power than *The Old Group* was. "We have come so far. We have progressed so much. We would never be like they were." But such reasoning excretes a camouflaged colonialism that is as repugnant to critical theory as universal morals. Isocrates notwithstanding, there seems no reliable (or even miniscule) historic evidence that one set of humans is inherently more moral than another and therefore inherently more capable of wielding power over others. It appears difficult to seriously recontextualize Isocrates's wholistic system without his prop of moral elitism appearing somewhere in the process, either externally in a sense of autonomous, superior moral norms or internally in the assumption of superior human souls and intellects (usually, like *us*). These elitist assumptions were the crucial bedrock of Isocrates's educational philosophy. Arguably, they remain present in many specific attempts to rehabilitate Isocrates as an educator for our time.

Welch's *Electric Rhetoric* embraces Isocratic community-centered, non-logical rhetoric as a normative structure for the emerging hypermediated world. This embrace is rooted in a view that some norms support racist, misogynistic, and imperialistic actions, and that subverting these particular cultural norms will cause such errors to wither. The goal is unambiguously and unironically laudable. But most of the criticism above applies directly to Welch's project. She fixes on no moral frame independent of community consensus via discourse, but she wishes "to self-consciously link language with power and action. . . . The beginning of that power and action lies in the production of discourse."[55] And students should, as a central part of their education, be provided "more opportunities for the production of discourse and training in how to make it more effective."[56] Welch seems to assume, as a matter of course, that students will use this power to support her own agenda

---

[55] Welch, *Electric Rhetoric*, 97.
[56] Welch, *Electric Rhetoric*, 98.

of addressing the erasure of women in history, contemporary racist visions, and the nationalist imperialism of the nineteenth and twentieth centuries.[57]

What if they don't?

And, much more to the point, why *should* they? What is it that makes Welch's view the *better* moral choice?

Without some assumption of elitist hierarchy—exterior to the system in some superior moral frame or interior to the system within the rhetor's elite superior soul—there is no reason that the call to produce more discourse along with the training "to make it more effective" under the Isocratic model could not serve oppressors as well as it serves liberators. The pressing questions are how to identify good rhetoric from merely powerful rhetoric, and is there a difference? Welch seems to relegate the answer to her own community's standards. But there is no reason that the power of the Isocratic system could not be focused on outcomes Welch (and many others, hopefully) would find repugnant—such as national imperialism. Certainly, for Isocrates, the final arbiter of all norms and the power of his elegant system were united in exactly such a nationalistic imperialism.

But perhaps that can be overlooked. Ekaterina Haskins, also championing Isocrates, acknowledges that his rhetorical vision is "complicated—if not tarnished—by the nationalism" present in it.[58] However, there is no need, per se, to throw out the baby of such an elegant rhetorical system with the bathwater of national imperialism, she argues. Critics have too easily taken this dark side of Isocratic nationalism as "a transcendental principle and not a series of statements crafted in response to a historical situation." The better Isocratic touchstone, according to Haskins, would be the "culturally sensitive, pragmatically oriented, and aesthetically influential" rhetorical performance that marks the elegance of his adaptable, powerful,

---

[57] That misogyny, racism, and imperialism are exactly the failings of the rhetor she is championing as a model of productive, effective discourse rooted in power is not lost on her, and she works to unveil, and thus disarm, the power of such broken views. The power of Isocrates's system will be taken up, but the racist and misogynistic blindnesses of Isocrates will be left behind and his nationalistic imperialism will be ignored, in Welch's revival. But this is a dangerous game. Unveiling a thing disarms its power only for those who share an already agreed upon hierarchy of values. That Welch assumes these values as common, and almost inevitable, is a mark of the era in which she was writing. See, e.g., *Electric Rhetoric*, 76–80 and 87–91.

[58] Ekaterina V. Haskins, "Logos and Power in Sophistical and Isocratean Rhetoric," in *Isocrates and Civic Education*, ed. Takis Poulakos and David Depew, 84-103 (Austin: University of Texas Press, 2004), 102.

responsive rhetorical system.[59] She champions this Isocratic rhetoric over other options because the Isocratic model is "a more socially productive approach to rhetoric" than what can be found in Aristotle alone, though "socially productive" is a notably amoral frame serving all ideologies—the racist as well as the antiracist—equally, and so we hear echoes of Welch.[60] And thus we seem to be back where we started.

Haskins's approach sounds, once more, suspiciously like a claim that either (a) we contemporary types are morally superior to the Greeks, and as morally superior people, we would never fall into their primitive uglinesses, such as national imperialism or (b) national imperialism could be, in the right circumstances, just fine.

The first option, however, seems to depend on that idea of a superior *internal* moral standard, which we have seen before. Haskins, like Welch, relies too heavily on Isocrates's assumption that there is, after all, a certain group of morally elite humans (surprise! it is *us*!) who will *properly* exercise power over others without those others needing to worry or even think much about it. We have already noted the absence of historical evidence for this position. But the option under (b) above is not particularly comforting either. It ties rhetorical morality to circumstantial victories, and as we have seen, this begs a legion of questions: Under what circumstances is national imperialism right? Under what conditions is lynching good? When is it permissible to deny a job to someone based on their race? Their religion? When is a human being permitted to lay claim to human rights? When are they not?

Haskins is emphatically not, of course, arguing directly for a rhetoric that could justify imperialism and other injustices, even in the hands of a rhetorical victory of one extremist party. Had the Klan won the culture wars of the American 1910s and 1920s, lynching, today, might be called a good thing, but it would not *be* a good thing. I suspect Haskins—and Welch—might agree with that assessment, even while championing Isocrates's rhetorical vision.[61] Both Haskins and Welch wrote in a more liberally optimistic time, when the need to justify such *prima facie* truths as

---

[59] Haskins, 'Logos and Power,' 102.

[60] Haskins, *Logos and Power in Isocrates and Aristotle*, 3.

[61] The assumptions of Welch's position—not Welch herself, of course—leaves less wiggle-room on this question. It is unclear how the view in *Electric Rhetoric* would extricate itself from this difficulty.

the immorality of lynching was unthinkable. But times have changed. They always do. That is the point.

Sincerely, Isocrates

Isocrates sought to produce statesmen of excellent rhetorical skill and public virtue. He sought to bring under the canopy of rhetorical education a synthesis and collaborative formation of both the soul and the social order, of the conscience and the polis. He saw in rhetorical education both a depth and a breadth that had escaped the earlier sophists. But he also sought to unify all of Greece under a banner of imperialism. Within his lifetime, he failed.

Isocrates maintained what might be seen as a hopeful sense of idealism through a long and tragic life. He believed in the old aristocratic way of shaping a soul so that it would become a better citizen with a broader, more encompassing, view. He acknowledged a complexity at the heart of the real world, but he never seemed overwhelmed by that complexity. A justified despair never materialized. In short, he was an absolutely committed patriot who believed in his country, perhaps more deeply than anyone else in his time. His sincere idealism led to remarkable achievements. The failure of his system in his own day should cast no blemish on that system. Its successes in later days might, if Vitanza is correct. But what Isocrates did achieve in his day was a rhetoric with an emphasis on power, moral authority rooted in community norms and traditions, and performative force. The strength of that perspective, and Plato's inversion of it, shaped education, defined rhetoric, and developed religious understandings and insights in ways that still cast shadows on our own culture, politics, religious views, and university life.

Isocrates was hardly the only citizen of Athens laying claim to the rising title of *philosopher*, of course. Plato also had a school of philosophy, and in it, he sought for exactly those absolute standards that Isocrates happily glossed over. What these two schools of philosophy had in common was their rejection of both the handbook tradition and the sophistic tradition of rhetoric. They both rejected the handbook tradition because it did nothing to actually form the soul—the crucial concern of philosophy. They both rejected the sophistic tradition because it formed the soul in the wrong way: as a self-interested, self-centered individual. But as thoroughly as these two schools of philosophy rejected both the handbooks and the sophistic crowds, they also rejected each other. Isocrates saw Plato as a notoriously pie-in-the-sky sort of character who was too clever by half, who did nothing to build the community, and who squandered himself in bothersome questions about abstract irrelevant pettiness. Plato saw Isocrates as an amoral (at best) sophist-writ-large with wasted potential and the depth of a puddle. But Plato's views need to be laid out a bit more clearly before considering this mutually acerbic critique in greater depth.

Chapter 5

Plato: Words as a Stairway to Heaven

THERE ARE PROBABLY MORE COMMENTATORS on Plato than there are readers of Plato. A simple internet inquiry for *Plato* in any of the standard search engines will supply ample evidence of the thesis. That said, there is no denying that Plato is challenging. He is complex, ambiguous, sarcastic, perfectly willing to live with tensions, and always *Other* to our contemporary sensibilities. He covers an enormous scope of topics, and, fittingly, there are a wide range of legitimate approaches, assumptions, and understandings of Plato's writings. Competing interpretations go back almost to Plato's own day, and any search for the final authoritative reading of Plato is doomed; certainly, this book makes no such heady pretense. But just because there are many valid readings of Plato, it hardly follows that every reading of Plato is valid. In the next two chapters, we want to grasp some of the fundamental basics of his views on rhetoric, education, and religion with a fair measure of confidence. We can then set these in comparison with both Gorgias and Isocrates in order, finally, to glance at the relevance of those views within our own era. The beginning of that task, however, is to set aside some clearly silly assumptions.

Plato Refuses to Dance with Descartes

Plato is more or less the archetypical philosopher in the contemporary mind, popularly associated with strict logic and metaphysical Truth with a capital T, while at the same time serving as "the father of Western rationalism," as E. R. Dodds refers to Plato, somewhat tongue-in-cheek.[1] Among contemporary scholars studying communication, Plato is widely assumed to have resisted the very idea of rhetoric because he valued a stale, finalized, absolute knowledge rather than the endlessly exciting sophistic sense of contingency, reinvention, and uncertainty which were championed by less up-tight thinkers. Such a portrait is familiar, easy to summarize, and wrong.

---

[1] E. R. Dodds, *The Greeks and the Irrational* (Berkeley: University of California Press, 1973), 64.

This popular image of Plato is hard to maintain when one turns from nineteenth and early twentieth century commentaries on Plato and picks up Plato himself, where one encounters very little certainty about anything at all. Indeed, in his *Letter VII*, Plato specifically disavows the possibility of knowing the deepest aspects of his philosophical insight.[2] Even at his most confident—arguably in the *Euthyphro*, where Socrates meets a young man bringing capital charges against his own father—Socrates remains qualified and contingent about his own judgment. In other writings, Plato is, by turns, angrily prophetic, intensely pious, comfortably bawdy, and frequently witty to the point of laugh-out-loud funny. He is a consistently complex, complicated, nuanced, and religious person. It is only under the pressure of changes in the Enlightenment view of education and the emerging Modernist philosophy of scientism (with its conviction that the results of the scientific methodology alone can properly justify human choices and beliefs) that Plato and his Socrates are turned into the sort of philosophers who champion absolute knowledge and logical certainty.[3]

Modernism is a fluid concept, and use of the title varies from field to field, so a small digression to define my own use will avoid unnecessary confusion. The term here and in later chapters references that period in which the loose confederation of ideals that make up the Enlightenment became stewards of a certain cultural orthopraxis in which human rationality, with a measure of autonomy foreign to most other eras of history, embraced itself as a final authority on human matters. Under these self-referential rubrics, it set itself the task of reshaping its social and physical environment. James Watt's 1776 steam engine is as handy a place as any to draw the line between the Enlightenment and Modernism, if one feels the need to draw such lines. The year is convenient because this device marks a significant transition in the growing domination of the *material* world

---

[2] Plato, *Epistle VII*, trans. Glen R. Morrow, in *Plato: Complete Works*, ed. John M. Cooper (Indianapolis, IN: Hackett, 1997), 341c. The letter may or may not be authentic; scholarship is divided. Even if spurious, the letter is universally acknowledged as ancient, and at a minimum it reflects the fact that, very close to his own day, Plato's works were understood in a way that does not reflect the popular contemporary image.

[3] The relationship between the Socrates of history, Plato, and the Socrates of Plato's writings is a vexing scholarly question. See Mark McPherran, *The Religion of Socrates* (University Park: Pennsylvania State University Press, 1999), 12–19, for one quick overview. I treat Plato's writings as expressions of his own convictions—with plentiful irony, dramatic staging, and crafted sarcasm, of course—without worrying overmuch about whether he is attempting at any particular moment to portray Socrates accurately or attempting to use the character of Socrates as a device to express views uniquely his own.

by human rationality, will, and craft. That same year, the largest *political* application of Enlightenment thought began with the Declaration of Independence by Great Britain's North American colonies, opening that strange cultural experiment, the United States, the end of which remains shrouded in darkness. These two events form a tidy if (as always) somewhat arbitrary boundary.[4]

The transition from perceiving Plato as a profound religious thinker (his reputation before the Enlightenment) to portraying him as an Enlightened rationalist was already well underway by the opening of the eighteenth century, and this new Enlightened (and then very *Modern*) Plato was designed to serve a specific political philosophy and colonial perspective.[5] Numerous texts in the late Enlightenment and early Modern age— Anthony Collins's *A Discourse of Free-Thinking*, John Gilbert Cooper's *The Life of Socrates*, and William Wotton's *Reflections on Ancient and Modern Learning* are fairly exemplary—reduce Plato to a more or less current peer of the authors.[6] The Modernist (and contemporary!) caricatures of Plato are not, of course, without some touchstone in reality, but they are far from nuanced or complete; in many ways, they mimic the criticism heaped upon Plato's portrayal of the sophists.

Plato is a philosopher, and certainly his philosophy concerns, among other matters, what he calls *epistēmē*, which is translated *knowledge*. But we must be careful not to turn Platonic *knowing* into something that imitates the contemporary post-Enlightenment ability to engage in data-retrieval or the contemporary vision of certainty rooted in the scientific method. Julia Annas succinctly notes that "Plato's search for knowledge

---

[4] Drawing the end of Modernism is an even messier task than sorting out its opening. Arguably, Modernism is a spent ideal by the end of World War I, though it might be stretched to the close of World War II. The cultural turmoil of the 1960s certainly reveals the popular embrace of perspectives that doggedly and dogmatically poke their fingers in the eye of Modernism.

[5] For a sense of the Modern and colonial uses of this secularized Plato, see my "From Here to Eternity: The Scope of Misreading Plato's Religion," in *Communication and the Global Landscape of Faith*, ed. Adrienne E. Hacker Daniels, 13–26 (New York: Lexington, 2016). Also, John J. Jasso, "Sympathy for the Devil: The Myth of Plato as the Enemy of Rhetoric," *Rhetorica* 37, no. 4 (2019): 351–81, provides a well-documented critique of the Modernist view of Plato as a rationalist thinker.

[6] See Anthony Collins, *A Discourse of Free-Thinking* (London: printed by Cornelius Crownfield of Cambridge University Press, 1713); John Gilbert Cooper, *The Life of Socrates* (London: printed for R. Dodsley at Tully's Head in Pall-Mall, 1750); and William Wotton, *Reflections on Ancient and Modern Learning* (London: printed by J. Leake for Peter Buck, 1698).

is not the post-Cartesian search for a state immune to sceptical doubt. Rather it is a search for understanding."[7] Plato is fairly clear about what he means by the word *knowledge*, and it is messier—and more tolerant of the messiness—than our truncated contemporary views often allow. Plato contextualizes *knowing* as a confident, foundational aspect of a philosophical pursuit that bluntly aims at understanding what matters, gaining religious insight, and living piously. In fact, the broad main claim of the next two chapters is that Plato, at least after the middle period of his work, includes a supernatural and divine facet as a necessary but not sufficient aspect in defining human reason.

In the *Republic*, Plato tells the story of a soldier named Er who has a near death experience.[8] The tale, notably, concludes the *Republic* and echoes its opening question about the source and definition of *justice*: whether it is best understood as a negotiated social construct by those in power or whether it has some fixed and substantial quality, independent of and indifferent to social opinion. In the dialogue, Er revives just before being burned on his funeral pyre and reports his vision of the afterlife. That vision is intriguing on several fronts, but at present the story interests us because it captures the very summit of what Plato claims to be about. The afterlife, according to the vision reported by Plato, is one where each soul is judged according to its choices in life. Those who were unjust in life are given a thousand years of troubling and arduous labor. They trek through the darkest bowels of the earth, suffering greatly and witnessing even greater suffering, and they return at last to their starting place. But the just souls travel lightly for their thousand-year journey, passing through the glory of the heavens in the presence of inconceivable beauty and goodness. They, too, after a thousand years return to the starting point where the two companies—both the unjust and the just—are united in a banquet. After the feast and rest, they prepare for their next life on earth, and each soul is given at that moment a chance to choose what life they will lead in their next birth. Some choose wisely, others choose poorly.

This choice, Plato warns, is the most perilous moment a soul can face:

> And because of this each of us must *neglect all other subjects* and
> be most concerned to seek out and learn those things that will
> enable him to distinguish the good life from the bad and always

---

[7] Julia Annas, *An Introduction to Plato's "Republic"* (Oxford: Clarendon, 1981), 212.

[8] Plato, *Republic*, trans. G. M. A. Grube and C. D. C. Reeve, in *Plato: Complete Works*, ed. John M. Cooper (Indianapolis, IN: Hackett, 1997), X.614–21.

to make the best choice possible in every situation. . . . And from all this he will be able, by considering the nature of the soul, to reason out which life is better and which worse and to choose accordingly, calling a life worse if it leads the soul to become more unjust, better if it leads the soul to become more just, and ignoring everything else. We have seen that this is the best way to choose, whether in life or death.[9]

There is no mincing of words here: there exists, we are told bluntly, a disciplined study which leads to wise choices in life and after death, and which must be pursued *to the neglect of all other studies*. That highest study to which all else must be sacrificed is philosophy, as Plato clearly states in the next passage: "if someone pursues philosophy in a sound manner when he comes to live here on earth . . . it looks as though not only will he be happy here, but his journey from here to there [*the afterlife*] and back again won't be along the rough underground path, but along the smooth heavenly one."[10] This is plain, unironic, religious talk. Gregory Vlastos brings the point home bluntly, saying we must face "a fact about Socrates which has been so embarrassing to modern readers that a long line of Platonic scholarship has sought . . . to explain it away: Socrates's acceptance of the supernatural."[11] A spiritual Socrates was difficult for Modernists to accept since philosophy, for most of them, came to mean the autonomous act of calculated rationality set loose upon a reality consubstantial with nature: a world of logical structures and material reactions without reference to spirits, gods, or miracles; one in which wonder is limited to questions of mere scale or complexity, but never offered to a transcendent (and in the later monotheistic traditions, personal) *Being-Outside-the-World*. Thus, when contemporary atheists or agnostics who lean toward materialism discuss the idea of wonder, they invariably talk about unimaginable material distances or material structures of unimaginable intricacy.[12] On the other hand, Postmodernist schools of thought reject a religious Socrates because the nature of religion establishes hierarchical claims

---

[9] Plato, *Republic* X.618c–e, emphasis added.

[10] Plato, *Republic* X.619c–e.

[11] Gregory Vlastos, *Socrates: Ironist and Moral Philosopher* (Ithaca, NY: Cornell University Press, 1991), 158.

[12] Examples of the former include the *Cosmos* television series (both Carl Sagan's and Neil deGrasse Tyson's); for examples of the latter, see Richard Dawkins, *The God Delusion* (New York: Houghton Mifflin, 2008), 31–50; or Sam Harris, *Making Sense* (New York: Ecco, 2020), 95–156, among others. For an excellent recent critique of the various contemporary blends of science, wonder, philosophy, and religion see the article by Ryan

of ontology and morality that limit individual agency and radical autonomy. But the religious element in Plato is, in the end, inescapable. Philosophy, for Plato, was the discipline of preparing one's eternal soul for encounters with an ultimate, divine reality that had its native being outside of nature, a foreigner to time and space. It was preparation for making the most important spiritual and metaphysical choices.

The observation is hardly original. Prior to the seventeenth century, Plato was routinely seen as a religious thinker and consistently (though, of course, not exclusively) viewed through his theological positions. The philosopher Proclus published his masterpiece, *Platonic Theology*, around the year 480 on the Christian calendar, and the work is widely viewed as one of the most substantive texts on pagan religious thought that has survived.[13] Almost exactly a thousand years after Proclus, we find the religious association with Plato is still very much intact. In 1482, Marsilio Ficino published his own masterpiece, outlining Platonic theological perspectives on immortality and emphasizing their superiority over Aristotelian theological views for the Christian thinker.[14] The consumption of Plato's religious perspectives by Enlightenment rationalism began in the century following Ficino and continued apace through at least the end of the nineteenth century. As Modernism began to fail, however, Plato's religious views began to come back into focus. Besides Vlastos, other contemporary scholars such as A. E. Taylor, Paul Elmer More, E. R. Dobbs, Thomas Brickhouse with Nicholas Smith, Pierre Hadot, Mark McPherran, Josef Pieper, Paul Ricoeur, Andrea Nightingale, and Vilius Bartninkas, to name just a few, have (with various emphases and drawing not always the same conclusions about its depth and worth) rediscovered and reemphasized Plato's religious vision and its identification with philosophy.[15]

While Socrates is unambiguously portrayed by Plato as a person guided by human reason, the portraits we have also show a person equally open to divine communication. For Socrates—and certainly for Plato—these two were not mutually exclusive.[16] Whatever Plato and his Socrates meant

---

Gillespie, "Cosmic Meaning, Awe, and Absurdity in the Secular Age: A Critique of Religious Non-Theism," *Harvard Theological Review* 111, no. 4 (2018): 461–87.

[13] See E. R. Dodds, *The Elements of Theology* (Oxford: Clarendon Press, 1933).

[14] Marsilio Ficino, *Theologia Platonica de immortalitate animorum* (Paris, 1482).

[15] The authors named cover more than a century of Platonic scholarship from 1911 through 2023. See the bibliography for references to each.

[16] Vlastos, *Socrates: Ironist*, 157, 171.

by "reason," they did not mean a process limited to a description of physical reality or a Modernist vision of human intellect performing calculations independent of those beings outside of nature.

If Gorgias found the divine too vapid or veiled to be worth his time, and if Isocrates found the divine to be an uninspiring but pragmatically useful aspect of social cohesion, Plato had a different view. Plato is (perhaps somewhat annoyingly) religious. Plato wants you to pray with him and ask Philosophia into your heart. He is looking for soul-serious converts from the shallow cosmology of Gorgias as well as from the mere perfunctory civic religion of Isocrates. The divine deserves to be taken more seriously than either of these allow, and when you come to confront the divine, according to Plato, you discover an orderly transcendent reality that makes justified demands on your intellect, will, and memory. Surprisingly, understanding the power and perimeter of language is a key to such religious insight and interior-formation.

The emphasis on language should not be a major surprise; Plato wrote in dialogues, after all, and if you were drawing up a template on how to start a decent Platonic dialogue, it would likely begin with people sitting around chatting about pretty mundane things like how much the last election sucked and who has a crush on whom, and what everyone's workout routine looks like these days.[17] This would go on a bit until Socrates says something like, "Ah! So then, the real issue is X. What does that word X mean, do you suppose?" And whether that X is being fair, or wanting sex, or setting the right economic priorities, or tending to our health, the conversation soon discovers that we are usually talking about things we do not understand very well. Or at all. And our ignorance, once named and examined and described in excruciating intricacy by Socrates, becomes a door through which we might, if we wish, glimpse other options. And almost inevitably, those other options are part of a divine realm of being and a more richly religious way of living.

Plato's stylistic choice of the dialogue means his presentations, unlike those of Gorgias and Isocrates, are not always so obviously thematic

---

[17] We sometimes forget that Plato was a decorated "wrestler" (Greek wrestling was a vibrant blend of fisticuffs and grappling) who competed in regional games that were rather like the Olympics, and who was known for his athletic prowess. The philosopher's actual name was Aristocles, and "Plato" is, in fact, a nickname ("Big Man") given to him because of his robust physique, according to Diogenes Laertius's *Lives of Eminent Philosophers*, trans. R. D. Hicks, Loeb Classical Library 185 (Cambridge, MA: Harvard University Press, 1925), III.4.

and transparently structured; they frequently meander (often enough into dead ends) in imitation of an unscripted conversation. It follows that pertinent comments often require a more intricate contextual review in order to be most fully understood. Thus, for the present text to engage in a broad sweeping survey (as suited Gorgias and Isocrates), picking up comments here and there, is perhaps less practical, even when trying to keep the discussion narrowed to the topics of education and religion within Plato's rhetorical frames. What can be done more profitably, perhaps, is to focus intensely on a narrower scope of his writing. In the remainder of this chapter and all of the next, we will be looking closely at two of Plato's more famous dialogues that are especially powerful examples of glimpsing divine things—justice itself and beauty itself—through the way we use our language. Those dialogues are the *Gorgias* and *Phaedrus*. The former takes on and critiques the vision of education and rhetoric that Plato attributes to Gorgias's educational perspective. The latter presents a discussion of rhetorical powers and limits that seems more specifically aimed at the great educator Isocrates—who is mentioned by name only in the closing of the dialogue.[18] We will look at each of these pieces before returning to a broader discussion of Plato's vision of words and the divine.

So, What Are You, Exactly?
A Reply to Sophistic Education

The focus of *The Gorgias* is captured in one particular bit of advice Socrates gives to his disciple Chaerephon. The two arrive at Callicles's house just after Gorgias, now an elderly man, has delivered some riveting demonstration speech. Callicles notes, rather wryly, the timing of Socrates's arrival and points out that Socrates and Chaerephon have missed Gorgias's display. Socrates offers polite excuses but states clearly that he is not interested in hearing one of Gorgias speeches, though he would be happy to hold a

---

[18] These two dialogues provide a crucial, but of course partial, view of Plato's ideas of language and rhetoric. For more extensive commentary, see Paolo Crivelli, "Plato's Philosophy of Language," in *The Oxford Handbook of Plato*, ed. Gail Fine, 481–506 (Oxford: Oxford University Press, 2023); Robin Reams, *Seeming and Being in Plato's Rhetorical Theory* (Chicago: University of Chicago Press, 2018), especially Ch. 6; and Raphael Demos, "Plato's Philosophy of Language," *The Journal of Philosophy* 61, no. 20 (1964): 595–610. For a broader collection of cuttings from Plato on the topic of language, along with a brief introduction, see Jean Nienkamp, *Plato on Rhetoric and Language* (Mahwah, NJ: Hermagoras, 1999).

conversation with Gorgias, if the elderly gentleman were willing to answer some questions about "what his craft can accomplish and what it is that he both makes claims about and teaches."[19] Callicles assures Socrates and Chaerephon that Gorgias would be happy to do so.

Socrates, suddenly delighted, declares this an excellent bit of news and, turning to his companion Chaerephon, blurts out, "Ask him, Chaerephon." This imperative seems to reference a perfectly obvious question, but if so, Chaerephon has missed it and (speaking for the reader, as well, perhaps) replies, "Ask him what?"

"What he is," Socrates instructs.[20]

Plato has moved immediately from what Gorgias "makes claims about and teaches" to what Gorgias himself *is*. The identification reflects an aspect of education we have already emphasized: learning is a process of inner formation, of internalizing lessons so that we ourselves become something different than we would have been without such education. In Socrates's questions, we meet the corollary assumption: what we teach comes out of who we are. We are what we study; we teach from what we are. This view of education will show up repeatedly in the discussion of what rhetoric is and what kind of person a student of rhetoric becomes.

Chaerephon, with one minor nudge, grasps the significance of Socrates's question and boldly moves ahead. We can note two things from this. First, Socrates sends his own student forward and seems to be confident in him. Second, Gorgias's student Polus is not sent forward, but intervenes in the opening of the conversation and inserts himself into the exchange. That difference is telling, hinting at the place ambition will play in this dialogue (a theme that will return in the *Phaedrus*). Chaerephon's opening demonstrates that he clearly understands the line of reasoning behind Socrates's question, and he brings Polus to tip his hand in short

---

[19] Plato, *Gorgias* 447c. I rely (unless otherwise noted) on Donald J. Zeyl's translation in *Plato: Complete Works*, ed. John B. Cooper (Indianapolis, IN: Hackett, 1997), though I routinely consult Robin Waterfield, *"Gorgias": A New Translation* (Oxford: Oxford University Press, 2008), as well as the Loeb Classical Library text and translation, no. 166, by W. R. M. Lamb (Cambridge, MA, Harvard University Press, 2001).

[20] Socrates asks a very similar question about another great sophist in *Protagoras* 311b–e. In that passage, too, the emphasis is on how education shapes the interior life, in this case with an emphasis upon who the student will become—what identity they will take on once they have studied wordsmithing with the sophist.

order—which Socrates quickly points out to Gorgias; clearly Chaerephon is the superior student.[21]

To see the significance of Socrates's opening question in the dialogue, we can observe his description of what he, himself, *is*:

> And what kind of man am I? One of those who would be pleased to be refuted if I say anything untrue and who would be pleased to refute anyone who says anything untrue; one who, however, wouldn't be any less pleased to be refuted than to refute. For I count being refuted a greater good, insofar as it is a greater good for oneself to be delivered from the worst thing there is than to deliver someone else from it. I don't suppose there's anything quite so bad for a person as having false belief about the things we're discussing right now.[22]

The last sentence is notable and echoes the cautions we have heard in the Myth of Er about setting correct priorities in our disciplined studies. Those things that Socrates says "we're discussing right now" are clear enough: the discussion is about how language, conviction, and interior formation are related to justice.[23]

The Gorgias divides comfortably into three major parts, depending on who Socrates is (for the most part) interacting with. The first section brings Gorgias himself to the front of the discussion, the second section has Socrates interacting with Polus, and the final division brings Callicles into the debate. These characters are hardly allegorical, but each has a coherent narrative perspective.

The caricature of Gorgias in the dialogue is a stand-in for a certain sophistic view of education and language, though the historical Gorgias is perhaps recognizable in the portrait.[24] Many of the views attributed to his

---

[21] Plato, *Gorgias* 448a–e. My judgment here is *contra* James Kastely, "In Defense of Plato's Gorgias," *Proceedings of the Modern Language Association* 106, no. 1 (1991): 99–100, where he argues that both students are inept and fail their teachers. Chaerephon is no Socrates, but his opening inquiry demonstrates a clear grasp of Socrates's method, and he seems to understand the core content of his master's question.

[22] Plato, *Gorgias* 458a.

[23] See, e.g., Plato, *Gorgias* 453d–e, 454d, 456b–457c.

[24] For a sampling of those who think the portrait in the dialogue is, while dramatic, fair and representative, see Renato Barilli, *Rhetoric*, trans. Giuliana Menozzi (Minneapolis: University of Minnesota Press, 30, 168–9; Kathleen Freeman, *The Presocratic Philosophers: A Companion to Diels, "Fragmente der Vorsokratiker"* (Oxford: Basil Blackwell, 1953), 366. For the alternative view, see Harold Barrett, *The Sophists: Rhetoric,*

particular brand of sophistry, with its emphasis upon the malleable nature of words, seem roughly consistent with what we have already seen in the small sample of Gorgias's original works that have survived.

In Plato's portrait, however, Gorgias claims to be improving the city and making it a more just place. Thus, if anything, Plato makes the dramatic Gorgias a bit more civically minded, but also a bit more naïve (or, perhaps, less forthcoming) than the few original sources we have from the historical Gorgias might suggest on their own.[25]

In the dialogue, Gorgias claims to seek a more just society—like Socrates—and believes he is contributing to that social program by teaching what he teaches.[26] He has the unquestioned assumption (and this is the root of his naïvete) that, of course, the noble, educated elites do what is right: they understand what is just, and they are trying their best to lead the state to justice. Socrates will make this assumption the focus of his discourse with Gorgias.[27] In that discourse, he will attempt to show that it is unlikely such men (*sic semper!*), skilled in sophistry, would be pursuing good because they have not pursued philosophy first, and philosophy is a prerequisite for understanding what the good is. By vaguely championing adaptable ideals without any grasp of the force, source, or substance of those ideals, this Gorgias is something of a caricature of the moral shallowness found in the Athenian educational enterprise as practiced by the sophists. In the end, Gorgias fails to provide any reliable advice about how to define justice, and the elderly sophist stumbles into a contradiction.

Polus—the young devotee of Gorgias who bursts in to defend his elderly master—will more or less repeat his teacher's error. He advances the argument, however, by stating plainly that the good of rhetoric is in fact that it provides power to get what you want. Polus is nothing if not overrun with the passionate self-confidence so common in the souls of young adults who have attended the best schools around. His contribution to the dialogue

---

Democracy, and Plato's Idea of Sophistry (Novato, CA: Chandler & Sharp, 1987), Ch. 5; Susan Jarratt, *Rereading the Sophists: Classical Rhetoric Refigured* (Carbondale: Southern Illinois University Press, 1991), 17–31.

[25] Cf. the closing section of Chapter 2 on Gorgias.

[26] Plato, *Gorgias* 454b.

[27] As he will later when he challenges Isocrates. Recall, this is an Athens less than a generation after the plague and soon after the horrors of the Peloponnesian War, The Thirty's reign of terror, and the proscriptions and mass executions of citizens. A belief that the noble elite naturally act justly might appear as a rather simplistic assumption in such circumstances.

sets up a rather obvious progression. First, Gorgias's character presents a civically minded, if somewhat naïve, view of *logos*, if we take the character's pronouncements seriously. Second, Polus, in his enthusiasm, introduces the idea that language is essentially a tool of power: rhetoric is a mechanism for getting what we want, and since *we* know what's best, we should have what we want.[28] The view attributed to Polus might be considered a sort of enthusiastic embrace that celebrates power when it is in the hands of the right crowd, meaning the elite gathering of "folks like us," of course. But Polus seems to unwittingly pull the curtain back from Gorgias's claims of civic improvement: the good of rhetoric, it turns out, is very much a matter of factional triumph, not civic justice.

Socrates more or less baits Polus by making claims that are increasingly astonishing. In the most famous example, Socrates suggests the art of rhetoric—championed by Gorgias and Polus as the most precious of all human skills—is actually rather like making and eating lavish desserts: a process that is sweet, pleasant, sticky, extraneous, and unhealthy. When this comparison leaves Polus flabbergasted, Socrates doubles down and says that the best way to use words is not to get your will, but rather to openly confess your injustice and to seek out punishment for your unjust acts. This view makes perfect sense, of course, if we remember the Myth of Er and believe Plato thinks the highest good is the discipling of the soul so it is drawn to what is true and good and capable of withstanding divine judgment, purged of what is false, evil, and spiritually repugnant. But not everyone in the conversation agrees with this project of moral improvement through penance.

From chocolate-caramel kataifi to what he believes to be psychological masochism is a leap too far for Callicles, the final and most interesting interlocuter. Callicles is by far the most consistent of the three debaters. Socrates remarks (and there is a sardonic note to the observation) that Callicles does not fall for sophistic tricks that play on popular sentiments as easily as Gorgias and Polus.[29] They were both tripped up, in the end, by their hypocrisy. Both claimed rhetorical prowess as the highest good, but each fell into the trap of setting something above rhetoric in their own discussion with Socrates. But Callicles, Socrates claims, is far too bold (the

---

[28] Polus, in many ways, sounds closer to the historic writings of Gorgias than the character Gorgias does, and this is also part of the dialogue's progression, I will suggest. Each of Socrates's three conversations is with a more transparent version of an arguably Gorgianic vision of the connection between power and language. In the end, Callicles is the most Gorgianic of all the characters in the dialogue.

[29] Plato, *Gorgias* 494d.

Greek word is *manly*) to be taken in by such a simple trick. Callicles agrees: he will not fall for such tricks. And he does not. Callicles embraces his toxic boldness to its bitter, consistent end.

Callicles argues that justice is a tool of the weak to keep the strong from taking their rightful place. The scam is this: certain ideas that advantage the weak are set up as *just*. This construct provides a social tool for weaker souls to corral and control those who refuse to embrace such *just actions*. The weak, wielding their petty moral codes and constructs of *justice*, manipulate those who are stronger. Callicles is hardly the last to forward such a suggestion. Rachel Barney notes that Callicles "inaugurates a durable philosophical tradition: Nietzsche, Foucault, and their successors in various projects of genealogy and 'unmasking' are all Callicles's heirs."[30] For Callicles, justice is the opium of the powerful: once it becomes an indulgence, the powerful fall into a dream-state that renders them impotent.

Try as he might, Socrates will not shake Callicles from his position: rhetoric is simply a tool for achieving one's interests and desires, and there is no higher guide than one's own will and desire; words are subject to nothing and rule most things. But if language is simply a tool of power, and if words are subject to no higher authority than themselves, then two opponents who are equally loquacious and equally committed to their own interests and conclusions can do little more than escalate the discourse of disagreement toward name-calling and eventually violence. Socrates the philosopher and Callicles the politician do not come to blows, but each holds out a threat of violence against the other. Callicles suggests that, were Socrates ever on trial for his life, he would easily be overcome and executed by the state. Socrates, who has been raising the stakes at every transition in the discourse, closes the dialogue by holding out a far more powerful threat of violence against Callicles: one brought by the divine realities that will judge the soul after death. The parallel threats that close the dialogue—somewhat abruptly—are almost certainly intended to echo past the discourse itself. Callicles's prediction regarding Socrates had come true, as any reader of the *Gorgias* would know. The parallel conclusion, to be drawn interiorly, is that Socrates's prediction about the afterlife might come true as well: final judgment might be just as real as Socrates's trial.

---

[30] Rachel Barney, "Callicles and Thrasymachus," *The Stanford Encyclopedia of Philosophy* (Fall 2017 edition), ed. Edward N. Zalta, https://plato.stanford.edu/archives/fall2017/entries/callicles-thrasymachus/.

In the end, this final focus of the dialogue reflects the opening question: What are you? Several options have been laid out. In the character named Gorgias, we meet a wealthy, privileged soul moving along without bothering to make inquiries into the depth, source, consistency, or consequences of its convictions and beliefs. This is certainly a character who (at least apparently) wants to build a vaguely better, more just, world, of course. But he never seems to have gotten around to defining *better* or subjecting his idea of *justice* to any substantive scrutiny. He lives, instead, the *vaciva vita*, an unexamined life of social privilege and shallow reflections. Second, we meet in Polus an enthusiastic soul who baldly plans to bend the world to his will. He will use his words. He will embody power, and he will have his way. He will use his power to make things *better*, though Socrates is still waiting on that definition of *better*. But Polus feels no need to define *better*. *Better* is just what people like him will do once they have power. By invoking the *better* and the *just*, Polus remains trapped in the matrix of socially constructed moral goals that he claims to have rejected but which still enslave him. According to some, he has not gone far enough. In Callicles, we finally meet the fully fermented, genuinely autonomous, perfectly amoral, and deeply jaded voice of self-interest; this is not someone who fails to consider the nature and definition of things like *good* and *justice*. Callicles has considered and rejected such petty ideas, seeing them as manipulative illusions unworthy of a man of his caliber.

Callicles recognizes what Polus does not: that Socrates is suggesting a transcendental critique for human action and for human language as well: an authority higher than and sitting in judgment of human acts, words, thoughts, and expressions of desire. The politician finds the suggestion a bit alarming in its stupidity. We come full circle here. Where we began with Socrates confronting the naïve foundations of the Gorgianic assumption, we end with amoral self-interest accusing Socrates of being naïve about the *real* world—by which Callicles means whatever political and material conditions embody the slurry of the present moment. Those material conditions compose what Socrates (and most religious believers throughout history) would call the world of shadows and illusions, not the real world, as we shall see. For Callicles, however, this is the only reality that matters.

Who is He?

In a number of ways, the historical Gorgias's original texts suggest a stronger affiliation between himself and the dramatic character of Callicles in this dialogue. Given that there is no record of Callicles anywhere outside this brief work, it is possible he is a fictional invention, but arguments from absence are always weak and never more so than in the ancient world. Fictional or not, however, Plato has intentionally opened the narrative by presenting the popular view of Gorgias as an admirable, eloquent statesman, while revealing that popular view to be shallow and ill-considered; the character of Gorgias is, then, not a critique of the historical Gorgias but of his Athenian reputation, situated at the opening of the dialogue. Plato then closes the dialogue with what he considers a more transparent portrait, in Callicles, of Gorgias's actual sophistic perspective.[31] These two sides of Gorgias's sophistic ego are used as brackets around Polus, the rash incautious student who tries—and miserably fails—to have both a program of socially-minded moral improvement and self-interested *Realrhetorik*.

Throughout the dialogue, Socrates behaves in a way that reflects the character of the person he addresses. With Gorgias, there is a presentation of polite, perhaps even deferential, disagreement. With Polus, he is brash and outlandish. With Callicles, he forcefully suggests a transcendent caliber of experience that trumps the temporal possibilities of power. In each case, Socrates has harsh words for anyone who makes the judgment that language can function well without reference to justice. In the *Phaedrus*, he will consider the possibilities not of the alienation of language from justice but of the substantive consequences (as well as the divine roots) of their collaboration.

Throwing Shade: The Opening of the Phaedrus

The *Phaedrus* falls naturally into two major divisions. The opening part, something less than two-thirds of the dialogue, delivers three speeches, the first two of which are blandly predictable after the first ten lines. The first speech is dull, repetitive, and uninteresting; it has the barest hint of middle-school wit. The second speech is passionate, impertinent, and

---

[31] Barney, in "Callicles and Thrasymachus," suggests Callicles is a fiction intended to mirror not Gorgias, but the darker side of Socrates: what he might have been without philosophy. Callicles's name implies an image of excellence, and the emphasis here might be on image rather than excellence.

not very interesting; it is possessed of some melodramatic flare. The third speech, straight out of the gate, is a different beast entirely and is likely to strike the contemporary reader as a blend between a bad fantasy novel, off-brand apocalyptic mysticism, and hallucinogenics; it is, as Plato intended, the one that stays with you. This trio of rhetorical prowess is introduced by a flirtatious homo-erotic conversation raising themes about the point of education, the scope of language, the purpose of memory, and the power of religion. Clearly, there is a lot to unpack here—so much to unpack that there is a long scholarly debate about the unity of the dialogue: whether it can be said to voice any coherent theme at all, or whether its two parts constitute two distinct rambles.[32] Even among those who hold the *Phaedrus* is in fact a unified whole, many find odd accoutrements in the dialogue here and there. Reginald Hackforth, for example, finds "the length and elaborate detail" of the third speech incomprehensible.[33] While it shines with "imaginative power . . . richness and grandeur," nevertheless, relative "to the formal structure of the whole, the great discourse is both too magnificent and too long; the balance of the dialogue is upset and the structural plan at least partially obscured," he laments.[34] Hackforth's concerns are misplaced, I will argue. It is precisely that third speech which, though it dominates the work as a whole out of necessity, provides the foundational religious understanding that serves as the mortar between every other part of the dialogue.

In the *Gorgias*, the vision of divine judgment appears at the very end of the very last scene and is a thunderclap that seems designed to try to startle the secular Callicles into a realization that, even if great power is the only thing that matters, he is not the only power nor the greatest; surrender to something other, higher, might be in order, even from his own

---

[32] For consideration of these questions, see Charles L. Griswold, *Self-Knowledge in Plato's "Phaedrus"* (University Park: Pennsylvania State University Press, 1996), especially Chs. 4 & 5, as well as William S. Cobb, *Plato's Erotic Dialogues* (Albany: SUNY Press: 1993),139–41; R. Hackforth, *Plato's "Phaedrus"* (Cambridge, UK: Cambridge University Press, 1972), 131–37; and the introductions to the dialogue in both Robin Waterfield's translation of *Phaedrus*, xliii–xlix (Oxford: Oxford University Press, 2009) and Christopher J. Rowe's *"Phaedrus": Edited with an Introduction, Translation, and Commentary*, 7–11 (Oxford: Oxbow Press, 2013).

[33] Hackforth, *Plato's "Phaedrus,"* 136. For the record, the third speech uses almost exactly one quarter (25.95%) of the total words in the Greek text.

[34] Hackforth, *Plato's "Phaedrus,"* 136.

assumptions.[35] In that discourse, which features power as the primary currency of language, Socrates presents the divine world, in a single stunning appearance, as the ultimate power. This is quite different from the *Phaedrus*. In the *Phaedrus*, the divine is everywhere. The gods are not brought in for the sake of dramatic punch at the end. Here, themes of sex, love, rhetoric, and religion are braided together, and the divine permeates the discourse.

The dialogue opens with Socrates strolling in the late morning near the gate of the city as the dashing young Phaedrus comes along.[36] There is a bawdy exchange of greetings and jests involving a scroll hidden under Phaedrus's cloak and a speech Phaedrus has just heard regarding how to choose a good lover. The speech, the youth notes, was given by the famous sophist Lysias. Phaedrus is utterly taken by the speech, has been studying it all morning, and is memorizing it. Its theme is a clichéd sophistic inversion of expectations, arguing (in this particular) that individuals should take as a lover those whom they do not love.

Socrates refers to himself as someone "who is sick with passion for hearing speeches,"[37] but refuses to listen to Phaedrus practice the speech when "Lysias is here, too," in the words of the original scroll.[38] Note that

---

[35] The introduction and presentation of divine judgment is a powerful adaptation of the Greek rhetorical trope called *biaios horos*, where an opponent's definitions, evidence, or assumptions are shown to lead to my own (not their) conclusions.

[36] The dramatic time of this fictional conversation is almost impossible to fix—and may, quite literally, be impossible. See Alexander Nehamas and Paul Woodruff, *Phaedrus* (Indianapolis, IN: Hackett, 1995), xiii; Hackforth, *Plato's "Phaedrus,"* 8; Rowe, *Phaedrus*, 13-14. Even assuming one can find a dramatic date of around, say, 410, when everyone mentioned in the dialogue would be both alive and in Athens, the relative ages of the individuals portrayed would simply not match the date. Phaedrus, who would have been in his late thirties or early forties at that time, is clearly presented in the dialogue as an easily influenced youth; Socrates directly addresses him as "child" (*pai*, the vocative of *pais*, 267c) and seems to include him in the set of "youngsters" (*neoi*) mentioned at 275b, though Rowe thinks these are more general statements on the "younger generation" rather than specific references to Phaedrus (11–12), and that in fact Phaedrus is portrayed in the dialogue as an adult. This perspective seems implausible to me. I assume a completely fictional time is represented in the discourse, crafted to assist the philosophic narrative, not reflect any measure of lived accuracy, and that Phaedrus is portrayed as a youth.

[37] Plato, *Phaedrus* 228b. Unless otherwise noted, I quote Waterfield's translation. I have also routinely consulted Alexander Nehamas and Paul Woodruff's translation in *Plato: Complete Works*, ed. John M. Cooper (Indianapolis, IN: Hackett, 1997), as well as the Greek text and translation in Rowe and the Loeb text and translation, no. 166 of the series, by Chris Emlyn-Jones and William Preddy, *Lysias. Symposium. Phaedrus* (Cambridge, MA: Harvard University Press, 2022).

[38] Plato, *Phaedrus* 228e.

Socrates rejects Phaedrus's spoken version in favor of Lysias's written version—an important point to which we will return. Once the scroll is revealed, Socrates and Phaedrus decide to find someplace comfortable where Phaedrus can read Lysias' speech, and Socrates can listen to the written words (with the implication, perhaps, of deciding what to do about the speech's thesis). They are walking beside the river Ilissus on the way to a shady spot in the distance that Phaedrus has picked out when the conversation casually turns to religion, and Socrates is asked whether he believes the stories of the gods.[39] His reply establishes the first important rhetorical and theological hinge in the dialogue. He opens by noting that some urbane, inflated sort of *hoi sophoi* often substitute natural explanations for divine actions.[40] They demythologize the myths, preferring an historical Boreas of a natural nature to anything so crude as an actual god. But such folks are too clever for their own good and "pitiable besides," Socrates says. The list of things that must be explained away with such a methodology is far too long and would end up consuming one's entire life—a point not to be passed over lightly: to discount the transcendent and the divine is, for a reflective person, a full-time job requiring a calculated attention given to every moment of life in order to insure the absence of anything too far beyond natural expectation. Socrates notes that he does not have leisure for such an enterprise and points out that he is making different use of the religious tales. Rather than trying to interpret the tales so that the religious narratives can be explained away, he is allowing those narratives to interpret him, so that he is able to understand himself. "I am incapable of obeying the Delphic inscription and knowing myself. . . . [And so] I investigate myself rather than these things, to see whether I am in fact a creature of

---

[39] Plato, *Phaedrus* 229c–230a.

[40] The term *hoi sophoi* is an ironic title for the pseudo-wise that Socrates uses here (229c) near the opening of the dialogue. At a later crucial juncture near the end of the dialogue (275b), he will use the even more pointed *doxosophos*. The term references a type of popular, impressive person who appears knowledgeable but lacks depth. It may imply someone in command of data without a grasp of context or someone captivated by fashionable and impressive presentation—precisely the sort of perspectives that enchant the young Phaedrus. See Griswold's comments in *Self-Knowledge in Plato's "Phaedrus,"* 206, and for a broader view of the concept, see Jennifer Whiting, "Fools' Pleasures in Plato's *Philebus,*" in *Strategies of Argument: Essays in Ancient Ethics, Epistemology, and Logic,* ed. Mi-Kyoung Lee, 21–59 (Oxford: Oxford University Press, 2014).

more complexity and savagery than Typhon, or something tamer and more simple, with a naturally divine and non-Typhonic nature."[41]

Just at this moment, Phaedrus and Socrates arrive at the plane tree Phaedrus had chosen for their destination, and they discover it is a place of divine presence with shrines and altars to various nymphs and, Socrates specifically points out, to Achelous. Achelous was the father of the Sirens.[42] Socrates immediately follows this observation by noting how the "whisper of the breeze chimes in a summery, clear way with the chorus of the cicadas."[43] By this point, the introduction of the dialogue has established a dramatic tension in the midst of a sacred, relaxed, and seductive setting with voices calling— some to self-discovery and submission to the divine, some to ambition and power, some to personal passion and ruin. Things might go in almost any direction. The following speeches lay out the options one might take.

Once settled in the shade of the tree, Phaedrus reads the first speech, composed by Lysias and recommending that a lover should be chosen on the basis of pragmatic considerations without regard to passion and love.[44] Lysias's speech, like the lover it recommends, is unimaginative and dull. A person who concludes that this is an admirable plan which will lead to great sex has to be a person who is almost unimaginably inattentive to life's offerings, and Socrates knows it. One can almost hear his slow, dull, mock applause at the end. Two things emerge from this. The first is that the character of Phaedrus is a bit of a trendy clod. He has been seduced by a speech that has virtually nothing to recommend it beyond its authorship

---

[41] Plato, *Phaedrus* 230a–b. Typhon was a diabolical giant filled with an ambitious lust for domination and was overthrown—barely—by Zeus before being imprisoned in Tartarus beneath Mount Etna.

[42] Throughout the dialogue, there is an unspoken tension between the Sirens and the Muses. Phaedrus's soul hangs in the balance as he decides which voices he will listen to.

[43] Plato, *Phaedrus* 230c. Later in the dialogue, we discover the cicadas are, according to Socrates, charged with reporting to the Muses the activities of human beings who honor them, and this will be the motive for Socrates and Phaedrus to continue their "philosophical discourse" in the second half of the dialogue (beginning around 257c). Philosophical speech "is the most beautiful and is concerned with the heavens and what is divine," as Emlyn-Jones and Preddy observe in their translation (458n89). There is much written on the significance of the cicadas in this dialogue. See, e.g., Pauline LeVen, *Music and Metamorphosis in Graeco-Roman Thought* (Cambridge, UK: Cambridge University Press, 2020), especially Ch. 3; Daniel S. Werner, *Myth and Philosophy in Plato's "Phaedrus"* (Cambridge, UK: Cambridge University Press, 2012), especially Ch. 6; and, more broadly, G. R. F. Ferrari, *Listening to the Cicadas: A Study of Plato's "Phaedrus,"* Cambridge Classical Studies (Cambridge, UK: Cambridge University Press, 1987).

[44] Plato, *Phaedrus* 231a–234d.

by a famous influencer. The speech is stylistically simplistic, and its main ideas (namely, that if you do not get your emotions mixed up with your love life then you will not be taken advantage of and you can more easily negotiate some basic friends-with-benefits transactions) are the sort of points that, once you grasp the fundamental thesis, will inescapably present themselves.[45] Socrates says as much: "These points are essential to the argument: do you think anyone would say anything different?"[46]

But another less obvious matter can be discovered here. In the dispassionate, dull, controlled written speech of Lysias, it is not Lysias who is the target of Socrates's mockery. Almost certainly, it is Isocrates who is the target. Isocrates has mistaken the power and goal of education and philosophy in exactly the same way the written speech here has mistaken the power and goal of eros and passion. This speech and Isocrates both represent the championing of that dispassionate, dull, controlled person with a soul as unlively and unvaried as a published text. This, Plato is pointing out, is the outcome of Isocrates's idea of philosophy. Nothing here reaches very far or very deep. And, at the end of the dialogue, we discover this is a bit of a shame, since Isocrates had real potential to be a real philosopher, but squandered it.[47] Once he has expressed his disdain for the speech, Socrates

---

[45] In our own day, the idea of calculated self-interest trumping romance is unusual, but the idea would have been, perhaps, a little less strange, per se, for the Greeks who were broadly acquainted with a suffocatingly patriarchal system of family life that did not generally involve romance as a motive for anything. Sex, within the family setting at least, was tied to its natural end, procreation, which was viewed as a social duty. Lysias's speech is an inversion of expectations because it brings this unemotional version of sex to a non-fecund setting that was broadly considered to be ruled by pleasure, passion, and desire: a boy in the early to middle teens was courted by an older potential mentor who had become enamored of the pubescent boy's physical "bloom," as the Greeks said. For more on the homoerotic aspects of Greek education, see Waterfield, *Phaedrus*, xi–xiv; William Armstrong Percy III, *Pederasty and Pedagogy in Archaic Greece* (Champaign: University of Illinois Press, 1996); Jennifer Larson, "Pederasty and Male Homoerotic Relations," in *Greek and Roman Sexualities: A Sourcebook*, 107–32 (New York: Bloomsbury Academic, 2012); and Andrew Lear, "Ancient Pederasty: An Introduction," in *A Companion to Greek and Roman Sexualities*, ed. Thomas K. Hubbard, 102–27 (Hoboken, NJ: Wiley-Blackwell, 2014).

[46] Plato, *Phaedrus* 235e.

[47] Plato, *Phaedrus* 279a. Socrates here, with sickly sweet sarcasm, notes Isocrates's great potential, provided he takes up a proper idea of education as true philosophy forming the soul to face the divine. The dialogue is set in a time when Isocrates was a young man; it was published when he was old, probably in his seventies. See Nathan Crick, *Rhetoric and Power* (Columbia: University of South Carolina Press, 2018), 194–95, for more on the association of the first speech with Isocrates.

goes so far as to suggest that he could make a better speech than Lysias on this same theme,[48] but then backs away until Phaedrus, with an oath and dare, draws him into the second speech.

Manipulative Middling Rhetoric

This second speech, certainly no example of rhetorical perfection, is still fascinating within the narrative for several reasons. First, Socrates begins his speech with an invocation—a prayer for help. The prayer is most likely a snide cut intended to parody the pretensions of sophistic discourse and perhaps the shallow, pragmatic civic religion of Isocrates, continuing his earlier criticism of his great rival in educational theory. In fact, a good case has been made that the whole of this middle speech is an ironic imitation of Isocrates's style.[49] Where the first speech had mocked the goals of his educational enterprise, the second speech mocks Isocrates's methods as an excessive melodrama, invoking shallow passions that lead to profound misunderstandings, as we will see. Despite the impromptu nature of the presentation, the language is rhythmic and self-consciously impressive, and Socrates will note, in a digression within the speech, that he is just on the border of religious ecstasy and epic inspiration. This comment, too, may very well be sarcastic: the form of poetry he speaks in and praises "was notorious for its affected language and florid music."[50] Or perhaps we are meant to understand that Socrates, under the adrenaline of his spontaneous performance, was in fact carried away into an intoxicating melodrama that swept him along, and he said much more than he had, in fact, planned. Regardless, this act of *hubris* will call out for correction. But a further interest regarding the opening invocation is to whom Plato is praying. The invocation calls on the Muses. And not just one. He invokes the full chorus of the Muses. All nine Muses were born of the Titan Mnemosyne, Memory, following a nine-night tryst with her nephew Zeus. In the opening of the

---

[48] We are, perhaps, meant to understand the boast as a claim that Plato can offer a richer education and truer philosophy than Isocrates. That boast will fail in the second speech, which will, once again, imitate Isocrates too closely. Only in the final speech, and with the help of the divine vision, will the Platonic education surpass the plodding pragmatics of his rival, Isocrates.

[49] See Malcolm Brown and James Coulter, "The Middle Speech of Plato's *Phaedrus*," *Journal of the History of Philosophy* 9, no. 4 (1971): 405–23. Their argument deserves more attention than it has received in the literature.

[50] Waterfield, *Phaedrus*, 83, comment on 238d *chanting*.

dialogue, we saw Socrates react negatively when Phaedrus attempted to deliver a speech from memory while the written copy was on hand. In the epilogue, Socrates will, in an apparent inconsistency, denounce writing things down rather than committing them to memory. To complicate things further, Hesiod tell us that the Muses, these daughters of Memory, offer "*forgetfulness* of evil" as a gift to the human race.[51] While the invocation of the Muses seems shallow in this middle speech, Socrates will, in the final speech, offer a direct tribute at a crucial juncture in the presentation to the actions of memory within the human soul. This later tribute is framed in conjunction with the Eleusinian Mysteries, and it is undoubtedly intended to be read as a sincere expression of Socrates's piety.[52] Clearly, memory is one recurring theme in this dialogue.

The force and power of memory is underappreciated in our own age where the motivation for remembering any specific fact is rather thin. That, after all, is what the internet is for: to store facts so they are not "cluttering up," as we say, our brains.[53] But memory in the ancient world is much more disciplined, orderly, and complex and is sometimes seen as a distant relation of magic. It would be a mistake to assume reductively that this association was because they were primitive in their understandings of memory while we get it right with our mechanistic database metaphors of memory; it is just as likely that we are naïve in our understanding of the potential and power of memory and the ancients are the ones who are closer to the mark.[54] The mechanics of memory—how to retain, organize, and access memories—was a basic subject taught in schools before the advent of the modern world, and memory was

---

[51] Hesiod, *Theogony*, in *Theogony, Works and Days, Testimonia*, ed. and trans. Glen W. Most, 2–155, Loeb Classical Library 57 (Cambridge, MA: Harvard University Press, 2018), 53–62, emphasis added.

[52] Plato, *Phaedrus* 250c. See also note 29, Ch. 6, of the present work.

[53] There is a popular perspective that attributes this "exiling" of memory to the presence of writing and that sees a tension between writing and memory. Mary Carruthers argues, not unconvincingly, that rather too much is made of this tension. See, e.g., *The Book of Memory*, 2nd ed. (Cambridge, UK: Cambridge University Press, 2008), especially 9–36. For the alternative view, see Yun Lee Too, *The Rhetoric of Identity in Isocrates: Text, Power, Pedagogy* (Cambridge, UK: Cambridge University Press, 2009), as well as Ekaterina V. Haskins, *Logos and Power in Isocrates and Aristotle* (Columbia: University of South Carolina Press, 2004) and Nathan Crick in *Rhetoric and Power: The Drama of Classical Greece* (Columbia: University of South Carolina Press, 2018).

[54] An attentive reader might note that I just moved the actions of the ancients into the present tense, grammatically. Remembrance moves the actions of the ancients into the present tense metaphysically.

considered one of the key elements, perhaps *the* key element, of intelligence. We have strong evidence of feats of memory among the ancients that are astounding to the modern mind. But it is crucial to note that memory was for them much more than a matter of data recall.[55] In the ancient world, especially, memory could be associated with an awakening of past events and rendering them *animated*, alive, in the present. Memory constituted for them "a kind of space within the soul . . . in which truths may be found and 'met with.'"[56] These "truths" which are met in the soul's memory are more than mere facts.

This *animation of the past* gave to events and persons who did not share our present tense a kind of causal power; they were, once *animated* by memory, an actual member of the council of this present moment, with a voice that could shape will and inform conscience about the current issues.[57] What was stored and accessed in memory became part of the soul's repertoire, a defining vein of its inner formation: "it was in trained memory that one built character, judgment, citizenship, and piety."[58] For this reason, rote memorization was generally frowned upon since such a mechanical use of the memory failed to animate the past: memorization was generally viewed as dead recitation rather than lived recollection: "Words without thoughts never to heaven go," Shakespeare tells us, hinting at a similar conviction some two thousand years after Socrates.[59] To merely recite memorized words or data without, in some measure, conjuring and animating some actual reality from the past seemed to them to be missing the main point of re-calling. The goal of recollection was invitational: realities, held

---

[55] Mary Carruthers's work on memory in the medieval era is the current scholarly canon on this topic, and though the ancient world differed from the medieval in various respects that remain unexplored, there was a great deal of overlap. See Beate Dignas and R. R. R. Smith, eds., *Historical and Religious Memory in the Ancient World* (Oxford: Oxford University Press, 2012). In addition to Carruthers's bedrock text *The Book of Memory*, already cited, there is also her *Craft of Thought* (Cambridge, UK: Cambridge University Press, 1998). See also fn. 59, below.

[56] Anthony Michael Pasqualoni, "Plato on Being, Time, and Recollection," ΣΧΟΛΗ 16, no. 2 (2022): 552.

[57] The Greek term for *animated* would be *empsuchon*—literally, *ensouled*, the term used by Plato at 276a in his discussion of memory and writing.

[58] Carruthers, *Book of Memory*, 11.

[59] Shakespeare, *Hamlet*, in *The Complete Works of Shakespeare*, ed. David Bevington, 1069–1120 (Chicago: University of Chicago Press, 1980), 3.3.98. Dead recitation of something that is not actually held within the soul is probably at the root of the "shame" of speech writers that Phaedrus laments (because it might cause Lysias to stop composing speeches) at 257c in the dialogue.

as treasures in memory, became, when they were re-called, enlivened members, invited into the present moment that (always) stood in need of counsel and direction. The gift of memory and the reward of recollection was the ability, then, to engage the past as an actual voice in the present. For us, memory is the act of throwing the mind back to an event within a fixed and unalterable past. For them, memory was the act of summoning a living reality into the present and granting that guest an authority of interaction and causality here and now.

Correspondingly, *forgetting* was an act of making the past barren and *removing* from that past reality the power to interact with the present. Hence the ancient emphasis on remembering the ancestors: if forgotten, faded and impotent; if remembered, lively and influential. These are broad cross-cultural concepts in the ancient world. For example, note the Hebrew prophet Jeremiah's proclamation that God will "remember their sins no more" (Jer. 31:34). The prophet is not suggesting the Almighty will fall into crass ignorance regarding some specific sin which took place last week or last century; rather, what is being highlighted here is the fact that the authority of Israel's sins to have an actual voice in the present, polluting their souls and national identity, is being obliviated. Hesiod's remarks regarding the forgetfulness of evil as one of the gifts of the Muses should be read in the same vein: good myths undermine the power of evil in the present by animating heroic good in the here and now.[60]

And this brings us back to Socrates's original preference for Lysias's written discourse over Phaedrus's verbal delivery from memory. One of the key lessons Socrates attempts to bring home to Phaedrus (repeatedly!) is the soul's need to unite itself to what is good and remove itself from what is not. If memory is an act of inviting a living reality to help shape the soul, then Lysias's speech, certainly, need not be committed to memory. That is, it need not be given the animated and vibrant participation with inner formation that is the task of Mnemosyne. When

---

[60] This theme of memory and forgetfulness plays a central role in dozens of invocations within the Psalms, both blessings and curses. See, e.g., Ps. 109:14 and 15 ("May the iniquity of his fathers be remembered"; "may his memory be cut off from the earth"); 25:7 ("Remember not the sins of my youth"), and so forth. Note, also, that when the poet Dante reaches the earthly paradise, he is bathed in the river of forgetfulness. Afterwards, he remains perfectly capable of recalling his past actions and the identity of himself and the souls around him. What changes is that the *sinfulness* of his life is no longer an authoritative voice in his will, and when he is afterward bathed in the river of clear thought, he is ready to ascend almost effortlessly to the heavenly paradise of which the earthly one is but an icon.

Lysias's speech comes up much later in the discourse, Socrates notes the piece might be reviewed, but only because "it contains a good number of examples which one could profitably look at, although one would certainly not profit from trying to imitate them."[61] On the one hand, dead memorization is a waste of effort. On the other hand, Lysias's speech is not the sort of thing Phaedrus should be committing to memory and *animating* within his soul. Committing the thing to memory within either of those frames is undesirable—better to just read the thing and be done with it.

But the invocation of the Muses at the opening of this second speech, given in a formal poetic structure and style, suggests—either quite ironically or quite improperly—that this middle speech will, unlike Lysias's, certainly be worthy to participate in that inner formation of one's soul. Of course, it is this very sort of *hubris* that will call forth Socrates's rejection of this speech.

In addition to this layered opening invocation, the introduction of this middle speech lays out a second significant point that must be held in mind. The speech begins by forwarding a standard Socratic aphorism: namely, that one cannot discuss a matter wisely unless one knows what matter is being discussed.

> Whatever the issue, my young friend, if you want to come to a correct conclusion there is only one place to start your deliberations. If you lack knowledge of whatever it is you are thinking about, you are bound to go wrong [*hamartanein*]. Now, most people fail to appreciate their ignorance of the true nature of any given thing, proceed on the assumption that they do know, and end up paying the penalty you'd expect, of agreeing neither with themselves nor with anyone else. I don't want you and me to experience what we criticize in others.[62]

A failure to define and understand the most essential qualities of any matter will inevitably lead to a failure to hit upon any understanding worth having. And so it is crucial, Socrates says, that they should proceed only after having established "a mutually acceptable definition of love—of what kind of thing it is, and what its powers are," and they should keep that definition in mind and refer to it constantly so that they do not go astray in

---

[61] Plato, *Phaedrus* 264e–265a

[62] Plato, *Phaedrus* 237c–d.

their discussion of love.[63] Of course, Socrates has, in this passage, laid out with thick irony the very error he is about to commit (discourse on his topic based on a shallow and insubstantial understanding of his topic) along with its result (going off course). The jaunty melodrama of the speech shows that Socrates is not taking the divine very seriously, and yet he is about to launch into an explication of the divine nature of at least one supernatural being, Eros. This will not go well.

In this middle speech, Socrates abandons the idea of informed self-interest found at the core of Lysias's presentation. Instead, Socrates begins by defining love as a species of desire that has been driven to excess, *hubris*, and he actually denounces the very idea of *erōs*, describing it as a sort of manipulative madness.[64] It is an "irrational desire" that is fed by "pleasure in beauty." Love overwhelms one's "reasoned impulse to do right."[65] This desire leads one into base jealousies and manipulations in order to get what one wants. If a young man chooses as his lover someone who is in love with him, the speech notes, that young man will be choosing a person "out of his mind" and he will find himself in a relationship with someone whom the passion of love has rendered "untrustworthy, bad-tempered, jealous [*phthonerō*], unpleasant, and harmful not just to his property and his physical condition, but even more so to the formation of his soul, which is in actual fact the most valuable thing there is or ever will be in the eyes of both gods and men."[66]

Throughout the speech, Socrates continues to amplify and intensify this denunciation of *erōs* before an abrupt ending that cuts short the flow of his impromptu performance: "You should realize that kindness is not involved in a relationship with a lover. . . . Lovers love a young man, like yourself, as wolves love lambs!"[67]

---

[63] Plato, *Phaedrus* 237d.

[64] Plato, *Phaedrus* 237a–241d.

[65] Plato, *Phaedrus* 238b, c.

[66] Plato, *Phaedrus* 241c–d. Here I take liberties with Waterfield's translation. His rendering of the Greek phrase *pros tēn tou psuchēs paideusin* as "to his mental development" smacks too much of the Enlightenment, while glossing too casually, by my lights, over the pious nature of Plato's language here, particularly given the divine prioritization placed upon that phrase in the following Greek clause. Emlyn-Jones and Preddy render the phrase "to the *education* of his soul" in the Loeb (emphasis added). Of course, the irony continues. This formation of the soul is being celebrated as the highest good, but in a context that arrogantly misconstrues the very nature of the divine, something Socrates will soon characterize as the worst possible use of discourse, at 242e.

[67] Plato, *Phaedrus* 241d.

When Socrates cuts off, Phaedrus objects that he was cheated out of half a speech; Socrates was just getting warmed up, he complains. This introduces a fascinating exchange, dense with ambiguity and cross references to the remainder of the dialogue. This interlude runs from 241d into 243e. It sees Socrates denouncing the speech he has just given, and it serves as an introduction to the motive and purpose of the dynamic third speech. Before turning our attention there, however, it is crucial to consider the interlude itself.

There is some tonal ambiguity to this important hinge in the discourse. It could be read as a sincere confession or as a self-conscious performance. The dialogue as a whole presents a clear image of philosophic seduction. Socrates is attempting, by several methods, to entice Phaedrus to abandon shallow and insubstantial things in favor of depth and substance. That is, Phaedrus is being called from the Siren culture of sophistic self-indulgence and into philosophy, that all-important discipline of interior formation which Musically prepares the soul to wisely encounter the divine realities and forget—make impotent, undermine—the power of evil. The consequences of Phaedrus's *vaciva vita*—his shallow life—are vividly portrayed in the second speech, where the presentation becomes increasingly excited about its own silly premise. But that excitement is based on a confusion about the very nature and significance of the divine realities that are at the core of the speech's theme, and so these confusions lead to inappropriate perspectives and impious actions.

By one reading of the style present in this interlude, Socrates was genuinely carried away by his own delivery of the speech and, when he realizes what he has been doing, breaks off the presentation and sincerely recants his own *hubris*, excess. A second reading sees Socrates as consciously and ironically in control of the entire second speech: there was no moment when he actually got carried away and "sinned against Love" (as he will say he did, in the interlude).[68] He was, instead, play-acting: consciously modeling a fault for the sake of teaching Phaedrus. In this reading, the interlude itself is a continuation of the performance about Phaedrus's trendy shallowness: the speech ironically demonstrates, and then the interlude self-consciously explicates, the nature of that shallowness and the proper response to it. Solid arguments can be advanced for either reading,

---

[68] Plato, *Phaedrus* 242e. The Greek is *hēmartanetēn peri ton Erōta*, translated "commit this offence against Love" by Waterfield. "Sinned against love" is Fowler's translation. The Greek *hamartanō* has an intriguing association in these texts. It most simply means to miss a target, but also implies a failure to discover the correct path or to hold onto something or someone. It also means religious or moral failure, sin.

but both readings emphasize the clear import of this moment as it models for Phaedrus the repentance that would be appropriate to any *vaciva vita*, since such a life is free of careful, deep, and moral reflection. But given the interlude's use of Socrates's most intimate religious perspectives and the strong subtext throughout the dialogue regarding how easily the soul is deceived and led astray by Siren sophistics, a view of the dialogue that portrays Socrates himself as, even in the midst of his self-conscious irony, somewhat seduced by his own display of shallowness (and thus carried too far by his own enthusiasm) seems marginally more reasonable.[69] Such a reading preserves both the intentional irony within his speech—an irony that went too far and became indulgent impiety—and the obviously sincere repentance in this interlude.

At the opening of his speech, recall, Socrates had noted that without a clear and genuine grasp of the topic being discussed one was bound to drift off course, to go astray (*hamartanein*).[70] In the interlude between the second and third speech, he notes that this is exactly what happened. He states, at 242e, that he has offended (*hēmartanetēn*) Eros. He names his offence: *asebēs*, impiety. The quality of the sin is broad enough that Socrates captures both his own and Lysias's speech in the net. Both speeches, focusing on the deepest realities but with only a shallow understanding of those divine realities, fail to hold to the correct path and inevitably become statements of impiety; and impious speech is the ultimate failure of human words, Socrates declares to Phaedrus.[71] If Socrates believes that rhetoric is an art of leading the soul (as he will define it at 261a) and that the point of philosophy is to prepare the soul for trafficking with the divine realities (as we have seen), it is only natural that a failure to speak properly about the divine is an ultimate *hamartia*, fault or failure.[72] Such a fault inevitably fails

---

[69] See, e.g., 242b–d where Socrates invokes his daimonion, his "supernatural sign," and lays out a dose of strikingly poignant self-awareness regarding his speech. Nothing is couched here in the conditional: there are no *ei* or *ean* clauses such as one could reasonably expect in explication of an example. We find that the speech *is wrong*, not that a speech of this sort *would be wrong*. This seems to be the grammar of penance, not pedagogy. An unwillingness to see Socrates as himself carried away and "sinning against love" feels a bit too hagiographic at one level, but it is a defensible and not uncommon scholarly view, and the text can be profitably read either way.

[70] Plato, *Phaedrus* 237c.

[71] Plato, *Phaedrus* 242d.

[72] Socrates defines rhetoric as the art of soul-leading at 261a and reiterates this as the function of language at 271d. In both cases, he employs the word *psuchagōgos*. The word references the spaces devoted to the acts of conjuring souls, guiding them from the realm

to hold onto what is most valuable, and so leads the soul astray. That is the worst act that words can perform.

Throughout the exchange in this interlude, Phaedrus is tentative and vague. When the declaration of impiety is made, Phaedrus remains qualified, agreeing that this would be a very bad thing, if—*if*—Socrates's assessment is, in fact, accurate. Socrates is (at least apparently) shocked: "What? Do you not think that Eros is the son of Aphrodite, and a god?" Phaedrus offers the tepid reply, "Well, that's what he's said to be."[73] Clearly Phaedrus remains within the camp of the merely clever; the display of his *vaciva vita* and its resultant impiety as outlined and embodied by Socrates has, so far, moved his soul no further than the belching of an ox.

Socrates, however, is thoroughly moved. Invoking not only the sacred sign that he says attends him from time to time, but also poetry and fear of divine judgment (he fears he will be struck blind for his refusal to look clearly at beautiful bodies and to speak truthfully about the allure of those bodies and the pious use to be made of that allure), he sets out to make restitution for his impious behavior by composing a palinode, a speech retracting and denouncing his former expression. Phaedrus is thrilled by an opportunity to hear yet another impromptu speech by Socrates, and this is his only display of intense emotion throughout the interlude except for his disappointment when Socrates had broken off the previous speech. The clear implication is that Phaedrus loves performances and is not very much concerned about content. It is merely spectacle that has captured him, so far. Socrates is about to out-spectacle Phaedrus's highest hopes in a final rhetorical attempt to move him from his *vaciva vita* and toward, instead, a *vita florentis*, a flourishing life of the sort offered by pious philosophy.

---

of the dead into encounters with the living. In some ways, this resonates with the sort of magical qualities one finds assumed around Mnemosyne. The Titaness Memory is capable of bringing the realities of the past into the present as actual participants, their power of temporal causality restored. A similar magic resonates within rhetoric, particularly around the goddess *Peitho*, who participates in both persuasion and seduction. The boundary between magic, memory, persuasion, seduction, religion, and reason is not always clear, if it exists at all.

[73] Plato, *Phaedrus* 242d. For these lines, I have relied on Emlyn-Jones and Preddy.

Chapter 6

Such is the Life of the Gods:
Language and the Divine

If Phaedrus is to be brought into contact with the divine life, he will have to, of course, find a new way to approach and examine himself and the world around him. The invitation to this new way of seeing begins with a delicate reframing of perspective in the opening of the final speech within the dialogue. Where the middle speech had denounced love as an irrational madness, the final speech praises madness—at least certain species of madness—as a rich gift. But this inversion is no sophistic witticism. Socrates here sets out, just as he did in the middle speech, to insist upon a careful definition of what it is the discourse will touch on. In this incident, however, he swears himself to truth in order to protect his ability *to see* clearly. In setting out in pursuit of a *true vision* rather than a clever one, he makes a subtle but significant distinction. Obviously, there is a sort of madness that is, in fact, *hubris*, an excess, something that goes so far that it severs the will and the intellect from the quality they supposedly seek. There is a certain kind of consumptive rationality that denies the very foundation of reason and leads those under its power to behave in ways that contradict reason. Take a few simple examples. Deference to the will of another can be a good thing, but it is possible to become so excessively deferential that a person ceases to have any ethical foundation of their own, at all. Or consider the fact that many of us know people so madly obsessed with some aspect of food—its quality or presentation—that the stress of going out for dinner with them brings on indigestion. And it is not difficult to imagine (or think of!) friends who become so irrationally obsessed with a game that they cease to *play* at all, and the very fun that was the point of the game is destroyed by their relentless focus on victory at all costs. And so it is with many good things.

To See or not to See: Excess, Meanness, and a Speech about the Unspeakable

If taken seriously, Socrates's definition of love in the middle speech would inevitably render love an unloving quality: an excess that, in its madness, destroys the very reasoned and reasonable acts and benefits of love itself, reasonable benefits hinted at in the interlude.[1] That is what *hubris* is: an excess that undermines and contradicts some reasonable *good*. And here that subtle reframing begins to come into sharper focus. Socrates never calls such irrational behaviors a *hubris* of reason. They are not a *hubris* of reason but a failure in reasoning—an error, not an excess, of intellectual activity. Holding this distinction about reasoning in mind, we can turn our attention to the third and final speech.

Socrates opens this last speech by naming four examples of a different sort of "madness."[2] These "madnesses" are religious prophesy, religious ritual (especially rites of purification and healing), divinely inspired poetry, and passionate, divinely inspired love. Each is attended by specific deities. These are, respectively, Apollo, Dionysus, the Muses, and Aphrodite with Eros.[3] Here, then, are four examples of divine madness, none of which deny reason but all of which color outside its lines. This sort of madness is not excessive

---

[1] E.g., Plato, *Phaedrus* trans. Robin Waterfield (Oxford: Oxford University Press, 2009), 243c.

[2] The term is inescapable, but when Socrates presents his noble madnesses, the contemporary reader might well envision these as a sort of Socratic way of being-in-the-world that is oriented toward a synthesis of the religious aspects and the reasoned aspects of the intellect. And, as we shall see, Plato considers religious vision to be an aspect of *theoria vera*, true perspective.

[3] Socrates sums up the four and mentions their attendant deities at 265b, near the opening of his famous discussion on collection and division, which runs from 264e to 266b (at least), a section Hackforth considers the central theme of the entire dialogue since it introduces new philosophic implications in Plato's fundamental course of reasoning. See R. Hackforth, *Plato's "Phaedrus"* (Cambridge, UK: Cambridge University Press, 1972), 136. The process of collection and division groups things that belong together and then distinguishes members of the group from one another. Griswold labels this the Platonic "method of knowing" and also spends some time on this section of the dialogue. See Charles L. Griswold, *Self-Knowledge in Plato's "Phaedrus"* (University Park: Pennsylvania State University Press, 1996), 186. I certainly do not disagree with Hackforth about the importance of the passage, but I do argue that the religious content of this third speech is necessary to contextualize properly Plato's remarks there, and this necessity is one reason Plato recalls the image of the gods and their gifts at that point in the dialogue: the divine is recollected at that very point in order to properly inform the following discussion.

reason; there is no such thing as being *excessively reasonable*.[4] But neither is it defective reasoning. There are certainly plenty of examples of defective reasoning available (and throughout the Platonic dialogues, Socrates is constantly showing those to us), but these are not among them. These examples of madness neither deny nor contradict reason. Instead, they supplement and enrich it, and that is their power. At 245b–c, Socrates states bluntly that human reason in which the divine way of being is incorporated into the intellect is the sort of reason preferred by the wise, though not the merely clever. The same point is made perhaps even more bluntly at 244d where Socrates says, "[T]he madness that comes from god is to be preferred to the sanity that comes from human beings."[5] This is the crucial, subtle distinction Socrates makes in the opening of this final speech. Even if your material calculations are perfectly rational (what was Callicles if not perfectly rational?), you may have omitted something valuable, and that omission prevents you from being entirely reasonable. Definition and clarity about the topic being discussed are essential; both the middle and the final speech begin with this insistence. But the middle speech defined love improperly, and, not surprisingly, that speech went off the rails. And so we see that reasoned definitions must be grounded in the ability *to see* the topic correctly. *To see* in Greek is *theōrein*, which gives us the English word *theory*. Brown and Coulter note: "But not just any theory can be advanced.... To satisfy the full-fledged Platonic requirement, it has to be the *true theory*. Thus it is perfectly possible for someone Plato represents to be half-right in this matter: rightly seeing the need for a definition, but failing to see the right definition."[6] That, of course, is exactly what Socrates did in the middle speech.

In the end, the worth of one's thought cannot be advanced without the correctness of one's theory. There is an irrational madness in spending one's life searching for novelists who are also koalas, no matter how intricately

---

[4] It is worth noting that for Plato an excess in pure *rationality* is possible, of course, where rationality is understood as merely cause-effect or means-end calculation. If, as Plato holds, reality is not simply (or even primarily) material, and if human reason is understood as the faculty for arriving at what is true, then a purely *rationalistic* approach to all things would be inappropriate and excessive. On the other hand, a *reasonable* approach, incorporating not just material calculus but also a harmonious and balanced blend of moral, relational, and aesthetic considerations, could not be.

[5] E. R. Dodds, *The Greeks and the Irrational* (Berkeley: University of California Press, 1973), especially Ch. 3, is probably the foundational contemporary starting point for this topic.

[6] Malcolm Brown and James Coulter, "The Middle Speech of Plato's *Phaedrus*," *Journal of the History of Philosophy* 9, no. 4 (1971): 408, emphasis in original.

developed one's theory might be regarding such creatures. Theory must be true to be valuable. But even when true, there is a type of perfectly reasonable "madness" that does not contradict, deny, or ignore the soul's intellectual vision, but merely stretches it via a cooperative inclusion of the divine. As Martha Nussbaum remarks, "Certain sorts of madness are not only not incompatible with insight and stability, they are actually necessary for the highest sort of insight and the best kind of stability."[7] Nussbaum holds that Socrates is, in the *Phaedrus*, championing only an aesthetic and artistic sort of inspiration, but that thesis is, in the end, too thin. As Michael Rinella convincingly argues, a merely aesthetic interpretation of the dialogue must simply ignore or gloss over the far too frequent, far too specific, and far too inescapably *religious* fulcra in the text. And for Plato's original audience, these religious elements would have been even more obvious and pervasive than for the contemporary reader.[8]

When Socrates opens this final speech, then, we have another clear indication that his idea of reason includes a sort of supernatural interaction, a divine element in our lives that a purely calculated rationality would not completely comprehend.[9] This religious element does not, however, contradict any true aspect of reality that is comprehended by reason, and in fact, incorporating this divine element into one's reflections has made the soul's intellect more reasonable. Socrates calls this religious element of the intellect a sacred madness, a "divine gift" that responds to human inquiry (in prophesy and oracles), that directs human action and identity toward wholeness (in ritual and festival), that softens the power of evil (in the *forgetfulness* of the Muses), and that heightens one's passionate encounters with beauty and love.[10]

---

[7] Martha Nussbaum, *The Fragility of Goodness* (Cambridge, UK: Cambridge University Press, 2001), 201.

[8] Michael Rinella, "Supplementing the Ecstatic: Plato, the Eleusinian Mysteries and the *Phaedrus*," *Polis: The Journal of the Society for Greek Political Thought* 17, nos. 1–2 (2000): 61–78; see also the discussions on the *Phaedrus* in Karl Kerényi, *Eleusis: Archetypal Image of Mother and Daughter* (Princeton: Princeton University Press, 1967). Kerényi is quoted at several important junctures in Rinella's article.

[9] The word *divine* is not, here, metaphorical, nor a symbolic (in the contemporary sense of that word) reference to a subjective aesthetic or vaguely spiritual experience. The divine in this context is clearly defined and tied to concrete religious expression.

[10] Plato, *Phaedrus* 244b. This *erōs* is clearly spiritualized in *Phaedrus*, but it must not be confused with either the ideals of a monogamous and preferential covenantal relation as found in Judaism or intimate friendship with God through the Incarnation as found in Christianity. Plato is talking about physical beauty and sexual desire, albeit as a distorted

Recognizing the value of these divine gifts which are organically connected to reason, are consistent with reason, but are larger than the intellect's unaided reach is crucial of course because this final speech will address issues that reason and speech—*logos*, reason itself—cannot reach. In one central passage, a key to the whole of the third speech (and, arguably, the entire dialogue), Socrates notes:

> The region beyond heaven *has never yet been adequately described in any of our earthly poets' compositions, nor will it ever be.* But since one has to make a courageous attempt to speak the truth, especially when it is truth that one is speaking about, here is a description. This region is filled with true being. True being has no colour or form; it is intangible, and visible only to intelligence, the soul's guide. True being is the province of everything that counts as true knowledge.[11]

Note, first, that there is a reality beyond the reach of language, *logos*, even language at its highest. If rhetoric (and language itself) leads the soul forward, that guidance may well be correct while at the same time incomplete: language can guide one correctly so far as it is able, but not so far as need requires. Socrates's soul does not live by *logos* alone. And a second crucial issue in this passage is seen in the fact that those realities which cannot be captured by words have two very specific qualities. They are not sensible realities and thus cannot be touched or smelled, seen or heard. On the other hand, they are within the reach of the intellect and can be apprehended through the actions of the mind—at least—and this is crucial— through the minds of the gods. For it is the life of the gods that Socrates is here describing, not the human life or even the human soul, liberated at death from the burden (as Socrates clearly held) of the body, though he will

---

and shadowy image of the soul's longing for a more substantive type of spiritual joy and divine nourishment.

[11] Plato, *Phaedrus* 247c–d, emphasis added. The remarks here echo what Socrates said earlier, at 246a, where he notes that the actual nature of the soul is indescribable but an image can bring some measure of understanding. At 265b–d, Socrates will refer to this third speech and its elaborate imagery as both a "light-hearted" hymn and a "playful" speech that narrates a persuasive point. He will in that same passage note that the speech was "appropriate and respectful" toward divine Eros. In Chris Emlyn-Jones and William Preddy's *Phaedrus* (Cambridge, MA: Harvard University Press, 2022), the two translate the phrase as "appropriate and pious fashion." The pleasantries of the style should not be taken to imply either insincerity or insignificance regarding the content in Socrates's mind.

soon suggest, at 248a–249d, that the human soul, if well-prepared by piety and philosophy, does have an ability to grasp true being, at least partially.

There is, then, a tension here between three demanding aspects of the final speech. First, there is "true being"—a reality that cannot be apprehended by the senses and is beyond the reach of words. We hear echoes of Gorgias's *On Being* here. Set against Gorgias's *nothing*, Socrates is offering a very, very real *something*. But if Gorgias and Socrates disagree over whether anything has being, there is an apparent agreement between the two, as well. Gorgias argues that, even if there was some true reality, you could never know it. Socrates admits that the true being cannot be apprehended by the senses. So what does it matter whether this true being exists or not? And that question sounds an awful lot like an invitation for Isocrates to join the conversation. He might very well reply that what matters about all this is what you can *do* with the *idea* of a true being as you educate an excitable and patriotic citizenry. But for Socrates, there is more to apprehending things than the senses; true being cannot be apprehended sensibly, of course. But it can be apprehended.

Second, then, while this reality is beyond words, it is, in fact, comprehensible by divine intellects, and true being constitutes the only content of "true knowledge." And so, the gods do comprehend such being.

But finally, while this reality cannot be apprehended sensibly, it can be apprehended even by the human intellect, at least partially, by attending to the divine gifts.[12] This is a dangerous claim. It might be taken to imply, as Vlastos notes, that Socrates believes there are two different types of *knowing*, one that constitutes rationally justified true beliefs and one that is a different sort of knowledge based on religiously justified true beliefs.[13] Vlastos rejects this epistemic dualism resoundingly.[14] His argument is, in essence, that Socrates does not submit *arbitrarily* to religious authority in the signs and omens of ancient Greece, despite his praise of the oracles and rituals as divine gifts. Rather, Socrates's praise is consciously taking these divine communiqués and making them a cooperative venture since "*only*

---

[12] Note Socrates's famous proclamation in Plato's *Apology*, trans. Harold North Fowler, Loeb Classical Library 36 (Cambridge, MA: Harvard University Press, 2001), 33c, stating that his calling to philosophize has been laid upon him by the god "through oracles and dreams and in every way in which any man was ever commanded by divine power to do anything whatsoever."

[13] Gregory Vlastos, *Socrates: Ironist and Moral Philosopher* (Ithaca, NY: Cornell University Press, 1991), 164.

[14] Vlastos, *Socrates: Ironist*, 167.

by the use of his own critical reason can Socrates determine the true meaning of any of these [religious] *signs.*"[15] Vlastos's argument is subtle and nuanced. He holds that Socrates is not (exactly) sublimating the religious to a cold calculated rationality, but rather offering a sense of dependency between intellect and divine communication, posited on a sort of *pistis*, a trust or confidence—a view to which we will return in the closing chapter.

That Socrates insists on human reason as an interpretive voice for religious signs is unquestionable, of course; Socrates would certainly say the same thing about *any* sign, written, spoken, or seen. What is most notable about the religious nature of these inputs into the human understanding of life, however, is not their status as signs that can be engaged by the soul's intellect but their religious nature itself. Socrates is certainly not claiming that experience of the divine (or anything else) is either a subjective awareness beyond reflective investigation or a *prima facie* truth beyond interpretation; he may be religious, but he is not a fundamentalist. Rather, Socrates might be better understood as one who insists that the divine elements of life must be properly balanced by the gifts of human reason. But by the same token, the gifts of human reason must be properly balanced by the divine aspects of life (some of which lay outside reason's full scope). This means the divine is a participant in human reasoning: a perfectly legitimate and often even a properly necessary element of any human life and every human choice that moves toward the *vita florentis*.[16] In short, Socrates is not calling for separate realms of knowledge, one religious and the other reasonable. What he does seem to believe, however, and what he insists on here, is that sense-making is truncated if the religious element of the intellect is truncated.[17]

---

[15] Vlastos, *Socrates: Ironist*, 167, emphasis in the original. See also Rowe's commentary on 242b.8–d.2 in Christopher J. Rowe, *Phaedrus* (Warminster: Aris & Phillips, 1998) for an additional sense of the way the divine signs and the intellect are integrated.

[16] It does not follow, of course, that these peers in crafting the *vita florentis* will not, in the clouded and clumsy material world, occasionally come into problematic tension. But in Plato the problem is the material clouding, not the defining core quality of either the religious or the rational. The tensions that do occur in the material world are to be addressed through the process of collection and division.

[17] Contemporary reflections on this topic of religion-in-reason as the mature organ of sense-making are numerous and multivocal. To cite just a few: Jürgen Habermas and Joseph Ratzinger, *The Dialectics of Secularization: On Reason and Religion* (San Francisco: Ignatius, 2005); Jürgen Habermas et al., *An Awareness of What is Missing: Faith and Reason in a Post-secular Age*, ed. Ciaran Cronin (Cambridge: Polity, 2010); Ryan Gillespie, "Reason, Religion, and Postsecular Liberal-Democratic Epistemology," *Philosophy & Rhetoric* 47, no. 1 (2014): 1–24; Jacques Derrida and Gianni Vattimo, *Religion* (Stanford, CA: Stanford University Press, 1996); Walter Jost and Wendy Olmsted,

All this raises, of course, the question of how religion functions within the soul, intellectually as well as in the realm of desire and of belief. How does Socrates see—how does he *theorize*—the human intellect interacting with those divine realities present to the intellect of the gods but materially imperceptible to mortals? The shortest answer is, "Not very well."

Socrates describes the gods' encounter with the full scope of true being in the embellished image of a religious festival procession.[18] The gods leave the material spaces of the cosmos itself and enter the realm of the Forms—true being, the ideal and perfect reality of The Eternal Things—to contemplate and comprehend them.[19] The gods move easily, at will, and under the full command of their powers. The image given for this harmonious arrangement is one where each god is standing in a chariot drawn by two sublime horses. The chariot itself is winged and, in response to the divine will, crosses the full scope of nature, rises up through the heavenly spheres, and passes outside of time and space to gaze on true being. The gods and their attendants proceed in a well-ordered fashion. Socrates's descriptive language implies both solemnity and festivity. Each god fulfills its role with perfection, and the whole company is, thus, properly ordered, cooperative, and unified rather like a perfectly formed image of the perfectly ornamented universe. Such perfection and unity are due, we are told, to the fact that, in the divine world, "meanness has no place."[20] The Greek

---

Rhetorical Invention and Religious Inquiry (New Haven, CT: Yale University Press, 2000); Michael Bernard-Donals and Kyle Jensen, eds., *Responding to the Sacred: An Inquiry into the Limits of Rhetoric* (University Park: Pennsylvania State University Press, 2021); Mark A. E. Williams, "St. Socrates, Pray for Us: Rhetoric and the Physics of Being Human," in *Rhetoric in the Twenty-first Century: An Interactive Oxford Symposium*, ed. Nicholas J. Crowe and David A. Frank, 81–99 (Newcastle-upon-Tyne, UK: Cambridge Scholars Press, 2016).

[18] Plato, *Phaedrus* 246a–248a

[19] There is a long and intricate debate on the Forms as a target of human knowledge or human belief or both. Plato makes claims in the middle books of the *Republic* that create special spheres of tension here and are interpreted variously. See Gail Fine, *Plato on Knowledge and Forms* (Oxford: Oxford University Press, 2003), Chs. 3 and 4, especially. Fine's position is known as the veridical interpretation, and she argues that Plato sees the Forms as targets of both human knowledge and human beliefs and that the sensible world is open to both experiences as well. Gorgias's writings, it will be recalled, argue that knowledge of even the sensible material world is never an actual reality.

[20] Plato, *Phaedrus* 247b. Plato's phrase "*phthonos* has no place the choir of the gods" practically became a moral aphorism in the ancient world. Matthew W. Dickie notes that references to the phrase rivaled a similar expression (on the same theme) from the *Timaeus* for "the number of times it is cited or alluded to in antiquity," casually listing

word rendered *meanness* is *phthonos*, and it references a competitive envy, grasping jealousy, begrudging nature, and base ambition.[21] These are not part of the divine life, and where they appear, Socrates will tell us in 248a–e, they are an indication that one has failed to grasp the divine things. This absence of meanness among the divine beings is perfectly reasonable, of course. The gods are heading out to gaze upon the perfection of the infinite and eternal realities. What possible sense is there in mean competition for an infinite reality? One cannot reasonably be jealous of the perfection and scope of your neighbor's garden if the two of you live in an infinite garden, equally perfect in every square millimeter, and you may fence in as much perfect garden as you wish. If your neighbor fences in an infinitely large garden, there is just as much garden left over for you—and for everyone else. That is the nature of an infinite and eternal reality. Among the gods, there is no malicious jealousy or base meanness. Why would there be? And there follows, thus, skilled and delightful cooperation, complete contentment, solemn festivity, and robust comprehension of true being. The gods know fully The Things That Really Matter.[22]

And so it is with the gods. But for the humans, well, not so much. Socrates's image of the human soul mirrors that of the gods in its general outline.[23] There is a winged chariot, also drawn by two horses, and the soul's reason stands in the chariot, driving it behind the procession of the gods. But the two horses of the human soul are not quite so sublime. One, true enough, is noble and longs to ascend and pass out of nature and see the true being of The Eternal Things: divine Beauty, Justice, Truth, and so on. But the other horse has no interest in any of that spiritual nonsense and wants to be left alone to eat oats, copulate, binge watch old reruns of *Mr. Ed* the talking horse,

---

more than twenty different ancient sources. See his "The Place of *Phthonos* in the Argument of Plato's *Phaedrus*," in *Nomodeiktes: Greek Studies in Honor of Martin Ostwald*, ed. Ralph Mark Rosen and Joseph Farrell, 379–96 (Ann Arbor: University of Michigan Press, 1994), 386.

[21] In Plato's *Apology* 18d, 28b, Socrates will cite *phthonos* as one of the motives of his accusers.

[22] This vision of the gods as ordered, just, possessed of self-motivated good, and free of *phthonos* is at odds, of course, with the transactional perspective found in much of the popular religion of Greece. The relationship between the theology of Socrates and the traditional religion is a complicated one. For the best introduction from various perspectives, see Rowe's commentary in his *Phaedrus* 229c6; Vlastos, *Socrates: Ironist*, Chs. 6 and 7; and Mark McPherran, *The Religion of Socrates* (University Park: Pennsylvania State University Press, 1999), Chs. 3 and 4, especially 144–85.

[23] Plato, *Phaedrus* 248a–c.

and mind its own pleasures.[24] The first horse responds in a lively fashion to the chariot's driver, while the second horse is ornery and impatient to get back to the barn and do as it pleases. The result is rather predictable.

Socrates lays out the human soul's encounter with true being by emphasizing repeatedly the arduous and incomplete nature of this encounter. Those who have been devout followers of one of the gods and thus had their souls formed and shaped into a likeness of that divine being (those who "have closely followed a god and have come to resemble" that divinity, Socrates says at 248a) will just barely manage to get their chariots high enough to allow their sight to break into the infinite and eternal realm. Even then, however, they will be in constant distraction and confusion, careening in and out of the supernatural sights, since half the soul's team of horses has zero interest in this sort of hard work and its benefits. Keeping the chariot on course, therefore, requires enormous effort.[25] Such souls will, nevertheless, catch glimpses of true being. Only glimpses, yes, but at least they have managed to see true being, and this ability to see (*theōrein*) correctly will assist them in remembering that reality later; with the correct theory, the worth of one's reflections increases, remember. But these souls who manage to glimpse the world of true being are among the very best examples of human lives, those who have disciplined themselves in the combination of rigorous reason and pious devotion. Reason and religion have combined to provide a glimpse of The Things That Really Matter, and souls like that are better able both to order and to understand their material lives here on earth. But those are the very best of us. What of the other human souls?

> The rest all long for the upper region and follow after, but they cannot break through, and they are carried around under the surface, trampling and bumping into one another as one tries to overtake another. So there is utter chaos, nothing but sweat and conflict. In the course of this confusion many souls are crippled as a result of the incompetence of the charioteers, and many have their wings severely damaged, but even after all this effort none

---

[24] Plato, *Phaedrus* 246a–b.

[25] I keep speaking of the "infinite and eternal realm" as if this were some self-contained dimension or a universe running parallel to our own. Though Plato himself uses this language in the final speech, it is clearly identified as a creative and imaginative crutch. The Forms for Plato are literally non-spatial and non-temporal; that is, they are *super*natural, outside of all aspects and dimensions of nature. For more on this discussion, see Fine, *Plato on Knowledge*, Chs. 3 and 4.

of them succeeds in seeing things as they really are before having to return and rely on specious nourishment.[26]

Emlyn-Jones and Preddy translate the closing phrase as "and away they go and feed on what they imagine nourishes them."

There are three things to notice in these descriptions of the human soul's encounter with true being.[27] First, in exact opposition to the gods' journey, many souls are beset with competitive envy, a base ambition, and a petty need to be ahead of the others. And so it is that, second, "none of them succeeds in seeing" true being, and, thus, they order their lives around "what they imagine" to be nourishment for the soul. But of course, what they imagine will nurture the soul actually impoverishes it, since such imaginings, like Plato's view of Eros in the middle speech, have been founded on no true vision of the divine world. The word *imagine* here, *doxastē*, is related to *doxa*, opinion, Plato's usual term denouncing that which falls short of genuine understanding. And so most souls are without understanding because they do not manage even to glimpse true being. But, third—some do. And that is crucial. Some human souls do have the potential to grasp, at least in part, true being so long as reason and religion are engaged in a disciplined, cooperative venture, preparing the soul for that encounter.

True being is inaccessible to the body and beyond the reach of words, but somehow capable of being present to the human soul. Caution is in order here. Socrates is not presenting us with "true being" as a simplistic and elaborate metaphor for merely thinking in vague and insubstantial abstractions. In this discourse on true being, Socrates is, as we have noted, invoking the Forms: the divine and perfected reality of The Eternal Things, fixed in their native environment, which is atemporal and aspatial; it is actually and literally *super*natural, outside of all dimensions of nature. But there are aspects of physical human experience that, incompletely and in ways sometimes misapprehended, re-present these Forms of true being to the intellect. How true being, foreign to time and space, can become present to a mind that is constantly locked into the input of sense data is, of

---

[26] Plato, *Phaedrus* 248b–c.

[27] Vilius Bartninkas, in his consideration of Plato's attempts to "cosmologize" the traditional gods, effectively reducing them to "bundles of the right kinds of cosmological characteristics," sketches the ideal encounter between the immortal human soul and the divine beings in this passage from the *Phaedrus*. See his *Traditional and Cosmic Gods in Later Plato and the Early Academy* (Cambridge, UK: Cambridge University Press, 2023), 9–16.

course, rooted in Plato's theory of memory. Before falling into the world of matter, the very best of the unbodied human souls had glimpsed true being, and those glimpses—even as glimpses they were overwhelming, intoxicating, and beyond all words—were imprinted upon the soul's memory. These memories, however, were locked out of awareness once the soul fell into the limitations of the material body.[28] But even the senses experience hints and shadows of these divine realities, and when that happens, the soul is stirred to recall—to summon again—an awareness of true being, and so these divine realities become present, active, and alive once more to the soul's reason. The most sensually powerful of these Forms is the true being of Beauty itself, and that is what the lover sees and desires in the beloved: the passion and desire of the soul to return to intimate communion with the divine reality of Beauty itself, beyond all telling.[29]

So far, so good. But life is filled with distractions, even for an ancient Greek philosopher who has no social media temptations. And there are myriad desires that come dancing before the soul. Do they *all* beckon us toward some sort of Eternal Truth hidden away in spiritual memory? What should a soul do, pragmatically and (especially) reasonably, to sort things and figure out what belongs in the set of the divine things? And, once these are properly organized, how does one get to know the specific nature of such divine realities?[30] Or, another way to phrase the question: how does one discover the correct way of seeing the world, the correct *theōria*, the correct theory of meaning and priority?

---

[28] Plato, *Phaedrus* 250a.

[29] Plato, *Phaedrus* 249c–252c. Note that at 250d, Socrates frames these passages as a tribute to the function of memory, and this tribute explicates how the nature of true being is animated in the human soul living on earth. This is done by awakening the forgotten images of Beauty itself which the soul had previously glimpsed while liberated from the body. The passages leading up to this "favor" offered to memory are heavy with language referencing the Eleusinian Mysteries. Socrates is here noting his status as an initiate, and he may or may not be intimating those mysteries as, perhaps, having some part in his explication of the human soul. How much the mysteries actually reflect the Socratic myth is simply unknown. See Rinella, "Supplementing the Ecstatic," especially 69–73; and Kerényi, *Eleusis*, especially 45–49; as well as the relevant notes and commentary in Waterfield's *Phaedrus* and in Rowe's *Phaedrus*.

[30] Plato's fundamental course of reasoning, usually called collection and division, is a process of grouping things that belong together and then distinguishing the members of the group from one another. That method should be recognized in the questions here. The broader and underlying question is what *theory*, what way of looking, guides that method, and how is the worth of any way of *seeing*, any *theōria*, to be explored?

To begin, one might remember that *knowing* in Plato's work should not be limited to recitation of abstract data discovered by objectified scientific methodologies or framed only by formal logic. *Knowing* has—especially in the *Phaedrus*—a relational aspect. But before we get to know the divine things, it is reasonable to ask how we are able to recognize them as divine things and bring them together in a single set. And on this front, Socrates's commentary has laid down two perspectives that should provide the first steps in reasoning about the divine realities by collecting them together. We have already been introduced to both of these guidelines.

First, there is the issue of *hubris*. We have seen that excess is a method for destroying the good it pursues and that it claims to value. Regardless of how much one adores eating chocolate éclairs, if one were commanded to begin now and ceaselessly consume chocolate éclairs forever, it would not be long before the pleasure of that delicacy would cease; indeed, it would soon become a torment. Shocking, admittedly, but upon careful reflection, one realizes that it is possible to have too much chocolate éclair in your life. The same thing is true of listening to Classic Rock. Or Bach. Or being alone. Or walking. Or sex. Or coffee. But it is not true of love. There may be, as we have seen, a failure to love *well*, but of loving well and being loved well *there is no excess*. The implication is that love—a proper, mature, wise, well-formed love—has its native home in the infinite and eternal, not in the here and now. The first broad guideline in recognizing true being, then, is the test of *hubris*: can the thing be had in excess? If so, it is excluded from the set of the infinite and eternal things; if not, that implies it exists as true being. And so, that is a thing worthy of philosophic attention as the soul prepares to encounter the divine. This, of course, is an inversion of Gorgias's argument in *On Nothing*. Gorgias had said that if some real thing has an essence that is infinite, that reality could never be contained in a finite space like the realm of the natural world, and it is, thus, unknowable—and therefore irrelevant. Socrates argues that if a soul encounters a thing that cannot be had in excess, that soul has discovered something with an infinite essence and has, thus, learned something about the infinite and eternal realities outside of nature, and this is (literally) infinitely relevant. It is, in fact, the goal of knowing and generates a knowledge that prepares the soul to encounter the eternal realities more deeply and more clearly.

Second, there is the issue of *phthonos*. Jealousy, meanness, and base ambition prevent access to the divine. If The Eternal Things are approached in that way, they evaporate. Again, a few simple examples may help clarify. If my primary focus in a relationship is on showing that you do not know how to love *as well as I do*—that, in fact, *you do not love well* at all and I am *more loving* than you are—then at that exact moment and to that exact degree, I have stopped loving. Genuine love cannot survive in an atmosphere of such base competition. The quality itself vanishes under the treatment it is being given. Likewise, I cease to be a peaceful soul if I am constantly fretting about the fact that you seem more peaceful than I am. I cannot both rub my joy in your face and still be actually joyful. If my only means to justice is through intimidation or torture, I will find that justice has left the room even if my side wins. When one reaches for the divine in a base way, one always discovers that it has moved out of reach. The second clue for gathering together the qualities of the divine, then, is this: these things are never within the grasp of mean ambition.

When those souls who never even glimpsed true being tumble back into the material world, *hubris* and *phthonos*—excess and grasping ambition—are exactly those sorts of things upon which they feed, supposing them to be nourishing: they give themselves over to base ambitions and gather (to excess) things that cannot, therefore, nourish the soul. In the *Gorgias*, we saw portraits of those who, despite a thorough and highly valued education, did not even understand what was at stake in their choices. They did not understand The Things That Really Mattered. But the *Phaedrus* offers guidance in identifying what belongs in that set of divine realities.

In *hubris*, then, we discover that the temporal things cannot bear the weight of being treated as an Eternal Reality; when forced into this role, they become a withering poison to the soul. In *phthonos*, we discover The Eternal Things will not bear the indignity of being treated like a temporal reality; when forced into this role, they simply abandon the soul. These two guides, then, serve as suggestive boundaries for the philosophic intellect as it begins the process of collecting together those things which have true being.

But if these tests suggest the set of things the philosopher should be examining, we are still left without any clear vision of how to examine them. If justice and love are both collected together under the heading of The Eternal Things, it still falls to the intellect to determine, for example, how love and justice differ from each other, what each actually is, whether conflict between them is possible in the material world, and if so, how these two divine realities should be mingled or prioritized in the event of such conflict. These are no simple questions, and the program and method that one must follow to address them remains hidden as we enter the closing reflections within the *Phaedrus.*

There is also a closely related second problem here, at least for most contemporary readers. It must be noted that the set of The Eternal Things is, for Socrates, a universal set. Understanding of these issues is healthful for the soul of all persons, inescapably. Every soul that attends to the divine realities with intellectual rigor and pious devotion will move toward the *vita florentis.* Every soul that fails to attend to these specific things in that way cultivates a *vaciva vita.*[31] But we must not mistakenly assume that these Eternal Things are, in essence, invitational abstractions each individual may define privately, and that the great majority of these varied and numerous private responses are all equally valid, accurate, and worthy of celebration. Such a contemporary view is not the one we find in the text. Socrates's radically different perspective is a vision in which The Eternal Things are unchanging realities with fixed facets, and any definition or description of these realities might be accurate in some ways while being inaccurate in others, just as a person calculating the volume of a tool shed with a steeply pitched roof might get some of their measurements or calculations wrong, no matter how confident they feel about their conclusions. Of course, in the same way, they might very well be right, regardless of any profound doubts about their answer. But there is, in the end one very specific and accurate answer; whether they arrived at that correct answer is a different question. But if a question with a definite answer is set before a person who lacks the

---

[31] That is, every soul *that has the potential* of being educated. The Greeks are famously misogynistic and classist. And while they do not have exact parallels to our very modern ideas of race, they clearly think of the non-Greek peoples as inferior to themselves. And so, naturally, the idea that soul-formation is open to everyone needs some qualification since the Classical Greek authors to whom we have access appear to believe that, on the whole, many souls are simply incapable of being educated and any higher instruction of the soul would be wasted on them. It will be another seven hundred years or so before Christian ideals will lead to a routine and basic form of soul education that is (hypothetically) universal, reaching to slaves, senators, women, freedmen, and all peoples through the *homilia* portions of their weekly liturgies, a method of inner formation taken over directly from Christianity's Jewish forebears. That said, Plato was an outlier in many regards, and he suggests in more than one place that education is perfectly proper for (at least some) women. See, e.g., *Republic* V, trans. G. M. A. Grube and C. D. C. Reeve, in *Plato: Complete Works*, ed. John M. Cooper, 971–1223 (Indianapolis, IN: Hackett, 1997), or *Laws* VII, in the same volume, 1318–1616. For more on the role of women and Plato's perspectives, see Emily Hulme, "First Wave Feminism: Craftswomen in Plato's *Republic*," *Aperion* 55, no. 4 (2022): 485–507.

skill to discover a complete answer— knowing, for example, what justice means in the aftermath of a war, or how to rear children so that they unfailingly receive only what is best for them in every situation, or other tasks beyond the skills most of us possess—what is one to do?

Taken together, these two challenges raise the question of how a philosopher might respond to some individual whose understanding of the divine realities differs from their own. How is the philosopher, for example, to interact with an individual who (rather like Phaedrus) seriously believes that they, personally, would never grow weary of endlessly consuming chocolate éclairs and that such infinite consumption would, in fact, be the pinnacle of purpose for them, a divine good, a god they would never grow weary of worshiping, and so they have decided to never stop eating éclairs and to eat nothing else, ever, starting right now. The reply that is most obvious to most of us—"Wow, let's see how that works out for you"—may need some philosophical polish. The philosopher who sets out to educate and be educated on the divine realities will need to know how to persuade someone to move toward better options. That same philosopher will also need to recognize when it is wise to change one's own views: what justifies being persuaded?

The theme of rhetoric and persuasion (or seduction; the Greek word is ambiguous), then, continues in the second half of the dialogue, but the method for how to critique persuasive recommendations and the relationship that rhetoric (famous for its versatility) has to the fixed and unchanging realities of the supernatural world remain as unclear to the reader as almost everything remains to Phaedrus. At the conclusion of Socrates's soaring final speech, Phaedrus manages to comment on only one thing: this speech was, he tells Socrates, "very impressive . . . much better constructed than your first one."[32] To the soul's divided nature and its struggle to see divine reality, to the function and intensity of erotic desire as a whispered memory pointing toward divine beauty, to the way *phthonos* cripples the soul's ability to contemplate the divine, to the nature of The Eternal Things as establishing the very divinity of the gods, to the whole domain of a glorious reality beyond the reach of *logos*—to all the sweeping vistas of this phenomenal meditation on the relationship between temporal life and The Eternal Things, Phaedrus makes not one reference.

---

[32] Plato, *Phaedrus* 257c.

Technically Seducing Phaedrus

So, what is Socrates to do? How can he persuade Phaedrus to break his éclair habit and move to healthier fare for his soul? Because, in the end, there is rather a lot on the line, individually and socially, when one moves from the fictional comedy of infinite éclairs to the all-too-real tragedy of limited justice and warped ideas of love (whether of God, neighbor, or country). Socrates begins, as would any good rhetorician or educator or spiritual guide, where Phaedrus's core interests lie. For over half of the dialogue, Socrates has attempted to reveal options and to inspire Phaedrus to look beyond the most obvious and flashy aspects of description, presentation, and performance in order to see, instead, a deeper source and higher task for *logos* in partnership with the divine. Socrates has offered Phaedrus a chance to discover something in the union of *logos* and *mythos* that could never be found in *logos* alone, much less in the union of two bodies, however intense or temporarily satisfying that erotic moment might be. But to all of Socrates's heroic efforts aimed at broadening his horizons, the young Phaedrus has replied, "Huh?"

And so, Socrates, at 257d, begins again, right where Phaedrus's interests and abilities have been unflinchingly focused. Socrates talks about how to put together a speech.[33] If that is all Phaedrus can think about, that is what Socrates will talk about—at least, to begin with. Waterfield notes that the whole dialogue takes a tumble, stylistically, at this point. There is, he says, "a distinct change of register, with the first part [of the dialogue] . . . being far more poetic than the rest—far more mad, one might even say,"[34] and he bluntly notes that "it is Phaedrus who lowers the tone."[35] Socrates is still trying to persuade Phaedrus to convert to the deeper life of philosophy, but after failing to entice interest by allowing him to glimpse, Eleusinian-like, the mythic mysteries that escape *logos* alone, he turns now to blunt mechanical consideration of the technicalities involved in assembling speeches. It is worth observing that the speeches fail to deliver the requisite seduction either because of their shallow content (in the first two) or because of the inattentive nature of the audience, who (in the final speech) fails to see the important things being said. At that point, precisely where

---

[33] As a contemporary parallel, one might think of a young person obsessed with producing social media content that will grow the set of followers on their social media platforms.

[34] Waterfield, *Phaedrus*, xi.

[35] Waterfield, *Phaedrus*, 96n257c: "*so much better . . .*"

rhetoric has failed, a philosophic exploration of speech-construction takes over, aimed at technical concerns and leading quickly to detailed questions about the foundations of such *technē*, or artistry. This obvious change in approach provides a clear clue that we are now considering new methods for exploring The Eternal Things. One clear method has already been shown to us: *mythos*—though with Phaedrus we may have barely noticed. Socrates, recall, told us quite bluntly that a soul setting out to explore the divine things will need the assistance of the mythic, the religious, the image, the Musical voice, the imaginative realm of longing and emotion to guide its journey. Now we are shown a different insight. Just as *logos* is inadequate in some measure, so is *mythos*. A soul ill-prepared to *see* such epic imagery and recognize it for the divine seduction that it is will, first, require a bit of intellectual shoring-up so that its *theōrein* is better suited to this rarefied vision. Philosophical discourse, not public speaking, offers this approach.

After a prayer that closes Socrates's palinode (including a plea for Lysias's conversion so that he might be a more true lover to Phaedrus), there is a brief exchange that establishes the core question unifying the last half of the dialogue: What does it mean to speak or write well or badly?[36] This is Socrates's final, barely veiled, attempt to seduce Phaedrus into opening his eyes to the divine realities and embracing a richer, more flourishing life that acknowledges the interwoven threads of *logos* and *mythos*, reason and religion.

Just as these issues begin to be addressed most directly, however, (around 258d) we are suddenly introduced to a digression about bugs. This part of the conversation serves as a mirror of the dialogue's opening introduction and so emphasizes the new beginning.[37] Socrates turns Phaedrus's attention to the cicadas that have been singing in the trees above them. The insects were previously mentioned in the first moment Phaedrus and Socrates arrived under the shade of the plane tree and found it a place particularly haunted by the divine. Upon their arrival, Socrates remarked on an altar to the father of the Sirens, and he almost immediately mentioned the cicadas above them. In this second introduction, we discover that cicadas are emissaries to the Muses, and this revelation comes just after another

---

[36] Plato, *Phaedrus* 258d–e.

[37] For a number of parallels between the introduction to the speeches and this second introduction opening the last forty percent or so of the dialogue, see Griswold, *Self-Knowledge*, 161-62. Also, see G. R. F. Ferrari, *Listening to the Cicadas: A Study of Plato's "Phaedrus,"* Cambridge Classical Studies (Cambridge, UK: Cambridge University Press, 1987), 204, and Waterfield, *Phaedrus*, xliii.

reference to the Sirens. The very song of the cicadas in the midday heat is so rich that it tempts one to lull away the time by napping, just as the song of the Sirens lulls one to destruction.[38] But it would be wise to resist this temptation and make a different choice.

The point is clear enough. Socrates will try, once more, to steer Phaedrus away from the ruinous seductions of the flashy but vapid Siren song and toward the divine realities lauded by the Muses. And if Socrates and Phaedrus manage to resist the Sirens, engaging instead in philosophical dialogue and discourse, the cicadas will reward them with gifts: the Musical emissaries will compliment Socrates and Phaedrus to the nine goddesses, reporting that the humans have given particular honor to Calliope and Urania by discussing philosophy rather than giving in to the temptation of "mental laziness."[39] These two Muses, we are told, are particularly "concerned with the heavens and with the way both gods and men use words."[40] Calliope was the Muse associated with epic poetry. Urania was the Muse concerned with the stars. Their pairing here is a transparent reference to the mythic and supernatural realms, and Socrates's invocation of these two specific Muses at this point serves as a clear reminder that philosophy is concerned with divine realities, with supernatural being. The implication is that the supernatural world is especially pleased with the sort of human philosophical discourse Socrates is offering. In the end, philosophical pursuits and *mythos*—that is, religious life—may differ, but not nearly so much as a contemporary mind is likely to expect, or perhaps even to wish, and it is not clear that they differ at all in Socrates's view.

The second introduction closes at 259e with Phaedrus's remark, "Then we have to talk."[41] The first introduction had ended with Phaedrus saying, "Very well, listen," just before launching into his performance of Lysias' speech.[42] The contrast between the arrogant proclamation, there, of his borrowed pseudo-wise speech and the willing surrender, here, to philosophical conversation in order to please the goddesses is stark. It may be the first incident in the entire dialogue to suggest Phaedrus is open to the mythic and philosophic, though he may be, even here, speaking tongue in cheek. Either way, Phaedrus has just leapt into the

38 Plato, *Phaedrus* 259b.

39 Plato, *Phaedrus* 259a.

40 Plato, *Phaedrus* 259e.

41 Plato, *Phaedrus* 259d. *Lekteon gar oun* is the Greek.

42 Plato, *Phaedrus* 231a. The Greek is *akoue dē*.

deeps, and there is more in his surrender to discourse than is dreamt of in his rhetoric, certainly.

While the first half of the *Phaedrus* provided, on the one hand, examples of flashy but sloppy thought (seen in the first two speeches) and, on the other hand, an imaginative invitation to engage with the sublime, mythic, and supernatural realities (in the final speech), the dialogue moves, now, to a more systematic and rationalistic approach. Socrates and Phaedrus return to the question of "what makes speech and writing good, and what makes it bad."[43] This inquiry leads quickly to a question about the *technē* of rhetoric. The Greek word *technē* invokes the idea of *art* or *skill* or a *system of craft*. It implies a set of abilities rooted in serious practice coupled with experiential knowledge containing at least some teachable guidelines and rules, all of which are present in a person whose nature—whose soul—is of the sort that is predisposed to such craftsmanship, someone who has some natural talent, we would say. When all of these come together, they produce a well-crafted end specific to that *technē*. A musician who has knowledge of music, who has a natural talent for music, and who has engaged in disciplined practice will produce beautiful music. Good health is produced by the knowledgeable, experienced, talented physician; good shoes are produced by a cobbler with all those advantages; beautiful paintings by the talented, knowledgeable, experienced painter; great meals come from chefs with the same qualities, and on and on. Given the question Socrates and Phaedrus have chosen to address—how to speak and write well—it is inevitable that they begin to explore the *technē* of rhetoric in order to find out what knowledge, what practices, and what inherent talents would constitute a speaker or writer of excellence.[44]

This *technical* focus will run from 259e to 274b, making it almost exactly the same length as Socrates's final speech.[45] In the first few exchanges, Socrates previews his main ideas about rhetorical skill and presents a powerful and unambiguous thesis stating his own position, a position he invites Phaedrus to explore and challenge.

The preview offers two basic points. First, we hear the familiar claim that speakers who do not understand the topic they are addressing are a

---

[43] Plato, *Phaedrus* 259e.

[44] The topic of *technē* was a core part of the debate in the *Gorgias* as well (the term appears some forty times there), and Socrates is accused of wearing the topic out by Callicles, 491a. Plato does, in fact, return to this theme regularly throughout his dialogues.

[45] Socrates's palinode is some 4,345 words in Greek; the discussion on *technē* is 4,468 words.

silly, perhaps even dangerous, lot.[46] But second, we are also invited to ask whether a profound understanding of a subject is valuable apart from a rhetorical *technē*. What, for example, is the point of developing a deep understanding of justice or goodness unless you can convince others of the value of your insight?[47] Understanding might not be, in and of itself, persuasive to someone else, and so goodness and justice would be weakened or even made impotent without the artistry of rhetoric employed to lead souls to proper convictions about these truths. Socrates agrees this is the case, so long as rhetoric can stand on its own as an actual *technē*, as opposed to some "knack, gained by trial and error."[48] But he seems doubtful. These two points result in his direct claim, stated as a personal challenge to Phaedrus, that "unless he practices philosophy to a sufficiently high degree of competence, he will never even get close to being a competent speaker on any topic."[49] This thesis makes sense, given Socrates's concern about preparing the soul for encounters with the supernatural world of the divine realities. If the only game of rhetoric is to manufacture conviction in the soul through words, then its goal is amoral.[50] The convictions it is producing might be either tyrannical and oppressive or just and liberating. The *technē* of "producing convictions" would be the same in either case and cannot, on its own, make any distinction between the two very different programs. And this is a major problem. If, however, an art of rhetoric could be shown to necessarily champion justice and lead a soul toward virtue and truth, that would be an art worth having. But the only way rhetoricians could perform this act of proper education, leading the soul toward truth and producing convictions that are virtuous, would be if they themselves have an understanding of virtue, if they themselves understand what justice is. But understanding justice requires philosophic discipline.

And so Socrates lays his cards on the table early in the *technical* discussion, stating plainly his position that a rhetorical *technē*, however fully developed, is inadequate on its own to produce a speech that is good since rhetoric, on its own, cannot discern goodness. This is not the first time we

---

[46] Note the discussion of going into battle on a donkey in Plato, *Phaedrus* 260a–d.

[47] This act of bringing others to see the deeper nature of justice or goodness is, of course, the very job given to the philosopher-king in the *Republic*. These ideal leaders would be able to imprint the power of the Forms on the souls of their subjects.

[48] Waterfield, *Phaedrus*, xxxii; *Phaedrus* 260e.

[49] Plato, *Phaedrus* 261a.

[50] Plato, *Phaedrus* 261a, 271a, 271c–d.

have been warned about the limits of human *technē*. Socrates has already told Phaedrus that "anyone who approaches the doors of poetic composition without the Muses' madness," believing that "skill [*technēs*] alone will make him a competent poet," is destined for poetic failure.[51] Knowing the rules of good poetry, practicing those rules, and even having a bit of talent will not turn one into a poet unless the composition is also *in-spirited*, animated, through some trafficking with the supernatural and divine. The same is true of speech. Skill and artistry require commerce with the divine realities to create an effect that is good or just, and any speaker without a soul that is alive to such commerce "will never even get close to being a competent speaker."[52] The type of education that prepares the soul to interact with the supernatural world—philosophy—is the knowledge and practice that is necessary to produce worthwhile speech.

This appears to be the claim Socrates invites Phaedrus to investigate and challenge. Once the claim is stated, Socrates immediately forwards a definition that rhetoric is "a kind of skillful leading of the soul by means of words, not only in public gatherings such as the law courts, but also in private meetings," and he states that the same set of skills is involved regardless of whether one "is dealing with slight or great issues."[53] Phaedrus is shocked by this since his education has prepared him to think of rhetorical skill as a thing operating strictly in the realm of political advantage and legal argument. That is, Phaedrus sees rhetoric as anchored to issues of power and victory. That the use of language might have something to do with the formation of the soul, addressing issues outside the seemingly high-stakes settings of Athenian political life, is news to him: he has not "heard of any wider use" for rhetorical education, as he tells us at 261b.

A number of relevant points emerge in the discussion that follows. While Socrates has already suggested (several times) that persuasive individuals who do not possess a philosophical understanding of a subject might cause troubles, he turns now to concerns about persuasive individuals who, in fact, do understand a subject like justice or goodness, at least in

---

[51] Plato, *Phaedrus* 245a. See Griswold's remarks on 162 on the limits of *technē*. The expectation in this passage is that, apart from some collusion with the divine realities, *technē* will fail. Compare this view with the one expressed by Gorgias, who states that *artistry* (*technē*) not truth (*alēthia*) is what actually matters; Gorgias, *Encomium on Helen*, in *Early Greek Philosophy, Vol. VIII: Sophists, Part I*, ed. and trans. André Laks and Glenn W. Most, Loeb Classical Library 531 (Cambridge, MA: Harvard University Press, 2016), 13.

[52] Plato, *Phaedrus* 261a.

[53] Plato, *Phaedrus* 261b.

part, but set out to use this knowledge to manipulate or deceive another.[54] The two images—the silly soul who bumbles into absurdity because it does not understand and the toxic soul who has some limited understanding but chooses to use that insight to manipulate others—cannot help but call to mind the first two speeches. Lysias's enlightened self-interest seems to stumble through love-logistics while missing the whole point of what intimacy and passion offer to a human soul. The middle speech, on the other hand, suggests a person who understands the passions of love at least in part, but that partial understanding leads to misunderstanding and then deceit and toxic manipulation. And, in fact, it is precisely the manipulative lover's limited grasp of what is true that empowers those deceits. If I sincerely set out to convince you that your kitchen table is planning to empty your bank account and run away to Patagonia with the toaster, there is a good chance I am only likely to convince you that I know nothing about kitchen tables and toasters. On the other hand, if I sincerely set out to convince you that your representative in government is taking bribes, this probability (even as a lie) is much harder for you to dismiss as utterly outlandish; we both know that politicians are, sometimes, corrupt. And since my lie has some resonance with known reality, it can be made much more convincing. Deception works "by means of similarities" to what is true, and those who best understand some situation are the ones best able to approximate what is true so that, with subtle adjustments and suggestive frames, they are more able to persuade me to form a conviction that is not true.[55] They are better able to deceive me. And so, by using their understanding of truth (politicians are often corrupt), a manipulator can make a lie seem far more probable; where they are without an understanding of truth (where they believe, for example, that kitchen tables are sentient), they are less likely to succeed.

Socrates also leads Phaedrus into a discussion on the mechanics of collection and division which picks up his thesis (that a high degree of competence in philosophy is a prerequisite to being a competent speaker on any subject whatsoever) and offers reinforcement for it. Collection and division (recognizing sets of things that, by their common nature, belong together, and then distinguishing the members of each set from one another according to their natural distinctions) are, we discover, how one manages to become "good at speaking *and thinking.*"[56] Socrates then re-

---

[54] Plato, *Phaedrus* 261d–262c.

[55] Plato, *Phaedrus* 262b.

[56] Plato, *Phaedrus* 266b, emphasis added.

veals that those who are skilled in this process are called dialecticians—that is, philosophers.[57] So the *technē* of rhetoric, if there is an actual *technē* of rhetoric, either must follow behind the method of philosophy or must be in some way consubstantial with that method of philosophy. And so, if a *technē* is knowledge, practice, and nature, then philosophy provides the knowledge needed for the rhetorical *technē*, practicing philosophy is the drill needed for the rehearsal of rhetoric, and the soul properly informed by pious philosophy is the one that has the nature required to speak what is true and needful. And it is not the art of rhetoric alone that is dependent upon the philosophic method of collection and division. Anything that can be taught as a *technē* will, in fact, be involved with this method.[58] Of course, if collection and division teach the dialectician how to speak and think clearly about things, that raises a serious problem for any autonomous *technē* of rhetoric.

In short, Socrates seems to believe that rhetoric is caught between a rock and a hard place. Without a dialectical road into the divine, rhetoric bumbles along like a fool, making itself a servant to passing trends and shiny misunderstandings filled with the sort of jargon-heavy "chattering and highbrow speculation" that offers only glitter-covered pseudo-skills for living well.[59] Rhetoric never rises above Lysias's speech. On the other hand, the rhetorician who is savvy and attentive or who has casually picked up some partial grasp of some aspects of some truths—well, such a person seems to be acquiring only the raw material to become an improved manipulator, rather like the "lover" of the middle speech.

In answer to both of these challenges, the *technical* discussion is peppered with references to the idea of *the whole*—that is, a broad awareness of how any specific aspect of a *technē*, from music to medicine to rhetoric, is to be applied *properly*, which means both contextually and skillfully.[60] The more precise and the broader this awareness, the better, of course, but all such awareness must be rooted in an experiential, self-conscious, and lived understanding of an art's abilities, limits, and goals.[61] The implication, in

---

[57] Waterfield notes in *Phaedrus* that in (what is sometimes called) Plato's "middle period," the idea of dialectic "took on a more metaphysical and mystical hue," though "there are grounds for thinking that Plato saw more similarities than differences between these different phases of dialectic": see the note on 101, addressing 266c, regarding *dialecticians*.

[58] Plato, *Phaedrus* 266d.

[59] Plato, *Phaedrus* 270a. I have here used Emlyn-Jones and Preddy's translation.

[60] Plato, *Phaedrus* 270c–d.

[61] Plato, *Phaedrus* 268a–271d. See also Waterfield's note at 270c.

the context of the discussion regarding the importance of collection and division, is that the dialectical method is a crucial aspect of sharpening this awareness and providing this view of a *technē's* wholistic and *proper* context. Near the beginning of an emphasis on the perspective of the whole, Socrates invites Phaedrus "to look and see, my friend, if you agree with me that there are holes in the fabric of the points we've already raised" regarding rhetorical skill.[62] The dialectic approach discovers, in what follows, the need for the broader perspective if one is to make valuable use of any aspect of a *technē*. This turn in the conversation winds down with Socrates praising the teachers of rhetoric in language thick with sarcasm. They are all knack and narrow technique rather than understanding and broad perspective. He then states that those who teach what presently passes for a rhetorical *technē* without the broader context that can only be found dialectically "thought they had discovered what rhetoric was when they had learnt only the necessary prerequisites."[63] These prerequisites are the things usually found in the handbooks of the time (and in public speaking textbooks today): the parts of the speech, the arrangement of evidence, sensible transitions, clear enunciation, the construction of compelling narratives, and so forth. But a real rhetoric—a rhetorical *technē*—would be able to see beyond such mechanical procedures and grasp a bigger picture. This view would be held by someone whose soul was talented in understanding the divine realities. Rhetoric might be able to be valuable, but only if it functions in concert with a soul that understands divine values and priorities. When the conversation turns, as it will shortly, to writing, we discover the same theme: writing has some purpose only when contextualized in a wholistic vision—a theory—of life that incorporates the divine. This is the recurring theme of the *Phaedrus* on every topic that comes up.

Pragmatically, since rhetoric is the art of leading the soul toward convictions, understanding the soul would have to be the primary task of a genuine rhetorician: "the soul is what he focuses all his efforts on, since it is the soul in which he is trying to produce conviction."[64] So a true rhetorician, like a true poet, like a true writer, is one whose primary study is how to lead the soul into cooperation with the divine.

---

[62] Plato, *Phaedrus* 268a.

[63] Plato, *Phaedrus* 269b–c.

[64] Plato, *Phaedrus* 271a. See also 261a, 270c.

Almost Impossible or Absolutely Undesirable?
Competing Theories

The *technical* discussion closes, then, with the presentation of two competing theories or visions of a rhetorical *technē*. These are described back-to-
back, with the first laid out in 271d–272b. This is Socrates's presentation of
the proper *technē* in light of all that has gone before. We discover that the
perfect *technē* for speech is one in which, not surprisingly, the sweep of
human souls is collected into the proper general types, probably in accord
with their religious predispositions. That is, the advice here likely echoes
the passages discussing the various types of noble madness and the attendant deities found at 250b, 252c–253c, and 265b–c. Most particularly, one
must learn what motivates and charms each of the various sorts of human
souls. Some are easily shaped on some subjects, while others are resistant
to change on that same topic but whose convictions may be directed more
easily in other areas. And, echoing the discussion on *the whole* above, it is
not enough simply to have an abstract understanding of these things because a true rhetorical artist would also possess the ability to see which sort
of soul is present in any given context, recognizing the specific sort of soul
inhabiting some very concrete person standing in front of the rhetor and
noting that this soul is of the sort more likely to be moved by emotion than
complex causal arguments, or vice versa. Book knowledge must become
experiential knowledge so that the rhetorician will be able to recognize the
particular example as well as define the general idea of each type of soul.

Once there is a thorough understanding of souls, the next step in
mastering the art of rhetoric is to recognize the host of possible types of
speeches and how they act to move a soul and which souls they most affect and in what way. And to this, one must add contextual circumstances
that also have to be grasped: when it is time to keep silent; when it is
time to speak briefly, and when the occasion suggests a longer appeal;
and which emotions would be best suited to each complex interaction of
soul, and topic, and situation, and how to arouse such emotions. There is
little wonder that so many have decided that Socrates has here damned
rhetoric by impossible ideals, setting the bar for a rhetorical *technē* so
very high so as to make it unreachable.[65] Perhaps, though it is difficult to
see how Socrates's requirements for a true rhetorician are so very much

---

[65] This is Waterfield's position. See his introduction to *Phaedrus* as well as his note at
258c.

higher than those laid out by Isocrates in *Panathenaicus*.[66] Nevertheless, if rhetoric is—in isolation from dialectic—an amoral force for producing convictions without connection to what is just and good and is, in the end, unwilling to undergo the rigorous demands of figuring out what justice actually is, then it is understandable that Socrates might want to increase rhetoric's load to the breaking point. There is no shortage of good minds who hold that position. And some lesser minds have leaned in that direction, as well. Once the Socratic view of the rhetorical *technē* is laid out, for example, Phaedrus remarks that this appears, indeed, to be the only way to achieve a *technē* of rhetoric, but he then notes that such "expertise does seem to be quite an arduous business."[67] Indeed. But there may be other options here, as we shall see.

Before exploring whether Socrates has only pretended to seek a *technē* of rhetoric while secretly planning to torpedo rhetoric as soon as it came into range, we need to note the competing *technē* laid out in 272d–273c. Here, Socrates sketches the standard view—whether from Gorgias's or Isocrates's school—which avoids "the long and circuitous route involved in referring things back to first principles" since, under this theory of rhetoric, an orator need not worry about the truth concerning what is good and just. In this art of rhetoric, the author of the discourse need only focus, instead, on crafting a believable perspective "because rhetorical skill depends entirely on one's speeches being infused throughout by probability."[68] Socrates suggests, and Phaedrus robustly agrees, that in this theory of rhetorical *technē*, the idea of *probability* presented here can only mean something like *whatever it takes to win the audience over to your side*.[69] For anyone interested in justice, the point seems to damn rhetoric, at least under this idea of a rhetorical *technē*, though it does allow the remote possibility that the core of rhetoric's focus, probability, may have other functions in other schools of thought. But within this second view of the rhetorical *technē*, the discussion of probability does sound suspiciously like a return to the theme of manipulation.[70] Socrates emphasizes this connection by noting that an argument of probability works "because of its similarity to the truth,"

---

[66] Isocrates, *Panathenaicus*, in *Isocrates, Vol. II*, trans. George Norlin, Loeb Classical Library 229 (Cambridge, MA: Harvard University Press, 1992), 30–32.

[67] Plato, *Phaedrus* 272b.

[68] Plato, *Phaedrus* 272d–e.

[69] Plato, *Phaedrus* 273a–b.

[70] Plato, *Phaedrus* 272e. Compare 262b.

suggesting that those with some grasp of the truth will be able to construct the best arguments to win people over to their side, just as they are in the best position to manipulate others—and probably those are the same thing.[71] But in all this, they must also be in a position to understand something of what is true; otherwise, they cannot persuade (or manipulate). Either way, then, whether the rhetorical artist is looking to persuade or manipulate (assuming those can be disentangled), some understanding of what is real and true and meaningful (at least to this audience) has to be present in the rhetorician's mind.

The obvious implication is that if the manipulators wish to be persuasive, they, rather like the true rhetoricians, also have to have an understanding of the sort of souls that are in the audience; the sort of circumstances that presently dictate the types of, length of, and emotional content of the appeals appropriate in this situation for this audience; the speech devices that can produce those effects; and the ability to present these devices with some forcefulness. In a passage that narrows Phaedrus's lines of escape from the demanding life of pious philosophy, Socrates offers this summary: "Now, a sensible person should not expend all that effort in order to speak and act in the world of men, but in order to be able to make speeches that are pleasing to the gods and to act, whatever he is doing, in ways that gratify them, to the limits of his abilities."[72] This is a familiar refrain in Socrates's conversations. While he always begins with the relevant particulars of any given moment, the consistent conclusion is that once a soul has become mature and reasonable, it prioritizes the divine and supernatural things as the ordering principle in the natural world of human concerns, decisions, and convictions.

Socrates closes his dismissal of the second *technē* by noting that a person looking for the art of rhetoric "shouldn't be surprised if the route is long and circuitous, because the goals for which the journey is undertaken are important, not the trivial ones you suppose."[73] It is harder to please the gods than to impress one's peers, but the goal of ordering one's speech and actions in accord with the divine world is what matters. The world of human power and the game of win-at-all-costs discourse is, by comparison, pretty petty stuff.[74] But the implication in the exchange here

---

[71] Plato, *Phaedrus* 273d. This phrase exactly echoes the discussion of deceit at 262b.

[72] Plato, *Phaedrus* 273e.

[73] Plato, *Phaedrus* 274a.

[74] Even if—perhaps especially if—you win, as Socrates emphasized in the close of the Gorgias.

is even larger. The trivial matters Socrates references are clearly the two main goals of rhetoric: victory in the law court and the establishment of policy in the assemblies. Assuming one genuinely wanted to have a just legal system and, further, that one sought policies to genuinely serve the common good of all those in the society, even these goals of human politics and social order are, when one stops to think about it clearly, better served by the genuine and demanding pursuit of the gods' perspective. In fact, without the pursuit of the divine, *logos* is reduced to a rather emaciated set of options. These are anchored, as in Callicles's world, to nothing larger than self-interest or (in Isocrates's world) state power. Rather than speech in search of words that are just, tapping into a divine justice common to us all, one is left with nothing more than words in search of a factional victory: just words as tools of petty power games where all moral appeals are manipulation of the strong by the weak. But if a soul has been "prepared to pursue the important" goals, it follows that even the "trivial goals" will be more likely to be achieved as well, we are told, since the only path to an actually just community lies through the discovery of actual justice itself, and that discovery is only found through the demanding discipline of participation with the divine life.[75]

Why Don't You Write This Down So You Can Remember It?

Phaedrus is overwhelmed. If he previously considered the pursuit of a true rhetoric to be an arduous matter, he now despairs. Certainly, this would be the best way to move forward "if only one could put it into practice!" he laments.[76] And Socrates immediately makes his next point in an uncharacteristically succinct way. In a single brief sentence, he states that any attempt to pursue the higher things—even as an attempt—conforms the soul to those higher things, regardless of "whatever happens" circumstantially.[77] The attempt itself, even if the goal is never fully realized, raises one above mere material things, and so the pursuit of what is beautiful and good and just forms the soul in such a way that every situation contributes to that

---

[75] Plato, *Phaedrus* 274a.

[76] Plato, *Phaedrus* 274a.

[77] Plato, *Phaedrus* 274a.

soul's increasing nobility,[78] regardless of "success or failure."[79] The implication is that the quest itself is good.

Once he has, in less than a single breath, made this point, Socrates immediately closes down the logistical question of how to build a *technē* of rhetoric because Phaedrus is, finally, ready to address a larger question.

Socrates asks Phaedrus if the youth understands how to approach language, either in practice or in theory, so as "to please god."[80] Phaedrus is at a loss: "No, I don't. Do you?"[81] Socrates is coy in his reply, and, suddenly, we are back to the realm of *mythos*, imagination, parables, and stories that might give us some guidance. And what guidance! If he and Phaedrus found the way to this insight—how to please god—"would we any longer have the slightest interest in mere human conjectures?" Phaedrus offers a hopeful hint that he is at last getting his priorities in order: "What an absurd question! Please tell me what you say you've heard" on this topic, he requests.[82]

And here we enter what is, apart from the flying chariots, perhaps the most famous part of the dialogue. Socrates tells the story of a god or demi-god, Theuth, who invents writing as a gift for humanity and submits it for review to his divine superior, Thamous. Thamous provides a rather harsh critique of this new technology. The following discussion between Socrates and Phaedrus compares writing with speech, especially speech in a private setting where there is a frank exchange and honest exploration of a theme—essentially, Platonic dialectic. In contemporary reviews, two points are often made at this juncture. The first is that writing is dismissed by Socrates because of its inability to offer clarification or answer questions that occur to the reader. The second is that writing is considered dangerous because it undermines memory. These are almost certainly not the primary points of the exchange from 274b forward (especially through 277a).

---

[78] In Greek, a form of *kalos*. The word is used here in the plural neuter, so *the noble (or beautiful, or good) things*—unless, of course, one wishes to read this as a substantive masculine, which might then be translated as the pursuit of "beautiful or noble or good men." See Rowe's commentary on this passage in his translation. The erotic *double entendre* tone of the dialogue has not been abandoned, but that joke is clearly subsumed here by the more spiritualized focus. Waterfield translates the word as "something fine," and Emlyn-Jones and Preddy also use the word "fine."

[79] The "success or failure" phrase is taken from a note on the passage in R. Hackforth's translation, *Plato's "Phaedrus": Translated with an Introduction and Commentary* (Cambridge, UK: Cambridge University Press, 1972), 154.

[80] Plato, *Phaedrus* 274b.

[81] Plato, *Phaedrus* 274b.

[82] Plato, *Phaedrus* 274c.

That writing cannot answer questions hardly makes it useless. It does make it, among other things, the wrong medium to pass along a *technē*.[83] Any *technē* will require an experiential knowledge communicated through physical demonstrations, lived questions, and a host of exchanges with someone who has embodied that craft: "No. Hold the hammer further back, like *this*" and "Tell me, master, how can I paint these shadows so they are more translucent?" and "See these pinholes? That means you overfired the bowl and the glaze was starting to break down." While it is possible to write up copious instructions, not every possible contingency can be covered in the instruction manual, and nothing can replace a master of the craft showing, adapting, and embodying the experiential knowledge of an art like stone masonry or painting or pottery or, for that matter, living a genuinely pious and religious life.[84]

No doubt this limitation found in written texts is a criticism of the educational and rhetorical handbooks, of course, but those handbooks have, by now, become little more than a dark icon for the wrong way to do life. For it is important to remember that this conversation between Socrates and Phaedrus is presently about how to use *logos* in order to please god. Phaedrus had lamented that he could not imagine how to put such a program into practice. Socrates is explaining that this pursuit is not like learning the parts of a speech or memorizing the nine templates for undermining your opponent. That stuff you probably can get from a book. But pursuing a pious life that seeks to encounter the divine things will not be learned from an instruction manual. A mentor skilled in that precise pursuit might be just what is needed to begin "putting it into practice," however.

And, truly, another downside to writing is that it can be a form of soulless memorization rather than animated memory. The written *logos* can be meaningless to a soul who is not prepared for it, just as the vision of *mythos* can fall flat on a soul whose theory is too shallow or whose attention is too dissipated to recognize the divine seduction present within it.

---

[83] Plato, *Phaedrus* 275c–d.

[84] Any enthusiastic hobbyist is familiar with this experience. In two hours at a craft fair or trade convention, you learn more about the art (whether it is calligraphy, restoring classic cars, or gardening) than you are likely to learn in a week of reading or even watching videos online. In the same way, a single dinner with Plato would almost certainly solve ten thousand scholarly questions about Plato's writings. For many of the same reasons that imbue such personal exchanges with value, gathering physically for communal ritual and liturgical celebrations is usually identified as a crucial part of most religious traditions, including in the pagan world of Socrates.

When watching a third-grader repeat the words of the Gettysburg Address or Martin Luther King's *I have a dream*, one has a vivid sense that this is not the speech of a soul who understands the larger, richer, and more painful vision of the whole from which those words emerged and who is, therefore, able to draw from the deeps of this well of suffering in order to re-collect and animate that watershed moment of meaning. Written texts are, as any teacher knows, quite capable of producing individuals who remain in the mindset of that third-grade performance though much older: individuals with a vast *doxosophoi*—a "spurious appearance of wisdom"—peppered with the most current jargon, which turns such individuals into "difficult company."[85] Pedantic book-learning or trendy taxonomy without the pain and peril of honest self-knowledge make for pretty unpleasant conversationalists, and these stand in stark contrast to those lively dialectical partners who, in the end, are honestly seeking a *technē* of spiritual life.

These limitations of writing, however, hardly mean writing is to be disparaged. Even if Socrates's remarks at 258c–d, where he seems to dismiss criticism of speech writers, are read as entirely ironic,[86] it is still the case that at least twice in the dialogue, Socrates specifically insists that Phaedrus read parts of Lysias' speech rather than recite them, and there are two other times when he requests readings without the direct comparison to recitation.[87] Neither reading nor writing is "*itself* something shameful."[88] But still, there is clearly criticism of writing.

Rowe's commentary on this crucial passage, especially 275a, provides a glimpse of how these various themes are intricately interwoven in this carefully crafted passage. As Theuth's gift of writing is being critiqued, the god Thamous observes that it is likely to give human beings "an appearance of wisdom, not the reality of it."[89] The word *reality* here is double-edged. The Greek is a form of *alētheia*, truth. But in the context

---

[85] Plato, *Phaedrus* 275b.

[86] The praise offered to some of the great politicians is clearly tongue in cheek, but the conclusion at 258d is more ambiguous.

[87] See Plato, *Phaedrus* 228d–e and 263e, as well as 230e and 262d. The phrasing in the first two references offer an especially pointed comment on the value of writing: " . . . when Lysias is here, too," in the written speech and "I'd like to hear the man himself." The implication is that what is written is, somehow, a genuine reflection of the soul that wrote it.

[88] Rowe's translation, 258d. The emphasis is original to the translation and captures something of the ambiguity in this passage.

[89] Plato, *Phaedrus* 275a. The translation is Rowe's.

of this discourse on memory, there is likely a second emphasis here. The Greek for *forgetfulness* is *lēthē*. The Greek word for *truth* here suggests a negation of forgetting: *a-lēthē*. The emphasis here is on the living reality of wisdom, rooted, on the one hand, in the negation of forgetfulness about the divine reality and so, on the other hand, in memory's animation of the divine world.[90] This connection between memory and the divine realities within the soul is also seen in the line just above this one, where Thamous notes that, as faith in writing grows, memory will be attuned to material signs—letters and words—outside of the soul rather than enlivening those spiritual qualities that are a dormant part of the interior life of the soul. The word for *remembering* in this passage is the same term Socrates had used in the final speech, at 249c, to describe how beauty in the divine world was made real and animate within the human soul through the process of recollection, overcoming the forgetfulness that clouded the soul at the time of its material embodiment.

Writing, it seems, can become an image of that fall into material forgetfulness: a sign of the wrong kind of forgetting and the wrong kind of remembering, set in contrast to the right kind of forgetting and remembering: the Muses' gift of forgetfulness of evil and the soul's ability to remember, and thus animate, the divine realities.

The criticism Socrates offers of the written word, then, is not so very far removed from the criticism he offers of those religious voices that prefer the tidy natural rationalisms they create over the supernatural realities beyond their control; he took these *doxosophoi* to task for failing to acknowledge a higher, and demanding, reality.[91] And the criticism is, furthermore, very like the criticism he heaps upon Polus and then upon Callicles in the *Gorgias*. The problem that frustrated Socrates there was the prioritization of an image of wisdom (in order to impress others and empower a political faction) above the pursuit of actual wisdom, even if it was costly for one's standing and social reputation. These misdirected ends, not rhetoric *per se*, were the problems. The failure to prioritize all these in the context of the whole of life was what frustrated him—especially since these views had omitted the most essential part of that wholistic vision of life: the divine realities. And so, the priorities were, necessarily, disordered. For whatever is named as the first priority in any vision (or theory) will inevitably be an

---

[90] See Rowe's commentary on this passage. He is not the first to make this association, as he himself points out.

[91] Plato, *Phaedrus* 229c–230a.

error if that vision misunderstands the most important priorities. But of course, the uncomfortable conclusion is that these *lesser things must, then, be ordered in relation to*—which clearly means *below*—the divine realities.

So, clearly, Socrates is not an absolute enemy to the written word itself. And in fact, at 276a, Socrates brings Phaedrus to acknowledge bluntly that writing can serve memory in the same way that physical beauty functions to re-collect the memories of beauty itself. The true written word, like a truly beautiful body, would be "a mere image" of things that have been animated—*empsuchon*, ensouled—by the author.[92] As he has at every turn since the conclusion of his palinode, Socrates immediately notes that such robust efforts would wisely be expended on the hard work of animating the divine for one's soul, not any lesser work such as, in this case, impressing one's audience.[93] And words physically written on a page can, like physical beauty, have some part in that process of ensouling the good. But writing (and its outcome, book knowledge) should, like physical beauty, not be confused with that larger end, with knowing, *ensouling*, the divine realities. The goal of pleasing god takes priority over all other goals and options. But in service to that goal, writing may have a place. Just as a poetic *technē* is dead without divine interaction, but helpful to the divine enterprise, so also writing is dead without a properly formed soul, but may be helpful to a soul that has properly animated the divine things.[94]

But we must not pass too quickly over Phaedrus's insight at the end of 276a. The youth seems to stumble into a moment of clarity at last. Socrates's point, a point of every religious mystic, is that the soul's encounter with the divine is always to be preferred to the images of those divine encounters, and Phaedrus is finally able to say this, in his own words, about the thing he himself values most: words.

For someone who has animated the divine realities, keeping them actual and lively within their own soul, writing can be a worthwhile but obviously lesser endeavor, a way of "storing up things to jog [one's] own memory" in later life, Socrates notes. "He'll happily watch these delicate gardens [of written words] growing, and he'll presumably spend his time diverting himself with them rather than the symposia and so on with

---

[92] Plato, *Phaedrus* 276a. The quoted phrase and the choice of the powerful word *empsuchon* are both, notably, Phaedrus's.

[93] Plato, *Phaedrus* 275b–d.

[94] At 248c, Socrates emphasizes the inadequacy of *technē* without divine commerce, but it is clear from 268c–e that rational, teachable elements have a contribution to make to the success of the arts. See Waterfield's note on the Muses in his translation at 245a.

which other people amuse themselves."[95] Phaedrus is, once more, drawn just a bit further in: "What a wonderful kind of diversion you're describing, Socrates—that of a person who can amuse himself with words, as he tells stories about justice and the other things you mentioned—compared with the trivial pastimes of others!"[96] Such a soul becomes not self-sufficient (that is hardly the goal), but at least more whole and complete because of its intercourse with the divine. The crucial point reiterated here is not that writing is stupid, but that the good found in writing, like the good found in rhetoric, like the good found in beautiful bodies, like any good found in any material experience whatsoever, is to be used to prepare the soul for and to spur it toward an encounter with the divine and that, furthermore, these lesser goods lose much of their significance when put to any other use.[97] In those cases, they cease to be *meaningful* because their fundamental relationship to reality has become distorted. Unless the soul chooses to pass through such pleasures and goods to the divine good itself, such pleasures wither into "specious nourishment," and that soul, after a great deal of hard work, perhaps even heroic work, is nevertheless a withered and broken thing trafficking in meaningless trifles.[98] Such a soul may be shallow and inattentive, like the lover in Lysias's speech, or petty and toxic, like the lover of the middle speech, or naïvely inconsistent, like Gorgias's character in the *Gorgias*, or pretentious and confused, like Polus, or grasping, greedy, ambitious, and self-centered, like Callicles; all these are merely species of the *vaciva vita*. What they are not, and what they cannot be, is whole and flourishing human souls because they have not submitted to the good. They have not united memory—the human quality that animates experience

---

[95] Plato, *Phaedrus* 276d. It is, after reading this passage, hard not to imagine Plato sitting around in his later years re-reading his dialogues.

[96] Plato, *Phaedrus* 276e.

[97] Any implication that Plato rejected writing because it ensconced a broader distribution of power that threatened his elitist rejection of Panhellenism—precisely why Isocrates accepted and celebrated writing—seems to me amiss on two fronts. First, Plato clearly did not reject or fear writing. Second, the distribution of power, whether rooted in the mediated technology of writing or in the broader force of arms or in the more limited force of public speeches seems to matter less to Plato than the question, equally applicable to each locus of power, of how such powers might be critiqued so as to assess their contribution to or thwarting of the soul's progress toward the divine realities. Compare with Nathan Crick in *Rhetoric and Power: The Drama of Classical Greece* (Columbia: University of South Carolina Press, 2018), 179–81 and 193–97.

[98] Plato, *Phaedrus* 248b. Of course, in Plato's vision, it does not follow that such souls will *appear* withered and broken, only that they *are* withered and broken.

and grants it permission to in-form and educate the immortal soul—to the timeless and divine realities.

So, how does one use *logos* in order to please god? By using *logos* to make lively and actual the divine things in one's own soul. This is accomplished by the soul's recognition that lesser things are lesser and will not nourish the soul except as hints, signs, and suggestive guides. They exist as material sketches and temporal evidence of supernatural and eternal things. Those eternal matters are more completely understood and embraced through the disciplined application of rigorous intellect and religious devotion. Shockingly, all this is exactly what Socrates had said in the final speech.

In Plato, truth constitutes a way in which the soul's intellect orders itself in relation to the divine beings. As such, truth is neither an objectified status independent of a mind nor a private sense of seeming independent of the unchanging divine. Rather, it is the relational nature of spiritual intellect and divine being. There is unquestionably some leeway in the phenomenological nature of that relationship, but it cannot be simply *whatever I feel comfortable with* or there is nothing to collect (or divide) and the intellect is adrift and has no actual relation to any reality beyond itself, and certainly not to that very Other being which is the supernatural. On the other hand, neither can these relationships be reduced to a fundamentalist assertion of *exactly this*, because the supernatural is simply beyond the scope of the analytical mind and can never be completely stated.[99] The divine is, in the former, merely a congratulatory title awarded to whatever the self prefers. In the latter, the divine is made into a moderately complicated puzzle that the self has already solved and now comprehends completely. Each of these two approaches to the divine realities are forms of a self-flattery that manage to side-step any actual relationship with what is greater than the self, reducing the nature of infinite and eternal being to the limited and temporal scope of my soul's desires and abilities. Very little extrapolation is involved before one concludes that both views are species of *hubris* and both invite *phthonos*. But it is not merely the soul's relationship to the divine that suffers under these views. No healthy relationship of any sort is possible in a frame that, on the one hand, requires the Other to become whatever I want it to be or, on the other hand, never allows the Other to be more complicated

---

[99] It follows, of course, that the soul's relationship to the divine will be both limited by the nature of that Other and not entirely comprehensible by the soul. This sets up a pretty puzzle: how does one explore the limits that the substance of the divine requires since that substance is beyond comprehension?

(or mysterious!) than I can fathom. A relationship under these rubrics can only exist with an entirely imagined being. Socrates is having none of it. He insists that the relationship to the divine is a relationship to an actual Other that is real and independent of the soul's preferences or choices, one that is larger than the intellect's abilities.[100] To be in relationship to the divine is to be in relationship with what is both superior to one's own being and beyond one's comprehension or control.

The divine beings certainly embrace scope and temporal potentialities: they can be encountered in many different specifics, but they have within them limits and eternal boundaries. In this relationship between the soul and the divine realities, then, there are necessarily specific and demanding requirements that prevent the soul from doing whatever it wishes, and there are always mysteries beyond the soul's full knowledge. The soul's intellect is, quite simply, too limited to engage the divine fully. But others might see some aspects of the divine I have not, and so seeking out their different perspectives may be necessary for my own understanding. The implication of these ideas, their deeper connection to Gorgias and Isocrates, and their contemporary implications remain to be explored.

In the preface to her *Aspects of Truth*, Catherine Pickstock forwards two claims she will spend the rest of her book explicating. Her first is that "truth is to be regarded as metaphysical rather than epistemological."[101] In other words, no mere brainwork will arrive at the fullest encounter of truth, for truth is transcendent. Her second point is that truth exists "as proportion between things and mind."[102] Here, her emphasis is on the idea that a mind never arrives at an encounter with truth if that mind is uninterested in the proper balanced response to the whole of reality, physical and metaphysical. These are complex philosophical and theological (Pickstock, like Plato, sees the two as inseparably overlapping) ideas, to be sure, but what is most important to us, at the moment, is Pickstock's view that "we live in an era in which pre-modern metaphysical approaches to truth are returning to view and to a renewed viability."[103] These heady premodern realities are not

---

[100] Recall the opening conversation of the *Phaedrus* on how one should relate to the gods. One does not explain away the divine if one takes life seriously. Rather, one allows the divine to explain the self.

[101] Catherine Pickstock, *Aspects of Truth: A New Religious Metaphysics* (Cambridge, UK: Cambridge University Press, 2020), ix.

[102] Pickstock, *Aspects of Truth*, ix.

[103] Pickstock, *Aspects of Truth*, x.

simply academic abstractions but practical contemporary partners in our struggle to make sense of things.

That is precisely the view of this book, as well. Throughout, we have attempted to see the pre-modern, even pre-Christian, perspectives on their own terms as much as possible. If the voices of pre-modern metaphysics are to be viewed as viable influences in the present, they need to be understood (and that was the task of these first six chapters), but they also need to be *remembered*. That is, they need to be animated and made living members of the present conversation once more. And so, in the final two chapters, we will engage those pre-modern views a good bit more conversationally in order to see what they might say to our post-modern and post-Christian (and, increasingly, post-secular!) views of education and discourse.

Chapter 7

"Who with Best Meaning have Incurred the Worst"[1]: How to Say Something Meaningful

EDUCATION IS, INEVITABLY, SOMETHING OTHER than crafting a reservoir of data that is easily retrieved. It is, inescapably, *inner formation*. At the very minimum, it teaches (or tries to teach) students to craft their intellects so they understand things they did not understand before. And it teaches them to practice certain skills that they need in order to accomplish that task of understanding. And, finally, it teaches them to lean upon their own natural talents and experiences in this process of exploration.[2] Most of the time, educators also specifically choose what material a student is supposed to be thinking about, at least in each particular class, and students would be wise to follow those directions rather precisely, of course. An astute literary analysis of that glorious scene in Dante's *Purgatory* where the author is bathed in the rivers of Lethe and then Eunoë will not, however insightful, earn a passing grade in a sophomore chemistry lab that set out to measure the density of an unknown liquid at different temperatures. Nor should it.

And so, given that the heart of education is a process of interior formation, and given that professors direct their students to contemplate specific material in a specific way during this formation, then it follows that an honest college professor cannot simply dismiss as nonsense the rage of parents and taxpayers who claim that schools and universities are indoctrinating students. Of course we are. In one very real way, that is why we exist. That is what we do: we offer teachings (*doctrinae*, in Latin) that students are supposed to *internalize* and make part of their souls. These *internalized doctrinae* are supposed to inform their intellect, become a vibrant part of their memory, and thus influence their perspectives and choices. That is simply our job as educators. So, perhaps we should stop arguing about

---

[1] Shakespeare, *Lear*, in *The Complete Works of Shakespeare*, ed. David Bevington, 1158-1216 (Chicago: University of Chicago Press, 1980), 5.3.5

[2] These three items—knowledge, practice, and natural talent—are, of course, the content of a *technē*.

165

whether that is what we are doing. Let us move on to argue instead about a much more important question: how well or poorly are we doing it?

If that question sounds suspiciously like the conversation Socrates and Phaedrus were having at the end of their dialogue—namely, how does one tell if one is doing rhetorical things well or poorly—that is no coincidence. Rhetoric was the core of "higher education" in Plato's day, and the question of whether educators are doing their job well or poorly is hardly an original inquiry that emerged for the first time in history during some Florida school board meeting early last month. We have, it turns out, been asking this question for rather a long time.

And Plato has raised an important point: what, precisely, are the criteria we will be using to determine if we are educating the next generation properly or poorly?

> Well, my friend, the people at the sanctuary of Zeus at Dodona say that the original prophecies there were spoken by an oak. In those days people weren't as clever as you young ones nowadays, and they were so foolish that they happily listened to oak and rock, as long as they told the truth. But perhaps it matters to you who the speaker is, or what country he's from.[3]

I have no shortage of students (and, it must be said, peers) who have come to believe that the first step in assessing the worth of any claim is to discover the ideological affiliations of the author. Once you know their ideological flag, you know whether you should laud or disparage, defend or dismiss (or attack) their discourse. But the core of Plato's vision, in contrast, is that the value of a spoken claim is independent of the identity of the speaker. It is tied, rather, to the truth of the claim. Plato is not encouraging naïvete, as is clear from his many cautions about manipulators. He, like us, knows full well that studies lauding the vast medical benefits of consuming dietary supplement Z4 are far more suspect if those studies have been conducted and paid for by the company that manufactures and markets dietary supplement Z4. Plato is clearly aware such manipulators—and far more subtle ones—are out there, and he will attempt to provide his students with a method for discovering and exercising caution about those who push agendas at the cost of truth, though his method is a perilous one, as we will see.

---

[3] Plato, *Phaedrus* 275b–c. I use Robin Waterfield's translation of *Phaedrus* (Oxford: Oxford University Press, 2009).

Nevertheless, the primary skills expected from an educated person are, for Plato, the ability to assess the truth of a claim (in addition to its provenance), along with the ability to possess and recognize the sort of interior character that prioritizes truth over agenda. Whether education is producing such persons tells us whether education is functioning well or poorly. There are two broad observations to be made in regard to the Platonic view. First, if the Platonic view is rejected, discourse of the sort required in a functional democracy is practically impossible. Second, the fixed nature of truth does not result in static knowledge of truth, even though what is true is unchanging. Both of these claims will require a bit of unpacking, and in that process of exploration we will find ourselves reviewing the approaches to educational formation we have examined so far. Gorgias, Isocrates, and Plato are hardly exhaustive educational perspectives, but they are fairly exemplary, and this is especially true if we toss in a bonus perspective like the practicalities of the handbook tradition. And the handbook tradition is perhaps the best place to start.

Specific, Profitable Training: Get the Job (Done)

Students do not show up in a university classroom as blank slates, obviously. By the time they are university students, the bulk of their education, and almost certainly the most important part, is behind them. It took place in the crafting of their priorities within their families and peer groups over the previous two decades. It took place in the stories they were told in movies and in books and in family outings. It took place in households where they experienced love, usually in the form of some clumsy, awkward, and imperfect parental and (if they were lucky) sibling affections. It took place in the unfolding of elementary school lessons in the classroom and in the sometimes brutal interpersonal dynamics of the playground. It took place in the unexpected discovery of some stunning book in the middle school library or under the inspiration of some high school teacher who absolutely loved what she taught. University students bring all this and more to their college campuses, and to be fair to the limited role of the university professor, it is pretty rare that anything on offer in a college will simply unmake all this past education and create some entirely new person. "Deep roots are not reached by the frost," the poem says.[4]

---

[4] J. R. R. Tolkien, *The Fellowship of the Rings* (New York: HarperCollins, 2002), 170.

Nevertheless, what happens in the university can be thought of as something of a capstone of education, and it is supposed to be, at some level, transformative. University comes into the life of young adults just about the time they are beginning to unpack the sharpest questions about their independence, their priorities, and their goals. It is in that context that the university offers, to most of those who pass through it, an opportunity (whether they seize it or not is up to each student) to synthesize, challenge, and solidify what has gone before. And students do, sometimes, discover new ways to understand their past and to approach their future and to define themselves in the present. University is usually the last broad formal educational experience, and in the liberal arts side of the university education, students are asked both to consider and to critique all they have learned so far. University education asks them, "How sure are you about this view of yours? On what grounds do you hold that to be true? What alternatives have you considered?" and "How do these pieces of your education so far fit together and relate, consistently, to one another?" and "Where do your beliefs and values fit in the bigger picture of what we know about the material universe? About the human experience of suffering and of joy?" and "What matters? What makes any life meaningful?" and "How do we account for the human propensity to act unjustly with such horrifying frequency?"

But it must be acknowledged that not all students are captivated by these questions, and those students are often interested mainly in the uses of a college degree to broaden their economic options or provide themselves with a sharpened toolset for crafting a career in a field they find valuable or even love. There is nothing wrong with that, of course, but the *technē* of vocational training, whether it takes place in high school or in college, and whether it targets a specific physical trade or professional skillset, is a somewhat different sort of learning from the education that aims at the broader *technē* of the liberal arts, where penetrating universal questions about the nature of reality itself, whether in the sciences or the humanities, are the focus. Loosely, the handbook tradition of the classical world, where the goal was simply to show the reader how to get by and make their way in a dangerous setting, might be considered something of a (very) rough parallel to those types of professional degrees on offer in universities; the parallel stretches no further than the emphasis on practical skills and successful outcomes, and nothing more than that should be read into the rough and ready comparison here.

While the handbook tradition was widely denigrated in the classical world, that is not my view of contemporary professional degrees. Such professional degrees may provide some context or historical perspective on their trades, and they often have exacting standards and demand both depth and broad overview of their subjects. Their final emphasis, however, is generally on producing a successful person with a desirable and employable set of skills and abilities. Business administration, journalism, pharmacology, public relations, film production, nursing, computer programming, forestry, engineering, dentistry, forensics, and a host of other university programs provide the culture with disciplined, skilled graduates who are justly celebrated and admired: they make our communities safer and richer, more lively and more valuable.[5] To point out the obvious fact that these courses of study generally differ in their methods and goals from the theoretical and liberal arts is to say nothing that disparages either educational path.

What does need to be pointed out, however, is that this process of educating citizens with a skillset that prepares them for professional participation in our common life may be moderately insulated from, but it is certainly not isolated from, whatever current theoretical questions are operating in the goals and methods of the broader liberal arts education at that moment. The general education courses within the American university system, for example, are specifically designed to acquaint each student with these broader liberal arts disciplines and introduce something of their theoretical perspectives. And those broader disciplines, methods, and perspectives will, also, generally influence all formal education outside of the university's liberal arts curriculum: high school, middle school, elementary school, kindergarten, and, for that matter, day care centers are—properly—the social battlegrounds when changes begin to

---

[5] Today, these courses make up the majority of college degrees awarded. Twenty percent of the bachelor's degrees conferred in 2021, the most recent data available, were given to business majors, a statistic that has remained remarkably stable for the last fifty years. Health professionals were awarded another 13% of the degrees in 2021, a percentage that has been steadily increasing over the last twenty-five years. A rough review finds more than half (conservatively, about 57%) of the bachelor's degrees awarded in the United States in 2021 were given in professional fields. The university has become the *de facto* vocational education center for white-collar jobs in America. See the September 2022 report from The National Center for Educational Statistics, Table 322.10: "Bachelor's degrees conferred by postsecondary institutions, by field of study: Selected academic years 1970–71 through 2020–21," *Digest of Education Statistics*, https://nces.ed.gov/programs/digest/d22/tables/dt22_322.10.asp.

break out of the liberal arts and simmer through a culture's formal structures for educating its rising generations. To pretend otherwise is either stunningly naïve or staggeringly insincere.

Furthermore, it must be recalled that any changes in educational goals, content, or procedure are, in public schools and state universities, blended with questions about the power and authority of the state to reach into the private lives of families in order to shape the content of their children's perspectives on issues as central as gender, sex, race, family, class, and religion. In other words, discussions of state-sponsored education cannot be separated from discussions of the right to privacy and the autonomy of the family unit. The question on the table—at least one of the big questions on even the kindergarteners' arts and crafts table—is how the power of the state will be used to inform and shape young souls. In a democracy which values individual choice and privacy, that is necessarily a contentious question at any time, but more so when cultural change is afoot.

So we have walked the labyrinth of professional education at the university level only to return to that school board meeting in almost any state where one can easily imagine a shouting match regarding the contents of a middle school library.[6] That debate is not insignificant, nor does it have an obvious solution, and if our deepest response is to roll our eyes and repeat

---

[6] On January 27, 2022, National Public Radio reported on a Tennessee school district that decided to remove all copies of the Holocaust series *Maus* from its libraries, despite the graphic novel having won a Pulitzer Prize; Associated Press, "Holocaust Novel 'Maus' banned in Tennessee School District," *PBS News Hour*, Jan 27, 2022, https://www.pbs.org/newshour/arts/holocaust-novel-maus-banned-in-tennessee-school-district#:~:text=ATHENS%2C%20Tenn.,minutes%20from%20a%20board%20meeting. On August 18 of that same year, NPR ran another story about a school district in Texas that had removed all copies of a graphic-novel of Anne Frank's diary, a number of books with LGBTQ+ themes and characters, and the Christian Bible from the school libraries; Wynne Davis, "The Bible is Among Dozens of Books Removed from This Texas School District," *NPR*, August 18, 2022, https://www.npr.org/2022/08/18/1117708153/bible-anne-frank-books-banned-texas-school-district. On June 2, 2023, the Associated Press published a story about a Utah school district that had also removed all copies of the Christian Bible; Sam Metz, "Utah District Bans Bible in Elementary and Middle Schools 'Due to Vulgarity or Violence," *The Associated Press*, June 2, 2023, https://apnews.com/article/book-ban-school-library-bible-fc025c8ccf30e955aaf0b0ee1899608a#. And on June 20, 2023, the *New York Times* published a story about the authors of a children's book which portrayed a family of penguins with two fathers. The authors were suing a Florida school district after it banned the book, along with some forty other titles, from its school libraries; Elizabeth A. Harris and Alexandra Alter, "Authors and Students Sue Over Florida Law Driving Book Bans," *New York Times*, June 20, 2023, https://www.nytimes.com/2023/06/20/books/book-bans-florida-tango-makes-three.html.

the clichés of our side because those people on the other side are so stupid that their words are not worth a refrigerated thimble of freeze-dried rat saliva, well, then, maybe it is time to take a deep breath and explain one's own expectations about how we are all supposed to live together. What, exactly, do we plan to do about such an amplitude of ignorance as is found on the other side?

The answer seems obvious. And, at present, it seems to be the same answer on virtually every side of multiple divides. The plan is, apparently, to make sure the Other Side withers on the vine and that their stupid and out-of-step and (let's be honest) wicked views are completely rejected by the next generation because that next generation has been *properly educated*.

It is an excellent plan. Isocrates would be proud. So would Gorgias. So would Plato. But, obviously, they would not all celebrate the same aspects of the plan.

Gorgias would likely be thrilled with the view of language as the superpower of the social order. The present concerns of the current culture war are nothing if not opportunities to define our social reality in the image or our own desires, rooted in nothing more than the protreptic force of our descriptions and the persuasive implications we imbed within the subtle (and obvious) frames of our discourse. Nothing is real—until we say so. But anything can be real, if we say so; this is the Prosperity Gospel for secular liberals: name it, claim it. Everything is up for redefinition, reality is but a slave to rhetoric, and the wittiest and most powerful discourse will win. It is enough to make a hard-core sophist giddy.

Isocrates would, perhaps, be somewhat more cautious. That caution might be based on the factious nature of the current culture. He might complain about the United States in much the same way he complained about Greece: petty regional and ideological divisions are preventing us all from uniting and realizing the full scope of our power. But perhaps it is not too late for us all to rally around a common hatred? United within, we could then dispose of the enemy without. The problem is that after some seventy years of uninterrupted US military mishaps—from Korea, to Vietnam, to Iraq, to Afghanistan—the panacea of militant imperialism is less palatable and moderately less marketable than it used to be.[7] And there is

---

[7] It is, perhaps, not completely a matter of chance that military recruits are largely taken from the less affluent segments of the American culture. For one intriguing perspective on the present US military recruitment challenge, see Thomas Spoehr and Katherine Kuzminski, "Bad Idea: Relying on the Same Old Solutions to Meet the Military Recruitment Challenge," *Defense360: A Project of the Center of Strategic and International*

no clear enemy against which our factions could unite. Of course, there is no reason to abandon all hope. Hating Russia is certainly back on the table. Or perhaps we might all unite around hating China? They do not make it difficult, Isocrates might observe enticingly. But whatever the future enemy, Isocrates would almost certainly appreciate the fact that both sides have figured out that the way forward is to seize the means of education.

Plato, too, would celebrate the insight that the way forward cannot be divorced from proper education. He just wants to know what you mean by *proper*.

The Greeks we have examined will need to be reviewed more carefully than these comic caricatures, of course. There is, however, nothing new under the sun, and these Greek voices will hopefully have contributions to offer to our present debates even from within their own perspectives, without shoehorning them too much into a world they would find utterly foreign. To that end, we will unpack the two observations offered above regarding the Platonic perspective: namely, that discourse is impossible without the Platonic view that relates words to a fixed reality independent of and indifferent to those words, and that this fixed nature of truth does not result in a static fundamentalist certainty about the fixed nature of truth.

Speechless: How the Unspeakable Makes a Word Meaningful

Plato's connection between what is transcendentally unspeakable and the possibilities of language is not intuitively clear, and that connection requires some context. I suspect little in Plato is, however, more relevant to the current world, and so the effort to understand Plato's thought on how speech is made meaningful is a worthwhile effort. To that end, we will return to Gorgias and to Isocrates—Plato's foils in the two dialogues we have examined—and review their positions and the current adaptations of their positions, focusing on their ideas about the uses of language. That practical focus will allow us the context to unpack the religious core of Plato's view of *logos*.

Studies, March 10, 2023, https://defense360.csis.org/bad-idea-relying-on-the-same-old-solutions-to-meet-the-military-recruitment-challenge/.

Talk about Nothing

Gorgias is never at a want for words. He can talk about literally nothing in a provocative way. But at the end of the semester at the University of Gorgias, are we any closer to having a more just community than we were at the beginning of the semester? Would that question even matter to Gorgias's students? Do the highest marks in this type of education go to those pupils who simply manage to most thoroughly disrupt the normative expectations, as Gorgias does in his *Helen*? Is all discourse simply a *paignion*, and the joke is on anyone who takes the idea of words like *justice* seriously? Is the valedictorian of this system of inner formation found in that knowing sort of student who ends up behind the curtain, pulling the levers of lesser people's naïve ideals and hopes? And, to ask a very Gorgianic question, is it not likely that we would all have a much more glowing appreciation of Gorgias if Plato had not sullied his reputation in that nasty hit-piece of his?

Let's begin with that last question. If Plato managed to undermine Gorgias's reputation for two-thousand four-hundred years by writing one dialogue in which the character of Gorgias himself speaks only four percent of the words and is actively engaged in the conversation on less than one in every five pages (and in none of the really juicy bits), then by Gorgias's own standards, Plato is the better rhetorician by several orders of magnitude.[8] But perhaps the problem is not Plato's fictional character assassination but Gorgias's actual perspective. Despite efforts to rehabilitate the sophist, there is a recurring difficulty with the core of his philosophical approach to language that has to be constantly papered over if one wishes to take both Gorgias *and* justice seriously. Specifically, in Gorgias's world, there is nothing to talk about. Or, more precisely, there is only nothing to talk about. Gorgianic discourse cannot be about anything because there is only nothing. And so, as we saw in Chapter 3, the purpose of words cannot be to communicate a description of some sort of transcendent reality or to offer an invitation to improve upon the present. What, in the University of Gorgias, could the word *improve* possibly mean? Answer: nothing. What, then, are words for?

Of course, devotees of Gorgias, especially those of the last fifty years or so, would be quick to suggest that all these questions have been crafted in a way that loads the dice, as all language does. I have, they would point out, stylistically framed the inquiries in order to slyly (or not) paint Gorgias in

---

[8] The *Gorgias* is some 27,824 words in Greek. Gorgias speaks around 1,190 of them, representing 4.28% of the total content. The Greek text in the Loeb runs to 137 pages. Gorgias's voice is heard on about twenty-five of those Greek pages.

the worst possible light. They might note that this proves Gorgias's point, in fact. His point is that words are what we use to build *ex nihilo* our systems of belief, expectation, and perspective. We make reality with our words. And thus, if we simply alter our wording, we change the way others think and what they expect, and, perhaps, how they act; we change what is real. I might agree that there is an element of truth in this observation that language frames expectations and inspires actions, of course. There is obviously such a thing as propaganda, manipulative spin, alternative facts, and disinformation that sets out to use words so that they swirl the intellect into vertigo, all while slanting the playing field to my ideological advantage.[9] But if that is what I have done to Gorgias, then the question that looms over Gorgias and his contemporary admirers is "so what?" At the University of Gorgias, anchored in nothing, all discourse—yours, mine, theirs—is precisely that sort of vertiginous slant. And any objection to my spin only means I successfully slanted the playing field to my advantage and away from your advantage. The other side can hardly suggest that by spinning the facts and slanting the table I somehow acted unfairly. Spinning the facts and slanting the table *is the game.* Calling out the fact that my spin slanted the table in my favor is only an attempt to make me seem untrustworthy and so slant the table in your favor. In the end, all words are simply protreptic propaganda whose spin is designed to win points for my side.

That is what words are for; that is their nature and their power. They are tools for spinning a perspective that is profitable to me within the void that is common to us all. They are how one becomes a player. This position is, indisputably, a possible way to order one's life, and such a world view might be lived out consistently. But it need not be. Contradictions within one's beliefs and views and actions can be consciously acknowledged and consciously dismissed as an inevitable part of the irony found in every system of discourse. I am, of course, attending exclusively to my own pleasures, interests, and agendas while speaking mostly about justice, for example, but that is merely the nature of communication in a world founded on nothing.

But a system anchored in nothing, where all meaning is manufactured *ex nihilo* and constantly updated by the cacophony of human speech, does not require even this level of self-awareness. I never face any requirement that I acknowledge or even notice a contradiction when acting, in one moment, as a proponent of the avant-garde skepticism that claims nothing exists beyond

---

[9] Whether this is the only use of words and whether they constitute reality are different questions, and those will be taken up shortly.

the shimmer of my words spinning and creating social reality while, in the next moment, sending feel-good memes about building a more just world. Contradictions need not be explained or examined, and they might even become a happy hidden defining habitude of life. To ignore is bliss.

That, indeed, may be one of the main points of the character of Gorgias in Plato's dialogue. Within the dialogue, we watch unexamined contradictions, of exactly the sort we have been discussing, play out. At one point, Gorgias argues that when some students of rhetoric use their skills to become manipulative and to do injustice, such behavior is not the fault of those who taught them rhetoric and the educators should not be held responsible.[10] But later, Gorgias argues that a person properly educated in rhetoric would necessarily understand what justice is, and they would inevitably lead others toward that very goal.[11] Socrates calls him on this contradiction: if those who are the product of Gorgias's education always pursue justice, then how could they be manipulative characters who act unjustly? But we never hear Gorgias's response to Socrates. First, Polus bursts in to defend his master at that precise point. But even after Polus's interruption, Gorgias himself never responds. In fact, at no later point in the dialogue does Gorgias offer any *substantive* contribution to the developing conversation. He simply drops out.[12] In many ways, it is fitting that the character of Gorgias remains politely (even pleasantly) engaged, but he never responds to (and seems to remain pleasantly indifferent toward) the contradiction at the heart of his own theory of rhetoric. Contradictions are, under the gaze of such skeptical visions of meaning as found in Gorgias's original works, simply unimportant. They are nothing to fret over. They are nothing.

Perhaps it is also fitting that at this point precisely, Polus interrupts, stumbling over his words in his indignation, to offer a heated defense of his teacher.[13] Emotional assertion and brash self-confidence aimed at preserving reputation become an alternative sophistic reply when theoretical contradictions and inconsistencies emerge within Gorgianic rhetoric in a way

---

[10] Plato, *Gorgias* 456e–457c. I rely unless otherwise noted on Donald J. Zeyl's translation in *Plato: Complete Works*, ed. John M. Cooper (Indianapolis, IN: Hackett, 1997).

[11] Plato, *Gorgias* 459c–460e.

[12] The character of Gorgias will speak again at 463a and e, 464a and b, 497b, and finally at 506a–b. In none of these sections do his remarks extend beyond a few words, and none of them affect the content of what is being discussed.

[13] Plato, *Gorgias* 461b–c. The wording here is intentionally clumsy. Polus is taken aback, and the phrasing reflects his incredulous and indignant tone.

that threatens one's power. And this point is not to be passed over casually or quickly. Gorgias's vision from within his own extant works offers a very limited set of responses when it is confronted with any challenge from an alternative point of view.

One response is to do nothing (as the character of Gorgias does in Plato's dialogue). If I live within the Gorgianic view, nothing is at stake, and so letting you have your truth and letting me have my truth is all well and good since truth is nothing. I may not especially like your truth, just as you dislike mine, but of course your truth is good for you. And my truth is good for me.

This is a noble sentiment when applied to, say, the question of whether one enjoys ginger beer. The sentiment is perhaps less transparently laudable when the question is human trafficking, or apartheid, or the presidency of Donald Trump.

And therein lies the first problem of nothing. There are, in the end, very limited options for public discourse in Gorgias. I might smile and banter and tolerate and make no waves and let be, because, in the end, there is nothing at stake. But, if I feel my own interests are at risk, I might need to break forth, rather like Polus (and later, with greater calculation, Callicles), and assert my own perspective by dint of passion, savvy spin, and, when necessary, misinformation and manipulation in order to make sure things go my way. But Gorgias's extant works provide neither a method nor a motive for engaging any other party on any other terms. What is offered is indifference for the inconsequential and no-holds-barred domination when an outcome I prefer is threatened.[14] Those are the options for public discourse within Gorgias's writings.

But there is a second problem with nothing. In Gorgias's view, I have nothing to work with, nothing to champion, nothing to guide me beyond my own pleasures and self-interests. My own idiosyncrasies and my own self-defined desires, isolated and liberated from others to any degree I choose, are the only foundation on which I can base my discourse and my decisions. This is what the character of Callicles sees so clearly and presents so clearly in his conversation with Socrates. Individual self-interest and self-defined pleasures are the sole measure of any definition of good that might be applied to me. But this inevitably means that with nothing but my

---

[14] For a more detailed expression of this view, see my "Substantive Discourse: Love, Justice, and Hierarchy as the Basis for Civility," in *Humility and Hospitality*, ed. Naaman Wood and Sean Connable, 33–46 (Pasco, WA: Integratio, 2022), esp. 41–44.

own experiential identity and idiosyncratic desires at play in the world, any challenge to my preferences—*every* challenge to my preferences—might easily be experienced as an existential threat to my entire *kosmos*. Gorgianic rhetoric provides us only with passionate assertion and savvy spin as a response to a significant challenge. But it also necessitates a way of being-in-the-world that renders virtually any disagreement, however apparently minor, into one of those significant challenges that must be viewed as an attack upon my entire way of life because it hinders me from achieving my preferred outcomes. And my preferred outcomes are the only content of my *kosmos*; there is nothing else.

Of course, I might occasionally compromise on some of my desires in order to form profitable alliances that assist me in achieving other desires of a higher priority. But in the end, what the Gorgianic system offers is some version of either indifference, because nothing matters, or absolute domination, because something matters to *me*. In the latter case, words are the way I wield the power to obtain my preferences, and the ends justify the means.[15] While power and secret agendas have had an undeniable part in human discourse (at least since Adam tried to spin that incident with the tree so that Eve took the fall), the Gorgianic view reduces all options to only power. In doing so, the system cuts us off from the possibility of exercising power in a way that *is just*. In a fundamentalist world grounded in the dogma of *sola potentia*—only power—power alone justifies a claim. Power alone defines justice. In this system, whatever situation is backed by the most power is just. On the Gorgianic view, any objection that the present status quo is unjust is always and only the tears of whiners who do not have what it takes to come out on top. The call for justice can be nothing else. All this echoes, but extends, our consideration of Gorgias's own works in Chapter 3. But Isocrates's reply to Gorgias does not differentiate him from Gorgias and Gorgianic nothingness quite as clearly as Isocrates seemed to think it did.

United We Fall: How Getting Along Agreeably May Not Be the Answer

Isocrates softens the Gorgianic vision by grounding a person's core values and defining identity not in individual self-interest, but rather in a

---

[15] Words are the primary way to wield power, though they work in conjunction with more material structures of power like violence or the police authority of the state, as Callicles makes clear.

broader cooperative community. The end of Chapter 4, however, found a series of serious limitations to that view. We need not repeat those complete arguments here, but it is perhaps worthwhile to recall the specific conclusions we drew in the close of that chapter, where we said:

> It appears difficult to seriously recontextualize Isocrates's wholistic system without his prop of moral elitism appearing somewhere in the process, either externally in a sense of autonomous, superior moral norms or internally in the assumption of superior human souls and intellects (usually, like *us*). These elitist assumptions were the crucial bedrock of Isocrates's educational philosophy. Arguably, they remain present in many specific attempts to rehabilitate Isocrates as an educator for our time. . . .
>
> Without some assumption of elitist hierarchy—exterior to the system in some superior moral frame or interior to the system within the rhetor's elite superior soul—there is no reason that the call to produce more discourse along with the training "to make it more effective" under the Isocratic model could not serve oppressors as well as it serves liberators. The pressing questions are how to identify good rhetoric from merely powerful rhetoric, and is there a difference?[16]

Isocrates's adaptive system is shackled to an inescapable vision of moral elitism that assumes we are better people than others, or it assumes that we know what is best for others, period. Frequently, it assumes both.

The moral superiority of such elitism is a coin polished on both sides, Left and Right. Whether Isocrates is seen as lending aid to a narrow fascist imperialism or to a broadly dissipated vision of post-Marxist *paideia*, his system seems to arrive at the same rather disturbingly oppressive location of a superior, absolutist ideology. That such ideologies, both on the Left and on the Right, have a tendency to end their narrative arc by shooting a lot of people who object to their conclusions needs, hopefully, no historic elaboration. But the macabre conclusion does need to be held in mind before arguing for any sort of *inherent* good within the Isocratic system of education and philosophy. And here we begin to see the ways in which a socially negotiated Isocratic code of norms in behaviors and attitudes mirrors rather disquietingly the Gorgianic problems with nothingness.

---

[16] Chapter 4, pp. 91–92.

Joining hands and uniting around a *cause célèbre* is a very fine thing to do so long as the cause being celebrated is a very fine cause. But it is not a fine thing to do *per se*. If the cause is not a very fine one—if it is, in fact, a dark and ugly one—then the united celebration only means a rather large number of people are all missing the point in the same way at the same time. United, we fall together. But as we saw in Chapter 4, Isocrates offers no basis for critiquing that cause around which we are rallying. And without a means to offer such a critique, his system of public discourse endorses the Gulag as quickly as jurisprudence, human trafficking as readily as human rights. Isocratic rhetoric is a free agent.

Once again, this is a viable path, but there is no way of knowing whether it is a good path. Nothing inherent within Isocrates's writings requires a deeper reflection about the social norms championed by my group, Left or Right. Isocrates never calls for the examination of the social or private conscience. Though he calls, consistently, for his students to live a virtuous life, the virtues he champions are the sophisticated aesthetics and unexamined cultural norms of well-heeled society. At no point does he offer any suggestion that these be examined, interrogated, challenged, justified, or even explicated. Aristocratic Athenian citizenship is the capstone of virtue. His system of both education and politics consistently reaffirms the embodiment of this way of life as the definition of *good*. Assuming one is operating in a relatively homogenous society, one can follow Isocrates's lead in both education and politics. One can simply rally around the cause (again, Left or Right) and ignore questions about the quality of what we are rallying around. Why would superior souls like ours need to bother with such petty explications and justifications for our insights? The very request that we do so is uncomfortable. The gods of Our Identity have spoken. Amen.

Second, in the Isocratic system, there is a push toward totalizing group identity in the same way that Gorgias's view pushed one toward totalizing private desire. We have seen that Gorgias's theory of language locks one into a sort of secular fundamentalism in which desire and self-interest are the only material to work with; there is nothing else. The result is that any challenge to my desires or self-interest becomes an existential threat to my whole *kosmos* because these desires define my world and everything that matters in it. Isocrates's theory of language creates a similar and in many ways more intoxicating fundamentalism anchored in the identity of our tribe and group. Those of us who have gathered under whatever flag is flying above our heads know absolutely who we are. And of course, how could

I be wrong about my own feelings regarding who I am? Error is unthinkable. We celebrate one another, reinforcing our infallible experiences of our united selves: there is nothing larger than our group. Our foundation stops at our sacred flag, but we need nothing more to guide us. But this means, just as it meant for Gorgias, that any challenge to our group—every challenge to our group—is easily experienced as an existential threat.

Gorgias's nihilistic system is founded on my unchallengeable knowledge of my own desires, and there is nothing more than that. Isocrates's broad educational system is founded on our unchallengeable knowledge of who we are, and there is nothing greater than that. Both of these forward arbitrary fundamentalist absolutes—*me*, in the case of Gorgias; *us*, in the case of Isocrates—that are the foundation of my way of being and, therefore, of what matters, what is meaningful, to me.

The single difference that most clearly separates Plato from both Gorgias and Isocrates is the question of how words are related to meaning. Plato presents Callicles, I have argued, as the logical conclusion of the Gorgianic view of language and education. I do not disagree with his assessment. If human language operates by making meaning *ex nihilo*, then it follows that the function of words, for any but the most naïve, would be to craft the sort of strategic circumstantial spin that allows me to act in my own self-interest, on my own terms, and with minimal interference from others. In such a world, the meanings made cannot be critiqued by any reference to anything outside of desire, passion, and careful calculations of what is most advantageous to me. Furthermore, since all language is solipsistic, every utterance I hear must be handled with a savvy understanding that it is an attempt to manipulate me. Every claim that something is *just* or *good* or *better* than something else is a statement that functions only as an appeal to the weak and sentimental underbelly of my psyche in order to soften me up and get something from me that the speaker or author wants.

Nothingness, taken seriously, reduces language to rhetorical nihilism. Contemporary sympathies for Gorgias often attempt to qualify and soften his position. Nihilism has, over the last seventy-five years or so, morphed into various expressions that attempt to sidestep the cruder implications of a foundational void. Religious naturalism of the sort celebrated by Ursula Goodenough or the perspective found in, for example, the sentimental nihilism of David Landers come quickly to mind.[17] They may be summed

---

[17] See, e.g., Ursula Goodenough, *The Sacred Depths of Nature* (Oxford: Oxford University Press, 2023) and David Landers, *Optimistic Nihilism* (Austin: IM Print, 2016).

up by the maxim, "Life is meaningless, but so what?" Life is, after all, sufficient for satisfaction and pleasure and perhaps even an occasional bit of psycho-somatic awe. Don't worry, be (arbitrarily, inexplicably, unjustifiably) happy. These are the people who made Nietzsche's madman break his midday lamp.[18]

The appeal of these perspectives seems, in the end, to assume a sort of moderately secure, moderately comfortable life with a modest measure of leisure. One can imagine how the maxims of such a view might feel especially apropos to some Saturday evening when one is just beginning a third bottle of above-average Cabernet, in the candlelight, with a small number of like-minded friends. Such sentimental nihilism might also be readily discerned in the popularity of recent films like Noah Baumbach's *White Noise* and Daniel Kwan and Daniel Scheinbert's *Everything Everywhere All at Once*. Tevya Turok Shapiro's appreciative review of the latter film sums it up this way: "There are infinite alternative universes where things could have turned out differently, but you live in this one. There's no point getting stuck on what could have been, no reason not to appreciate the good things in your life; everything's bullshit anyway, so why not just be kind?"[19] Or, one might add, cruel and domineering, if that is more to your liking? And,

---

Anti-foundationalism, yet another philosophical outgrowth of nihilism, has also had a profound influence on views of rhetoric, education, and religion. The history of that movement, which seeks to justify one course of action as better than another but without any transcendent foundations, is beyond the scope of the present study, but individuals such as Jacques Derrida, Richard Rorty, Stanley Fish, and Gianni Vatimo, to name just a few of the most famous anti-foundationalists, have all shown an intriguing interest in religion and religious language. For insight about these views and critical consideration of them, see Ryan Gillespie, "Normative Reasoning and Moral Argumentation in Theory and Practice," *Philosophy and Rhetoric* 49, no. 1 (2016): 49–73, as well as his "Cosmic Meaning, Awe, and Absurdity in the Secular Age: A Critique of Religious Non-Theism," *Harvard Theological Review* 111, no. 4 (2018): 461–87.

[18] The Madman, in Friedrich Nietzsche's *The Gay Science*, trans. Josefine Nauckhoff (Cambridge, UK: Cambridge University Press, 2001), sect. 125, meets a group who claims to reject God but who refuse to acknowledge the consequence of that rejection. Frustrated, the madman—who is a prophet—casts down his lantern and extinguishes its light.

[19] Teyva Turok Shapiro, "'Everything Everywhere All at Once' is a Dazzling, Must-Watch, Sci-Fi Spectacle," *Daily Maverick*, March 13, 2023, https://www.dailymaverick.co.za/article/2023-03-13-everything-everywhere-all-at-once-is-a-dazzling-must-watch-sci-fi-spectacle/. As for *White Noise*, written and directed by Noah Baumbach and distributed by Netflix (Production Houses: NBGG Pictures, Heyday Films, and A24, 2022), the closing scene is perhaps the most consistent ending to a film that I have ever seen: the grocery store dance is both sentimental and meaningless.

with Plato waiting in the wings, it is only fair to ask what Shapiro means by *good things* and how she settled on that meaning?

Sentimental pointlessness aside, however, the most common attempt to tame Gorgianic nothingness, especially within the academic world, might well be various versions of the Isocratic idea of community.[20] Group interactions become a source of identity which is then used as a counterweight to Gorgianic vapidity. Meaning is not anchored to nothing, in this view, but rather to an already woven set of expectations, definitions, and vaguely considered decisions that constitute social order and the boundaries of reality. Within the community, meanings are the artifacts of interaction. Public discourse takes strands of possibilities and weaves them into resplendent and appealing aspects of an identity to which members of the community are drawn. Discourse then proceeds to show new ways to weave, specify, and make conscious these strands; new meanings emerge. The process marches on. In this view, nothingness is upgraded to consensus and the meaning of anything—all the meaning of everything—is a constant renegotiation of each particular circumstantial moment. Why would such a web of negotiated meaning and identity not be enough for us?

We have already noted that an Isocratic philosophy of education has no way to critique the aspects of identity to which a community might respond, and this fact alone might give us pause. But a second problem is how such a system deals with disagreement between identities which are championed by different fragments of the community or different communities that cannot avoid one another. In Gorgias, public discourse is limited to indifference or domination. In Isocrates, public discourse fares no better. Isocrates's various identity groups are limited to the same options that confine the individual in Gorgias's vision. The groups can ignore a view when it is deemed irrelevant, but if they perceive any view as a challenge to their core identity, then the options for discourse are rather stark: the other group must be unmade because it threatens my unchallengeable knowledge of myself and the very core of who we are together.

---

[20] Indeed, some version of the *community* aspect of Isocrates's view is almost always at the core of the sentimentality used to soften Gorgianic nihilism in popular culture. This is true even when worshiping at the altar of natural religion, where our connectedness to nature is generally emphasized. For examples of this sort of tree-of-life community emphasis in film, one need go no further than James Cameron's *Avatar*, Godfrey Reggio's off-beat *Koyaanisqatsi*, or Andrew Stanton's *WALL-E*, to cite a few quick and obvious examples.

In their contemporary manifestations, both the Gorgianic and Isocratic perspectives see rhetoric as a form of creating meaning and identity. Gorgianic theory believes such creation is an *ex nihilo* act. The Isocratic view holds that such constructions are the result of creations woven from past social interactions and, thus, contributions to future social interactions. In both cases, the meaning of a word like *right* or *justice* is artifactual. That is, it is manufactured and has no limit, no referent, no source of meaning independent of our discourse. Even in Isocrates, the word justice is merely a sound signifying something our group agreed to. But that sound might end up referencing anything when we are done with it.

It is difficult to overemphasize the importance of this constitutive view of rhetoric and its implications for our ability to use language meaningfully. One can review the writings of the historical Gorgias as well as the writings of the historical Isocrates as well as the contemporary adaptations and celebrations of either of their theories. In none of these is one provided with any way to make any moral statement that does not become a Toddlerism: *I want this.* And if all we have to work with is *I want this* while you want *that*, our options for discourse have dwindled to manipulation and name-calling until one of us is strong enough or angry enough to hit the other. Or shoot them. For the other must be struck down. Silencing them is a justified act of self-defense because their discourse threatens to tilt the table in a direction that drains from me those defining qualities of the self which are all I have.

A reader need not be exceptionally attentive to realize that Platonic views of a divine and transcendent reality are about to be examined as an alternative to this discursive cul-de-sac found in Gorgias and Isocrates.

Now We're Talking

In the Platonic view, some realities have a divine perfection. The nature of this perfection means the thing must be unalterable in all of its defining qualities. Any change to a perfect circle's circularity degrades its perfection, of course. Change it enough, and you cease to have anything that might be recognized as a circle at all. Obviously, then, perfection necessitates the idea of an unimprovable reality, as well.[21] If a circle can both

---

[21] This argument, applied by Aristotle to being itself, ends in the Aristotelian conclusion that there is an ultimate god, beyond the reach of nature, who is the "unmoved mover"—that is, an unchangeable state of perfected being contemplating only itself, since contemplation of any lesser being would introduce imperfection to its thought and ungod it. This god is, perhaps, more like a principle of being than a personal being, though Aristotle is

change and improve, then it was not a perfect circle to begin with. And so the divine realities are fixed and unchangeable precisely because they are divine and perfected: any alteration, therefore, would inevitably unmake the perfection—that is, their very nature. But if a reality is perfected, that reality must be indifferent to our words about it; discourse cannot change or alter a divine reality; even if words had that power, they could only alter the divine reality by destroying it. One might talk a circle into growing a corner, but only by making it cease to be a circle. Fortunately for human speech, circles are a notoriously uncompromising audience: the fixed and indifferent quality of the divine perfections is the lynchpin of the Platonic idea of true rhetoric. It is not difficult to understand why.

The meaning of a word like *justice*, under the Platonic view, is liberated from its slavery to a manipulative Toddlerism, which is its only possible function under Gorgias's self-interest or under Isocrates's community consensus. In the Platonic perspective, *justice* exists as a perfected and therefore unalterable divine quality. But if *justice* is really the goal, and if any alteration to the definition of justice moves that goal further from me, then it follows that I would want my understanding and use of the *word* justice to reflect as much as possible the actual quality of justice itself. That divine quality is fully contained and perfected in the thing itself; the task, then, is to discover, describe, and apply that perfected quality in this imperfect moment. Not creation but discovery and description are the focus. Such description can be done well or poorly, accurately or inaccurately, depending on how well or how poorly one understands the defining quality of the divine and perfected reality of *justice*. And, in fact, Plato provides us the only conditions that allow for statements about *justice* that can be critiqued as accurate or inaccurate. If one describes *justice* poorly, then one's invocation is of a degraded vision of justice. Describe it poorly enough and you are no longer talking about justice at all, no matter how persuasive you are.

One might attempt to describe the Gulag as *just* with as much eloquence as one can muster, just as one might try to carve an otter from a two-ton block of granite using only a pigeon feather and a belief in oneself.

---

somewhat ambiguous on that front. Whether personal or principle, the highest form of human life, according to Aristotle, is to contemplate this perfected being. The unmoved mover is discussed, among other places, in *Metaphysics*, trans. Hugh Tredennick, Loeb Classical Library 271 (Cambridge, MA: Harvard University Press, 1935), XII, beginning around 1071a. The significance of human contemplation of the final god as the highest good is discussed in his *Eudemian Ethics*, trans. H. Rackham, Loeb Classical Library 285 (Cambridge, MA: Harvard University Press, 2004), VIII.1249a–b.

But in both cases, the enterprise is doomed. Granite will not respond to the feather regardless of one's confidence, and justice will not describe the Gulag regardless of one's eloquence. But this outcome, where justice is barred from describing the Gulag or the Trail of Tears or human trafficking is possible only because the actual quality of *justice* is not within my reach. I cannot both alter it and possess it, for alteration is always an unmaking of the perfected thing.

And so we are now in a position to ask of Plato a question similar to the one we posed earlier to Gorgias. Under such a scheme, what are words for? With definitions already fixed and unchangeable, present in a realm of supernatural being that has no time and no space, what is the purpose of language? We have already anticipated the answer to this, of course. In the Platonic system, rhetoric is mimetic. Its goal is to re-present as much of the divine reality as can be squeezed into words.

This mimetic quality does not confine and restrict rhetoric but instead liberates it. The Platonic view invites discourse to be something besides an attempt to spin facts, create alternative facts, manipulate others, establish arbitrary priorities, or aggregate power. Granted, the Platonic view does not require all interlocutors to abandon such Toddlerism (how could it?), and that is one of many reasons that extreme caution is in order. There are players out there. There are liars who manipulate others under the pretense of honest inquiry and discourse. But the Platonic view, nevertheless, offers something that cannot be found in Gorgias or Isocrates: the potential for an honest discussion based on the startling fact that there is now something to discuss. But in mimetic rhetoric, with words now anchored to realities independent of those words and my own psychological state of desire, a host of new rhetorical possibilities emerges. For example, terms like *justice* can now be accurate or inaccurate descriptors of a phenomenon. And if I develop a habit for recognizing the true descriptions, I might become a better person. I might even come to know something of what the word *better* means. If I call the Gulag *unjust*, I speak truthfully, and the utterance means that something truthful is presented to the soul's intellect. There is, in such speech, an opportunity to expose the soul to a clearer theory of the divine realities. When I describe the Gulag as *just*, the opposite happens: the soul's vision is clouded and its ability to understand the divine is restricted.

In both Gorgias and Isocrates, we have seen that language is severed from any substantive critique of a claim that some situation or action is *right* or *just*. At the same time, both Isocrates and Gorgias tend to exacerbate and totalize views that differ from one's own, framing difference as an existential threat. Both of these troubles emerge from a view that sees rhetoric as the source of meaning, constituting social reality. In such a constitutive view of rhetoric, moral language is only an expression, however emphatic, of privately preferred outcomes, of desire. By way of contrast, the Platonic view allows discourse to become a possibility precisely because it limits words to an (inevitably incomplete) attempt to engage divine realities. But such engagement does not result in fundamentalist certainty. Ironically, such uncompromising certainties are the domain of the Gorgianic and Isocratic systems. There, and only there, can one be absolutely certain about one's claims since those claims are always and only expressions of a desire presently felt; a self-referential statement of that sort is, naturally, infallible. The Platonic system, on the other hand, allows no such certainty and, in fact, requires a specifically qualified view. I am certain only that my own view is not complete, and therefore I need other perspectives: yours. I know only that I do not know fully. But rhetoric is about precisely those sorts of possibilities, not certainties, and so, in the end, Plato's search for divine realities is the source of rhetoric. Gorgias's and Isocrates's subjective certainties provide no atmosphere in which rhetoric can actually function.

By now, however, we have come to the threshold of that second issue in Platonic discourse: that this fixed nature of truth, possessed by the divine realities, does not result in a static fundamentalist certainty about those divine realities.

Various Sacred Veils: The Rhetorical Gift of Ignorance[22]

We have made the argument (or Plato has) that unless language is shackled to a metaphysical reality, it cannot be free, just, or meaningful; it can only be narrow, sleazy, and manipulative. Ironically, the more *logos*— word and thought—is set free from the divine world, the pettier and more pointless it becomes. But the more tightly *logos* is linked with the divine,

---

[22] "The divine ray is unable, by any means, to bring light to us unless it is hidden, covered with the covering of various sacred veils." Pseudo-Dionysius, *Celestial Hierarchies*, vol. 1, archived at *Hodoi Elektronikai*, managed by Alain Meurant, Université Catholique de Louvain, updated 20 Jan. 2010, http://mercure.fltr.ucl.ac.be/Hodoi/concordances/denys_areopagite_hier_cel /ligne05.cfm?numligne=1&mot=82#debut. The translation given here is mine. Pseudo-Dionysius was a Neo-Platonic philosopher of the fifth century whose works had a significant influence on Medieval theology.

the more robust and valuable it grows. And we have seen Plato provide us with some guidelines for identifying what belongs in the set of these divine realities to which language needs to be linked. The eternal things are inexhaustible and cannot be had in excess. But they are also noble and cannot be pursued with a possessive, ambitious envy. Even after the divine realities are recognized, however, they are not fully known, and so the goal of discourse is to discover and describe them in as much detail as possible. Language, then, is a force that seeks to engage divine reality as it is in its perfection, mimicking, re-presenting the eternal things as much as possible within the temporal order.

Does such a Platonic engagement influence and direct those change-able moments that are lived out in my daily life? Of course. Language, then, might be allowed a certain Isocratic leeway. Language is certainly a tool that reinforces social identity and weaves social priorities and negotiates social norms and expectations. To state that language is how we navigate such things is only to state the most obvious truism possible. But com-pare the Platonic view's justification of these priorities and identities to the creation *ex nihilo* of defenses for my self-interest, or the weaving and spin designed to provide an advantage for my group. Both of these latter, reflecting Gorgianic and Isocratic constitutive views of justification in lan-guage, treat your feelings about justice as something I can use when carving out my own advantages. And enhancing my advantage is the only means for critiquing discourse; efficacious self-interest becomes the only critical method available to anyone who wishes to pass judgment on speech, policy, or even facts. In the more mimetic vision from Plato, however, our words about justice are a lens—scratched and somewhat distorted, but real—that allows us to critique choices based on a divine status that applies to both of us and to both of our perceived advantages. There is common ground, in other words, with those who disagree with me as well as those who are on my side of the disagreement. In the present era, the mimetic mechanics of that common ground are worth examining more closely.

The first advantage of a mimetic rhetoric anchored to divine reali-ties is that differences in descriptions of these realities are not so quickly totalized: disagreements with my own view might emerge without being immediately experienced as an existential threat. A middle ground appears, a sort of "wait a minute" space where clarification can be sought. In this ap-proach, a challenge is not inevitably an assault. It is an invitation to, maybe, learn more about what I, myself, value: "Wait a minute. You said you valued justice, and so do I. But I do not see how this cause (or policy or perspective) you are championing is just. Explain this to me." The possibility of an existential threat is still very present, but it is mediated by that independent reality that is indifferent to our words, to our preferences, and to our way of life. That divine space serves as a common ground where we both can meet. If we both say we love and desire justice but disagree about what justice looks like in this situation, the first thing to talk about is *justice* itself, not the other's character or agenda. Let's see if we can find where our descriptions of justice differ. Perhaps you have seen something I missed. Maybe I understand something you overlooked. Maybe both. But this exploration and explication of justice as a reality neither of us controls and both of us desire will very likely mean that we will also discover even more places where our perspectives on justice agree. And that agreement enlarges the hole in that wall of disagreement between us. This is no guarantee of a peaceful outcome, but it opens the possibility of discovering that we do not need to shoot each other quite yet. Maybe not at all.

Closely linked to this advantage of a guaranteed meeting ground in moments of conflict, there is the fact that divine realities invite a hesitation about violence precisely because the realities under consideration are by nature supernatural. Any honest member of such discourse must begin, then, with the realization that they do not—cannot—have the ability to understand and describe this reality completely or perfectly. No poet has ever worthily sung the divine things, and they never will, Socrates said.[23] It necessarily follows that since the object of our discourse is both a divine and perfected reality and, at the same time, inadequately grasped by any one group or person, then talking about one another's vision may be a shortcut to learning more truth about what I claim to value. And so discourse—actual discourse, not a manipulative imitation of discourse—is the Platonic first response to disagreement precisely because it is anchored to the divine. Assuming I genuinely do love the divine realities and I genuinely do want to understand more completely their unchangeable nature, then disagreements and inconsistencies between our views now invite a shared contemplation of the divine by both of us. If we accept the invitation, that act of shared contemplation might expand our understanding about a common reality that will not bend to our desires, that we both claim to admire, and toward which our words are reaching, however incompletely.

---

[23] See Plato, *Phaedrus* 247c.

It certainly does not follow that agreement will be inevitable or that every perspective I listen to will be worth learning from. Sometimes people believe really shallow and stupid stuff, and they talk about it. But under the necessary ignorances of the Platonic system, my own default definitions of *shallow* and *stupid* are pretty narrow, actually, and do not often include the really big questions. And so, it is worth pausing here for a quick examination of the soul's conscience. If throughout this discussion, the image in my mind is of those other people finally seeing how right my side is and getting straightened out a bit, then there is a good chance the point of the discussion has been missed. Try imagining discourse that results in one's own perspective being corrected. And if the response to that last comment is, "Yeah, tell them to do that. That's what they need to hear," well, then maybe we need to just go back to the opening of Chapter 5 and start over with Plato from the very beginning.

If I claim to love justice, or truth, or righteousness, or any other divine reality, the opportunity to leave my own views for a richer and more accurate understanding of those divine truths should be a joy. "And what kind of man am I? One of those who would be pleased to be refuted if I say anything untrue and who would be pleased to refute anyone who says anything untrue; one who, however, wouldn't be any less pleased to be refuted than to refute. For I count being refuted a greater good."[24] Though the divine is unwavering, it cannot result in unwavering certainty because the divine is beyond my grasp. That is why Socrates can correct others but also why he can be corrected. Outside of mathematics, certainty is always unflinching Gorgianic ego or Isocratic ideology. But with certainty off the table, the only other option, as we will see, is that condition of life the Greeks knew as *pistis*, which is translated *faith*.

One encouragement to engage in public discourse, then, is our ignorance—that is, our incomplete understanding of the divine. Every embodied soul is, in relation to this divine realm, a student in need of education, in need of inner formation. And every other student in the classroom who claims to understand something that I do not understand about this lesson is a potential teacher. Potential. That they see things differently does not mean they see things more clearly. They may. They may not. We would need to sit down and talk together and hear what insights they have to share, and we would need to weigh those insights properly and carefully. That is the point.

---

[24] Plato, *Gorgias* 458a.

With public discourse anchored, then, to the divine realities that cannot waver, discourse rather than spin is possible. But since every grasp of the divine realities is partial, discourse is also desirable, because discourse is how our understanding of the divine sharpens. Our views can become clearer precisely to the degree that they increase our true understanding of those divine realities we want to see fully.

But we actually have to want to see them—and on their own terms, not for the use we can make of them.

The Whole, the Whole Whole, and Nothing but the Whole

Desire, then, is hardly something Plato finds problematic in and of itself. It bears remembering that the whole of the *Phaedrus* is built around the playful consideration of how one might go about seducing a potential lover. That said, desire is, famously, the naughty horse in the soul's chariot. Desire must be, if the soul is to get anywhere important, powerfully reined in by the soul via an intellect that is desperately trying to train all material desires to conform to the divine procession, imitating the example and cooperating with the authority of the god this soul is struggling to follow. And so here is a pretty picture that addresses a question that has been lingering over the conversation since the middle of Chapter 6, one which we have hinted at and danced around but never addressed directly. Briefly, how is one to explore the eternal realities once they are identified? We noted above that one of the purposes of words was to discover and explicate the infinite and eternal divine as it is relevant to the present. And we saw that such an explication would be, always, incomplete. And we said we needed to be able to discuss and critique differing views of these infinite and eternal realities. But how? How is one to explore a reality outside of time and space and so arrive at some worthwhile, clearer, but limited understanding of the divine world? Even here, we can only address these questions suggestively (seductively?).

The temptation is to reply *philosophy* and then move on. And certainly the Platonic answer is *philosophy*, but Plato's idea of philosophy needs to be remembered. Philosophy in Plato is an intellectual discipline that prepares the soul to interact properly with the divine world. Early in our discussion of Plato, we noted the way he and his Socrates had been turned into Enlightenment icons, eventually portrayed as pure rationalists focused on absolutely provable things which would then get labeled *knowledge*. In that era, any field incapable of providing absolute proof for its conclusions (and thus providing knowledge about the world) was increasingly viewed as a suspect space where more or less groundless private opinions were tossed about in the unseemly context of being taken seriously by adults. Rhetoric itself wasted away in an elocutionary desert, reduced to talking about vocal inflection and the angle of the elbow in gestures during a speech's concluding appeal. It certainly had nothing to offer in the realm of thinking clearly. The Enlightened Modernists were going to do all the clear thinking using an analytical and scientific model. This view hit its heyday around the year 1900 (give or take) when the prominent belief was that everything, absolutely everything but especially human nature, was going to get better and better and better and people would evolve, psychologically and socially, into inevitably nice creatures and we would all do good and be good and live well and get along, because we would *know* things.

Those expectations did not pan out.

Little wonder, then, that the field of rhetoric enthusiastically embraced a Gorgianic and Isocratic vision of language as these reappeared in the last half of the twentieth century, dancing on Modernism's grave. After that long exile in the elocutionary desert, here were flowing springs of theory that seemed to attribute real power to words. This post-modern embrace was, I have suggested, short-sighted and little better than the Modernist option, leaving words spinning around the smallest orbit of my own infallible experience of my own subjective desires. But rhetoric is always a third-wheel and a foreigner in the land of certainties, whether it is the objectified and self-correcting certainties of science or whether it is the subjective and self-centered certainties of me and my feelings. The native realm of rhetoric is and has always been on the wide plains of a confidence that can be challenged, not the narrow alleys of a certainty that is established, whether scientifically or subjectively. In other words, rhetoric belongs, perhaps more than anywhere else, in the realm of the human soul's reach for the divine, where even success leaves one without absolute knowledge and unbending certainty but only confidence, conviction, *pistis*, faith.

In Plato's chariot there is a wholistic vision where intellect corrects that part of desire which leans away from a higher good. That higher good can be intellectually defended as higher, better, superior. This confidence about what is *better* and how to lead the soul there is supported by two contributing streams that help shape intellect. First there is that other horse.

Something in the soul actually does, in the end, want to see a beauty too large for it and to surrender to a truth both more simple and more expansive than the purely analytical mind knows what to do with. Lynching is wrong. Part of the soul understands this and offers its contribution to help sharpen the intellect. But second, there is the god in front of you whom you are following. There is *mythos*. This is not a vague subjective aesthetic nor a spirituality without religion, but an ordered, disciplined, solemn, religious, ritual procession that has happened before and will take place again just like this. Such ritual is the very icon of *kosmos*, order and ornament. There is, in other words, a corrective and mentoring authority in the structures of religious life and religious festival and religious ritual.

Here, again, we have echoes of Isocrates's community, certainly, but under the aegis of an ordered tradition necessarily braided into a partial understanding of divine perfections that are real and independent of my opinions and understanding. Here is a religious relationship that has proven itself capable to guide one toward good, to offer reliable advice on how to live a flourishing life, to explicate an actual divine reality. It has established this authority over centuries of reflection and in a flurry of different circumstances. A spiritual but not religious life offers little more than ginned up subjectivity that may or may not lead somewhere. Religious life offers a structured path that, like it or not, definitely makes demands, establishes boundaries, disciplines the wild horse, and has a proven track record of pointing the soul toward the divine. Yes, we all know that all religious organizations, like all organizations, are full of hypocrites and suckers and failures and far worse, but we are not here talking about Hindus or Catholics or Muslims. We are talking about Hinduism and Catholicism and Islam. But if the soul's intellect is supported by religious authority and tradition in its understanding of how to get to the divine, the soul's passions are also disciplined and trained by the intellect and the authorities that point to the *vita florentis*. And those authorities—their consistency and vibrancy, and certainly their hypocrisies and evil acts—are consistently under review by the intellect and the desires and the expectations of the faithful.

In other words, there is a system of checks and balances between the various parts of Plato's chariot and its participation in the divine procession toward the divine. This system results in a Whole, an interactive sense of what the divine is like, how to approach it, how to engage it, and where one might find it. Such a Whole takes both the natural and the supernatural seriously. It operates by finding itself in a complicated relational dance between desire and understanding and authority, both divine and political. It is *mythocentric*, which is to say submissive to specific religious discipline and supernaturally aware. It is *logocentric*, which is to say reasoned, rational, and self-aware. It is truthful, which is to say *philosophical* and *theological*. It is uncertain and tentative, which is to say *rhetorical*.

This system of checks and balances between intellect, desires, and authority will emerge in Aristotle as *logos*, *pathos*, and *ēthos*, which he collectively calls *pisteis*, the plural form of *pistis*, meaning assurance, faith, or conviction. Faith, belief, confidence, conviction: these emerge in those moments when clear thought, disciplined emotion, and proven authorities provide "wholistic" and unified reasons to believe, accept, trust, embrace a conclusion where certainty is not possible. And what is uncertain covers a lot of ground—and most of the really interesting moments in life. Tomorrow is always more risky, for example, if one loves.

Rhetoric was correct to be embarrassed by its subjugation to a shallow modernist and enlightened philosophy of analytical certainties. It was perhaps too hasty to take up the secularized psychological and social certainties of a post-modern Gorgias and Isocrates. Perhaps it is time to review the possibility that a pre-modern philosophy, combining both absolutes and uncertainties in equal measure, might, as Plato suggested, be a very fine basis for a true rhetoric. This true rhetoric would be saddled with lessons in how to think clearly, not conclusively, about real things that really matter but cannot be proven. A true rhetoric would, then, be rooted in the relational truth that is present in the interaction of *mythos, reason, words, desire, community,* and, yes, *power*. In the realm of faith—that is, in the realm of a true rhetoric—there is no room for a fundamentalist domination of any one of these aspects. True rhetoric is saddled with the inexhaustible (not impossible) task of explicating the divine. But precisely (and only) because it is the divine that is being explicated, true rhetoric is capable of actual and meaningful discourse in its native tongue of faith, confidence, and belief—but never certainty.

Chapter 8

The End: Where to Begin

ARISTOTLE NO DOUBT WOULD DISAGREE WITH that version of Plato created by the Enlightenment for the Enlightened. How much he disagreed
with Plato is a very different question.[1] But Aristotle—his *Ethics*, his
Metaphysics, and especially his *Rhetoric*—are not the focus of this chapter.
Aristotle has only made his brief cameo appearances here and at the end of
the last chapter as a reminder that the conversation of this book is hardly
self-contained. As Plato's most famous student, Aristotle had a great deal
to say. And the discussion goes on. Education and rhetoric and the gods
are part of Cicero's work. Plotinus, Philo, Proclus, Avicenna, Athanasius,
Augustine, Anselm, Scotus, and Aquinas—to choose just a few names that
come quickly to mind—add more than a few ripples to the conversation.
And if we have leapt from Plato to Florida school board meetings, it bears
acknowledging, as we close, that such a leap, though certainly justified,
is not without its complications and laughably broad omissions. But one
cannot say everything all at once, and what has been said is not nothing,
Gorgias notwithstanding.

Using the Past to Look Ahead

We have met three thinkers from Classical Greece whose views of language,
whose thoughts about education, whose relationships with the divine all
differ from one another. They all differ from us as well. And yet their perspectives are not so bizarre as to be incomprehensible nor so foreign as to
be without echoes in our world. My own fifth grade English lessons, though
taught by an ancient Ms. Harris, could have been designed by the more
ancient sophist Gorgias: we were given a series of paragraphs that served as
templates which were to be written out (by hand, of course) verbatim, more
than once. Next, we rewrote each sentence in every paragraph, replacing all
the nouns, adjectives, and verbs in that sentence, but leaving all the other

---

[1] See, e.g., Lloyd Gerson, *Aristotle and Other Platonists* (Ithaca, NY: Cornell University
Press, 2017).

elements—transitions, adverbs, punctuation, prepositions—exactly as they were, all while making sure each individual sentence still made sense. Once the basic forms of the sentences were grasped, we were tasked with writing our own new paragraphs that combined, but rearranged, adapted, and imitated, various sentences from any of the paragraphs. The result was staggeringly pretentious but stunningly fluid fifth-grade prose on, say, the importance of a good breakfast. Such essays, filled with periodic sentences, sounded as if they were composed by an earnest Winston Churchill or Franklin Delano Roosevelt, our usual models. It is difficult to imagine a more Gorgianic system, logistically. To this day, Gorgias's *Palamedes* always sounds to me as if it were being read in Ms. Harris's stiff elocutionary voice in that stuffy fifth grade classroom.[2] And the idea of templates for a student to imitate is not gone, as witnessed by the quite popular *They Say / I Say* series.[3] These are logistics, of course, that are easily separated from Gorgias's philosophic view, though that view remains part of the broader liberal arts education as well as popular culture, as we have seen.

But if the Gorgianic method and outlook still has occasional echoes in education, Isocrates has been part of every class any of us have ever had once it set out either to offer epideictic praise of the normative system or to forward ideological challenges to those norms. Isocrates saw education as the fountainhead of community, and he recognized that one of its core tasks was to enculturate the identity and priorities of some recognizable *us* that would flock together. For better or for worse.

And Plato saw the educational task as one of figuring out what *better* or *worse* might mean so a person would not lose their eternal soul and might have a chance to contemplate the heavenly things and live with others in a way that was meaningful. Are students today graduating from high schools and universities and graduate schools with the sort of character that prioritizes truth over agenda? Do they recognize the difference between the two? Are they capable of discerning other souls with that same priority? Are they able to assess the truth of a claim with integrity and honesty even when spoken by those with whom they disagree? These are the questions

---

[2] In a final tribute to Ms. Harris, this sentence is modeled on one from George Orwell's "Politics and the English Language," in *George Orwell: Collected Essays, Journalism, and Letters*, vol. 4, *In Front of Your Nose, 1945–1950*, ed. Sonia Orwell and Ian Angus, 127–40 (Jaffrey, NH: David R. Godine, 2019).

[3] Gerald Graff and Cathy Birkenstein have a number of books that teach original composition through various templates suited for differing tasks. See, e.g., their *They Say / I Say: The Moves that Matter in Academic Writing*, 5th ed. (New York: W. W. Norton, 2001).

that tell us whether educators are doing their job. The critique of education is more complicated, of course. But these are the first steps toward any
meaningful assessment.

Beyond education, we have also looked at the ancient views of *logos*,
of language and thought and the relation of these to reality, and here we
see an even sharper divergence—the defining difference, really—between
the three thinkers. Gorgias dwelt in a world of uncertainty. But when we
come to Plato, we also find uncertainty. And yet, Plato's uncertainty offers guidance toward something comprehensively meaningful. Gorgias's
uncertainty offers only the opportunity to exercise private power that is
ultimately meaningless. Not fully comprehending a divine reality is different from there being nothing to comprehend, it turns out. The former is an
invitation to explore and discover new aspects of meaning; the latter is a
doom of pointless power-hoarding. And so, while both Plato and Gorgias
traffic in ignorance, they are spending very different currencies. And something quite similar is true when we look at Isocrates.

Isocrates sought to reinforce and rebuild a fallen community around
the familiar refrains of class and ethnic superiority. The Greeks are the better
people. And the Athenians are the better Greeks. And the well-heeled, well-
educated Athenians are the very best Athenians. And so, power belongs
in their superior hands, naturally. Thus will we repair the damage done
to us and restore the glory taken from us. And that refrain is as chilling
as it is familiar. After the terrors and chaos of his youth, Isocrates appears
desperate for a return to a stable and functioning community on almost
any terms, but (very fortunately), the most reasonable terms available are
the ones that put *us* in charge of things. Plato, on the other hand, sought to
remember what community was for and what made it worthwhile in the
first place. And in the end, he hit upon the disorienting conclusion that
the only health for any earthly community was found in the exact degree
that it sought, truthfully and sincerely, to participate in the procession of
divine reality. And not a "divine" sort of "reality" but an actual reality that
was actually divine: infinite, eternal, unchanging, present to the gods, comprehended by the gods, contemplated by the gods. Gathered together in
quest for justice, not as I want it to be but as the gods know it to be, humans
discover—there and only there—the possibility of a just communion, the
substance of community.

These, then, are the most fundamental views of Gorgias, Isocrates,
and Plato (whose mentor was executed for taking these views seriously,

remember). And, arguably, by moving closer to their foundational perspectives, we find more in common with them, almost as if such options for understanding words and thought were "inherent in the very germplasm" of being human.[4] We recognize Gorgias's self-asserting ambition as a response to a small life within a meaningless world. We recognize Isocrates's relentless urge to connect to others and his insecure need for *us* to be better than *them*. And we also understand Plato's intense requirement that unless the divine is actually there and actually sought, we cannot say or do anything substantive. We recognize all of these calls. We hear some unfocused versions of them constantly. We hear them in our own souls' fears and ambitions, in Superbowl commercials, in classroom lectures, in sermons, in supporting actors' monologues on Netflix, in the lessons of YouTube Yoga teachers, in campaign speeches, and in podcasting influencers and movies and CNN editorials and the songs on the radio and uncles holding forth at Thanksgiving dinner.

But if we have seen something of the past and if we have found its echoes and shadows in the present, it is important to recall that this book was never intended to be a complicated scavenger hunt. The goal of the text, stated plainly in the Preface, was not to collect dead data about a dead past nor to rally around and highlight once more the limitations and blind spots of these past minds, as catalogued by our present sensibilities. The goal, rather, was to engage the past minds to try to hear their relevant comments regarding our own limitations and blind spots. One such comment is, perhaps, an imprecation of our own views about words and the divine. We seem terribly comfortable passing fairly expansive judgments on political and moral issues in a way that our own views of language simply cannot support, for example.

I have argued that our contemporary theories of rhetoric and public discourse lean on Isocrates and Gorgias, and in doing this, they leave us cut off from meaningful critique or even meaning. If we are satisfied with such a world, we need do nothing. Our subscription to MeMeMe.com, where our own desires are the final word about everything that matters, will automatically renew at midnight tonight. But if we believe that we live in a world where human trafficking and the Trail of Tears are unjust in a fixed and unalterable way, rather than merely unpalatable to me and my group at this particular moment, then we will need to search for alternative theories

---

[4] Kenneth Burke, *Counter-Statement* (Berkeley: University of California Press, 1969), 219.

that provide alternative ways to ground those judgments. We need to think of language in a way that allows us to talk about those judgments. We need words that are just, not just words about our preferences, however deeply felt or impressively presented. We need to consider Plato's suggestion that the actual divine is *necessary* to rhetoric.

I do not necessarily claim that Plato is correct, *per se*. First of all, it must be noted that very little, if anything, presented in this book argues *directly* for the truth of Plato's view. I have only pointed out that if his views are true, then and only then can words traffic in a meaning that is larger than manufactured idiosyncratic self-expression. Certainly, I have critiqued Plato more favorably than the alternatives in the analysis chapters of the book, and I am, myself, a type of Platonist. But Plato's theory, empowering the possibility of discourse to make substantive critiques by linking language to divine realities and therefore fixed and transcendent meanings, does not constitute an overwhelming argument that Gorgias and Isocrates are wrong. It may only suggest that Plato was too cowardly to stare into the abyss. And Plato's view, even if it is closer to the truth, is not without some difficulties of its own, of course.

But, second, it must also be remembered, as we noted at the outset of this chapter, that a Platonic perspective is something that quickly came to embrace more than Plato, and we have not opened that larger conversation in this book. If Platonic thought is poised to make contributions to the contemporary debates, then it will be in the voice of a pre-modern Platonism larger than Plato, and it will include not just Pagan but obviously Christian (at the very least) metaphysics. This will bring its own challenges. If *logos* grows more robust the more closely it is anchored to the divine, then the Christian theology of the Incarnation (where a literal and specific gendered human being in body, word, and thought is also the self-causing God of all being) becomes the most meaningful foundation for an embodied theory of rhetoric possible, a point I suspect will not receive universal acclaim in the world of communication studies any time soon. But neither is such a claim quite as reductive and totalizing as it might at first appear. The entire phenomenological "Theology of the Body" from John Paul II requires a constant personalization of experience within the limits of unalterable divine realities. And it requires this in the context of a relationship with an ultimate supernatural and personal divine being. That relationship is, then, reflected in every embodied interaction of the individual as they go about being-in-the-world. And John Paul's writings are hardly the only example of a very contemporary vision of Platonic thought peppered with philosophical reflections after Modernism passed away. One might turn just as easily to Christos Yannaras's *Person and Eros*, which argues that meaning cannot be approached without *logos*, of course. But he then complicates this by arguing that *dia-logos* is the only actual connection to the substance of what transcends us, and so being and truth are both fundamentally relational and require *ec-stasis*, the standing away from any objectified sense of self and the recognition of a second presence in *logos*, the *dia-logos* in which one surrenders self to the very different Other and self is found in the *eros* of that opposite.[5] Like John Paul, Yannaras acknowledges, challenges, and extends Heidegger.

In other words, the last century or so has seen new approaches to the ontology of relationships and the phenomenology of truth that are potent and cannot be ignored by any honest soul.[6] Even if Plato is remembered—and remembered in the old way: made animate and allowed to participate as one actually present and causally potent in this moment—he will not be the final word. Catherine Pickstock notes that such an invitation, even fully realized, "may involve a reversed enrichment" of any pre-modern voices brought into the present, with that reversed enrichment growing out of "a newer sense of the importance of body, language, time and community" that has appeared in recent decades.[7] In other words, to invite Plato to enter, actually, into our present time hardly guarantees Platonism a philosophical checkmate in two moves. To invoke a Platonic response to the limits of Gorgias and Isocrates in our current views is a beginning, not the end, of a complicated contemporary conversation.

Nevertheless, Plato himself is the foundation of Platonism, and this book has attempted to call attention to Plato himself as a glossed-over and neglected starting point for addressing today's problems and building today's theories of language and rhetoric. If one believes (as I do) that the pre-modern Platonic tradition has some correctives to offer a post-modern, post-Christian, post-secular, post-ironic world, then understanding something of Plato's original writings is the logical starter kit for this new adventure.

---

[5] Christos Yannaras, *Person and Eros*, trans. Normal Russell (Brookline, MA: Holy Cross Orthodox Press, 2008).

[6] One might, e.g., look at Catherine Pickstock, *Aspects of Truth: A New Religious Metaphysics* (Cambridge, UK: Cambridge University Press, 2020) as well as the various essays in John Milbank, Catherine Pickstock, and Graham Ward, eds., *Radical Orthodoxy* (London: Routledge, 1999).

[7] Pickstock, *Aspects of Truth*, 31.

Perhaps the time is right to sit down and reconsider Plato and his legacy, focusing on what these might have to offer the present as well as what the present might have to offer them, but starting always from the view that *the pursuit of the actual divine—while understanding and admitting that we will never fully comprehend it—is the true rhetoric.*

Once More unto the Breach, Or Close Up the Wall with Our English Dead: Nothing Again

In what is perhaps his most famous parable, Nietzsche's madman, the prophet of the void, calls out his invitation to retool the human being from the ground up, severed from any divine constraint, treating human nature in the same way we have treated all other aspects of nature: taking from it and leaving in it whatever we choose on the basis of any desire we see fit to have.[8] In the story, the call to create anything we like from the raw act of being human fails to resonate with his audience, even though he presents that call to those who have, ostensibly, already rejected the divine. But these weakling atheists have not considered their severance from the divine as profoundly as they should, and they do not see its implications as clearly as they might. They are sentimental nihilists. They will not or cannot fathom the necessary obligation of their beliefs, and so the madman—which is to say, Nietzsche—declares that he has come too soon.

The parable closes with the madman forcing his way into various churches where he begins to chant an inverted liturgy of the dead. Rather than "*Requiem aeternam dona eis, Domine* [Grant eternal rest to them, O Lord]," Nietzsche's madman begins the chant "*Requiem aeternam deo* [Grant eternal rest *to God*]." The command in this inverted liturgy is clear: be done with your hypocrisy. The question is equally clear: why have you not *really* put God away? And so, the madman, because he arrived too soon, must make do with retooling the old ways in which human beings acted while waiting for the day when he can refashion the very act of being human. The madman will do what he can until his time comes. Then he will do more.

Perhaps his time is now. Pragmatically, the ability to retool the human being from the ground up has never been more within our grasp, and our technology for altering the act of being human, body and soul, individual

---

[8] Friedrich Nietzsche, *The Gay Science*, trans. Josefine Nauckhoff (Cambridge, UK: Cambridge University Press, 2001), 119–20.

and corporate, grows daily. If our hesitation to seize the means of being human is linked to our vague community sentimentality or to some environmental awe in the face of the mere mechanics or scale of nature, then we need to consider that, perhaps, such hesitation is no more than a failure of nerve. Why have we not *really* put God away?

Alternatively, perhaps this is not the time for Nietzsche's madman, but Plato's madness. Perhaps we have not *really* put God away because we suffer not from some cowardly hypocrisy, but rather from a vague metaphysical hangover that has left a fuzzy buzzing (almost like a chant) in the back of the brain. Ambrosia packs a lingering punch, for sure, but the crew that brought that bottle to the party? They might be worth having over again. They were a little crazy, admittedly, but they knew how to party. Our Platonic pre-modern drinking buddies certainly saw the divine realities differently than we do. For one thing, they saw them. They certainly saw the relationship between those realities and demi-divine creatures like ourselves—embodied beings with eternal souls—differently than we do. Perhaps they saw these things better than we do? Perhaps we need to have them back over and crack open another bottle (or two) of Ambrosia? Perhaps their voices should be re-collected, re-called, re-membered, and invited to become an animate and living voice in the present? The question is hardly an irrelevant ivory tower dream of speculative abstraction.

There are questions about our very humanity these days. What *is* it? What is it *for*, if anything? What are we *allowed* to do to it? What *should* be done to it? What should *not*? And what will my answer to any of these questions be grounded on? Gorgias's sense of savvy self? Isocrates's amoral happenstance of cultural consensus? Plato's divine realities?

Who we choose to talk to about all of these questions, and what we conclude about them, about our embodied humanity, about whether we really should do to human nature what we have done to the rest of nature, will matter perhaps now more than it ever has before.

Unless you pick Gorgias. Then it won't matter at all. Nothing will.

Bibliography

Allen, Amy. *The End of Progress.* New York: Columbia University Press, 2017.

Annas, Julia. *An Introduction to Plato's "Republic."* Oxford: Clarendon Press, 1981.

Aristophanes. *Wasps.* Translated by Jeffrey Henderson. Loeb Classical Library 488. Cambridge, MA: Harvard University Press, 1998.

Aristotle. *Art of Rhetoric.* Translated by J. H. Freese. Loeb Classical Library 193. Cambridge, MA: Harvard University Press, 1975.

Aristotle. *Eudemian Ethics.* Translated by H. Rackham. Loeb Classical Library 285. Cambridge, MA: Harvard University Press, 2004.

Aristotle. *Metaphysics.* Translated by Hugh Tredennick. Loeb Classical Library 271. Cambridge, MA: Harvard University Press, 1935.

Aristotle. *On Sophistical Refutations.* Translated by E. S. Forster. Loeb Classical Library 400. Cambridge, MA: Harvard University Press, 1978.

Aristotle. *On the Soul.* Translated by W. S. Hett. Loeb Classical Library 288. Cambridge, MA: Harvard University Press, 1957.

Aristotle. *Politics.* Translated by H. Rackham. Loeb Classical Library 264. Cambridge, MA: Harvard University Press, 1932.

Armstrong, Karen. *Fields of Blood: Religion and the History of Violence.* New York: Anchor, 2015.

Associated Press, "Holocaust Novel 'Maus' banned in Tennessee School District." *PBS News Hour.* Jan 27, 2022. https://www.pbs.org/newshour/arts/holocaust-novel-maus-banned-in-tennessee-school-district#:~:text=ATHENS%2C%20Tenn.,minutes%20from%20a%20board %20meeting.

Barilli, Renato. *Rhetoric.* Translated by Giuliana Menozzi. Minneapolis: University of Minnesota Press, 1996.

Barney, Rachel. "Callicles and Thrasymachus." In *The Stanford Encyclopedia of Philosophy*, Fall 2017 edition, edited by Edward N. Zalta. https://plato.stanford.edu/archives/fall2017/entries /callicles-thrasymachus/.

Barrett, Harold. *The Sophists: Rhetoric, Democracy, and Plato's Idea of Sophistry*. Novato, CA: Chandler & Sharp, 1987.

Bartninkas, Vilius. *Traditional and Cosmic Gods in Later Plato and the Early Academy*. Cambridge, UK: Cambridge University Press, 2023.

Baumbach, Noah. *White Noise*. Written and directed by Noah Baumbach. Production Houses: NBGG Pictures, Heyday Films, and A24. Distributed by Netflix. Released 2022.

Benoit, William. "Isocrates and Plato on Rhetoric and Rhetorical Education." *Rhetoric Society Quarterly* 21, no. 1 (1991): 60–71.

Bernard-Donals, Michael, and Kyle Jensen, eds. *Responding to the Sacred: An Inquiry into the Limits of Rhetoric*. University Park: Pennsylvania State University Press, 2021.

Bizzell, Patricia, and Bruce Herzberg. *The Rhetorical Tradition*. 2nd ed. Boston: Bedford/St. Martin's, 2001.

Boyarin, Daniel. "The Scandal of Sophism." *Common Knowledge* 13, nos. 2–3 (2007): 315–36.

Brazier, Mary A. B. *A History of Neurophysiology in the 17th and 18th Centuries: From Concept to Experiment*. New York: Raven, 1984.

Brazier, Mary A. B. *A History of Neurophysiology in the 19th Century*. New York: Raven,1988.

Brickhouse, Thomas, and Nicholas Smith. *Plato's Socrates*. Oxford: Oxford University Press, 1994.

Brown, Malcolm, and James Coulter. "The Middle Speech of Plato's *Phaedrus*." *Journal of the History of Philosophy* 9, no. 4 (1971): 405–23.

Burke, Kenneth. *Rhetoric of Religion*. Boston: Beacon, 1961.

Burke, Kenneth. *Language as Symbolic Action*. Berkeley: University of California Press, 1966.

Burke, Kenneth. *Counter-Statement*. Berkeley: University of California Press, 1969.

Bury, J. B. *A History of Greece to the Death of Alexander*. New York: St. Martin's, 1967.

Carruthers, Mary. *Craft of Thought*. Cambridge, UK: Cambridge University Press, 1998.

Carruthers, Mary. *The Book of Memory*. 2nd ed. Cambridge, UK: Cambridge University Press, 2008.

Cherniak, Christopher. *Minimal Rationality*. Cambridge, MA: MIT Press, 1986.

Chesterton, G. K. *Orthodoxy*. Garden City, NY: Image, 1959.

Cicero. *De Officiis*. Translated by Walter Miller. Loeb Classical Library 30. Cambridge, MA: Harvard University Press, 1990.

Cicero. *De Natura Deorum*. Translated by H. Rackham. Loeb Classical Library 268. Cambridge, MA: Harvard University Press, 1951.

Cobb, William S. *Plato's Erotic Dialogues*. Albany: SUNY Press: 1993.

Cole, Thomas. *The Origins of Rhetoric in Ancient Greece*. Baltimore: Johns Hopkins University Press, 1995.

Collins, Anthony. *A Discourse of Free-Thinking*. London: printed by Cornelius Crownfield of Cambridge University Press, 1713.

Collins, James. *Exhortations to Philosophy*. Oxford: Oxford University Press, 2015.

Cooper, John Gilbert. *The Life of Socrates*. Printed for R. Dodsley at Tully's Head in Pall-Mall, 1750.

Cooper, John M., ed. *Plato: Complete Works*. Indianapolis, IN: Hackett, 1997.

Crick, Nathan. *Rhetoric and Power: The Drama of Classical Greece*. Columbia: University of South Carolina Press, 2018.

Crivelli, Paolo. "Plato's Philosophy of Language." In *The Oxford Handbook of Plato*, edited by Gail Fine, 481–506. Oxford: Oxford University Press, 2023.

Davis, Wynne. "The Bible is Among Dozens of Books Removed from This Texas School District." *NPR*. August 18, 2022. https://www.npr.org/2022/08/18/1117708153/bible-anne-frank-books-banned-texas-school-district.

Dawkins, Richard. *The God Delusion*. New York: Houghton Mifflin, 2008.

Demos, Raphael. "Plato's Philosophy of Language." *The Journal of Philosophy* 61, no. 20 (1964): 595–610

Depew, David, and Takis Poulakos. *Isocrates and Civic Education*. Austin: University of Texas Press, 2004.

Depew, David. "The Inscription of Isocrates into Aristotle's Practical Philosophy." In Poulakos and Depew, *Isocrates and Civic Education*, 157–85.

Derrida, Jacques, and Gianni Vattimo. *Religion*. Stanford, CA: Stanford University Press, 1996.

Detienne, Marcel. *The Masters of Truth in Archaic Greece*. Translated by Janet Lloyd. New York: Zone, 1996.

Dickie, Matthew W. "The Place of *Phthonos* in the Argument of Plato's *Phaedrus*." In *Nomodeiktes: Greek Studies in Honor of Martin Ostwald*, edited by Ralph Mark Rosen and Joseph Farrell, 379–96. Ann Arbor: University of Michigan Press, 1994.

Dignas, Beate, and R. R. R. Smith, eds. *Historical and Religious Memory in the Ancient World*. Oxford: Oxford University Press, 2012.

Dillon, John, and Tania Gergel. *The Early Sophists*. New York: Penguin Classics, 2003.

Diogenes Laertius. *Lives of Eminent Philosophers*. Translated by R. D. Hicks. Loeb Classical Library 185. Cambridge, MA: Harvard University Press, 1925.

Dodds, E. R. *The Elements of Theology*. Oxford: Clarendon, 1933.

Dodds, E. R. *The Greeks and the Irrational*. Berkeley: University of California Press, 1973.

Engler, Barbara. *Personality Theories*. 9th ed. San Francisco: Cengage Learning, 2013.

Enos, Richard Leo. *Greek Rhetoric before Aristotle*. Prospect Heights, IL: Waveland, 1993.

Ferrari, G. R. F. *Listening to the Cicadas: A Study of Plato's "Phaedrus."* Cambridge Classical Studies. Cambridge, UK: Cambridge University Press, 1987.

Ficino, Marsilio. *Theologia Platonica de immortalitate animorum*. Paris, 1482.

Fine, Gail. *Plato on Knowledge and Forms*. Oxford: Oxford University Press, 2003.

Ford, Andrew. "Sophists Without Rhetoric: The Arts of Speech in Fifth-Century Athens." In Too, *Education in Greek and Roman Antiquity*, 85–109.

Fournier, Michael. "Gorgias on Magic." *Magic, Ritual, & Witchcraft* 8, no. 2 (2013): 119–31.

Fox, Michael V. "Ancient Egyptian Rhetoric." *Rhetorica* 1, no. 1 (1983): 9–22.

Fredal, James. *Rhetorical Action in Ancient Athens: Persuasive Artistry from Solon to Demosthenes*. Carbondale: Southern Illinois University Press, 2006.

Freeman, Kathleen. *The Presocratic Philosophers: A Companion to Diels, "Fragmente der Vorsokratiker."* Oxford: Basil Blackwell, 1953.

Gerson, Lloyd. *Aristotle and Other Platonists*. Ithaca, NY: Cornell University Press, 2017.

Gillespie, Ryan. "Cosmic Meaning, Awe, and Absurdity in the Secular Age: A Critique of Religious Non-Theism." *Harvard Theological Review* 111, no. 4 (2018): 461–87.

Gillespie, Ryan. "Normative Reasoning and Moral Argumentation in Theory and Practice." *Philosophy and Rhetoric* 49, no. 1, (2016): 49–73.

Gillespie, Ryan. "Reason, Religion, and Postsecular Liberal-Democratic Epistemology." *Philosophy & Rhetoric* 47, no. 1 (2014): 1–24.

Gillespie, Ryan. "Religion and the Postsecular Public Sphere." *Quarterly Journal of Speech* 102, no. 2 (2016): 194–207.

Goodenough, Ursula. *The Sacred Depths of Nature*. Oxford: Oxford University Press, 2023.

Gorgias. *Defense of Palamedes*. In Laks and Most, *Early Greek Philosophy, Vol. VIII*, 186–217.

Gorgias. *Encomium of Helen*. In Laks and Most, *Early Greek Philosophy, Vol. VIII*, 166–85.

Gorgias. *On Nonbeing* or *On Nature*. In Laks and Most, *Early Greek Philosophy, Vol. VIII*, 218–43.

Graff, Gerald, and Cathy Birkenstein. *They Say / I Say: The Moves that Matter in Academic Writing*. 5th ed. New York: W. W. Norton, 2001.

Griffith, Mark. "'Public' and 'Private' in Early Greek Institutions of Education." In Too, *Education in Greek and Roman Antiquity*, 23–84.

Griswold, Charles L. *Self-Knowledge in Plato's "Phaedrus."* University Park: Pennsylvania State University Press, 1996.

Habermas, Jürgen, and Joseph Ratzinger. *The Dialectics of Secularization: On Reason and Religion*. San Francisco: Ignatius, 2005.

Habermas, Jürgen et al. *An Awareness of What is Missing: Faith and Reason in a Post-secular Age*. Edited by Ciaran Cronin. Cambridge: Polity, 2010.

Hadot, Pierre. *What is Ancient Philosophy?* Translated by Michael Chase. Cambridge, MA: Harvard University Press, 2002

Hammond, N. G. L. *A History of Greece to 322 BC*. 3rd ed. Oxford: Oxford University Press, 1986.

Hammond, N. G. L. *The Classical Age of Greece*. New York: Harper and Rowe, 1975.

Harari, Yuval. "Homo Deus: A Brief History of Tomorrow with Yuval Harari." University of California Television (UCTV), 24 April 2017. Video, 57:11. https://www.youtube.com /watch?v =4ChHc5jhZxs.

Harris, Elizabeth A., and Alexandra Alter. "Authors and Students Sue Over Florida Law Driving Book Bans." *New York Times*, June 20, 2023. https://www.nytimes.com/2023/06/20/books/book-bans-florida-tango-makes-three.html.

Harris, Sam. *Making Sense.* New York: Ecco, 2020.

Haskins, Ekaterina V. *Logos and Power in Isocrates and Aristotle.* Columbia: University of South Carolina Press, 2004.

Haskins, Ekaterina V. "Logos and Power in Sophistical and Isocratean Rhetoric." In Poulakos and Depew, *Isocrates and Civic Education*, 84–103.

Herodotus. *Histories.* Translated by Robin Waterfield. Oxford: Oxford University Press, 2008.

Hesiod. *Theogony.* In *Theogony, Works and Days, Testimonia*, edited and translated by Glen W. Most, 2–155. Loeb Classical Library 57. Cambridge, MA: Harvard University Press, 2018.

Homer. *The Illiad.* Translated by Robert Fagles. London: Penguin, 1990.

Horkheimer, Max. "Traditional and Critical Theory." In *Critical Theory: Selected Essays*, translated by Matthew J. O'Connell, 188–233. New York: Continuum, 1973.

Hulme, Emily. "First Wave Feminism: Craftswomen in Plato's *Republic.*" *Aperion* 55, no. 4 (2022): 485–507.

Hume, David. "An Enquiry Concerning Human Understanding," sec. 4, part II, 29. In *Locke, Berkeley, Hume*, ed. Mortimer J. Adler, *Great Books of the Western World*, vol. 35 (Chicago: William Benton).

Hutto, David. "Ancient Egyptian Rhetoric in the Old and Middle Kingdoms." *Rhetorica* 20, no. 3 (2002): 213–34.

Isocrates. *Against the Sophists.* In Norlin, *Isocrates, Vol. II*, 159–78.

Isocrates. *Antidosis.* In Norlin, *Isocrates, Vol. II*, 179–366.

Isocrates. *Busiris*. In Van Hook, *Isocrates, Vol. III*, 100–33.

Isocrates. *Panathenaicus*. In Norlin, *Isocrates, Vol. II*, 367–541.

Isocrates. *Panegyricus*. In Norlin, *Isocrates, Vol. I*, 116–243.

Isocrates. *To Demonicus*. In Norlin, *Isocrates, Vol. I*, 2–37.

Jaeger, Werner. *Paideia*. Vol. 1, *Archaic Greece; The Mind of Athens*. Translated by Gilbert Highet. Oxford: Oxford University Press, 1973.

Jarratt, Susan. *Rereading the Sophists: Classical Rhetoric Refigured*. Carbondale: Southern Illinois University Press, 1991.

Jasso, John J. "Sympathy for the Devil: The Myth of Plato as the Enemy of Rhetoric." *Rhetorica* 37, no. 4 (2019): 351–81

Johnstone, Christopher Lyle. *Listening to the Logos*. Columbia: University of South Carolina Press, 2009.

Jost, Walter, and Wendy Olmsted. *Rhetorical Invention and Religious Inquiry*. New Haven, CT: Yale University Press, 2000.

Joyal, Mark, Iain McDougall, and J. C. Yardley. *Greek and Roman Education: A Sourcebook*. London: Routledge, 2009.

Kastely, James. "In Defense of Plato's Gorgias." *Proceedings of the Modern Language Association* 106, no. 1 (1991): 99–100.

Kennedy, George A. *Aristotle, On Rhetoric: A Theory of Civic Discourse*. 2nd ed. Oxford: Oxford University Press, 2006.

Kennedy, George A. *The Art of Persuasion in Greece*. Princeton: Princeton University Press, 1963.

Kennedy, George A. *The Older Sophists*. Edited by Rosamond Kent Sprague. Indianapolis, IN: Hackett, 2001.

Kerényi, Karl. *Eleusis: Archetypal Image of Mother and Daughter*. Princeton: Princeton University Press, 1967.

Kerferd, G. B. "Gorgias on Nature or That Which is Not." *Phronesis* 1, no. 1 (1955): 3–25.

Kilmer, Joyce. "Trees," *Poetry Foundation*. Accessed October 4, 2022. https://www.poetryfoundation.org/poetrymagazine/poems/12744/trees.

King, Alexander, and Marin Ketley. *The Control of Language: A Critical Approach to Reading and Writing.* London: Longmans, Green, and Co., 1939.

Kramer, Jillian. "Structure and Chemistry Dictate How Cicada Wings Repel Water and Kill Bacteria." *The Scientific American*, September 1, 2020. https://www.scientificamerican.com /article/structure-and-chemistry-dictate-how-cicada-wings-repel-water-and-kill-bacteria/

Krentz, Peter. *The Thirty at Athens*. Ithaca, NY: Cornell University Press, 1982.

Laks, André, and Glenn W. Most, eds. and trans., *Early Greek Philosophy, Volume II: Beginnings and Early Ionian Thinkers, Part I*, Loeb Classical Library 525. Cambridge, MA: Harvard University Press, 2016.

Laks, André, and Glenn W. Most, eds. and trans. *Early Greek Philosophy, Vol. VIII: Sophists, Part I*. Loeb Classical Library 531. Cambridge, MA: Harvard University Press, 2016.

Lamb, W. R. M. *Lysias*. Loeb Classical Library 244. Cambridge, MA: Harvard University Press, 1988.

Landers, David. *Optimistic Nihilism*. Austin: IM Print, 2016.

Larson, Jennifer. "Pederasty and Male Homoerotic Relations." In *Greek and Roman Sexualities: A Sourcebook*, 107–32. New York: Bloomsbury Academic, 2012.

Lear, Andrew. "Ancient Pederasty: An Introduction." In *A Companion to Greek and Roman Sexualities*, edited by Thomas K. Hubbard, 102–27. Hoboken, NJ: Wiley-Blackwell, 2014.

Leff, Michael. "Isocrates, Tradition, and the Rhetorical Version of Civic Education." In Poulakos and Depew, *Isocrates and Civic Education*, 235–54.

LeVen, Pauline A. *Music and Metamorphosis in Graeco-Roman Thought*. Cambridge, UK: Cambridge University Press, 2020.

Lewis, C. S. *The Abolition of Man*. New York: Macmillan, 1955.

Lewis, C. S. "On the Reading of Old Books." In *God in the Dock*, edited by Walter Hooper, 200–207. Grand Rapids, MI: Eerdmans, 1970.

Liddell, H. G., R. Scott, and Sir Henry Jones. *Greek-English Lexicon*. Oxford: Clarendon, 1996.

Lombardo, G. P., and R. Foschi. "The Concept of Personality in 19th-Century French and 20th-Century American Psychology." *History of Psychology* 6, no. 2 (2003): 123–42.

Lu, Xing. *Rhetoric in Ancient China, Fifth to Third Century B.C.E.: A Comparison with Classical Greek Rhetoric*. Columbia: University of South Carolina Press, 1998.

Mahaffy, J. P. *Old Greek Education*. New York: Harper & Brothers, 1882. Reprinted 1997. Folcroft, PA: Folcroft Library Editions.

Marrou, Henri I. *A History of Education in Antiquity*. Translated by George Lamb. New York: Mentor, 1964.

Marsh, Charles. "Millenia of Discord: The Controversial Educational Program of Isocrates." *Theory and Research in Education* 8, no. 3 (2010): 289–303.

Mastin, Luke. "Pre-socratics." *The Basics of Philosophy*, June 1, 2023. https://www.coursehero.com/file/107569056/359588813-Philosophy-Basicsdocx/

Maximus Tyrius. *The Dissertations of Maximus Tyrius*. Translated by Thomas Taylor. London: Whittingham, 1804.

McComiskey, Bruce. *Gorgias and the New Sophistic Rhetoric*. Carbondale: Southern Illinois University Press, 2002.

McLaren, Peter, and Nathalia Eugenia Jaramillo. "Not Neo-Marxist, Not Post-Marxist, Not Marxian, Not Autonomist Marxism: Reflections on a Revolutionary (Marxist) Critical Pedagogy." *Cultural Studies ↔ Critical Methodologies* 10, no. 3 (2010): 251–62.

McPherran, Mark. *The Religion of Socrates*. University Park: Pennsylvania State University Press, 1999.

Metz, Sam. "Utah District Bans Bible in Elementary and Middle Schools 'Due to Vulgarity or Violence.'" *The Associated Press*, June 2, 2023. https://apnews.com/article/book-ban-school-library-bible-fc025c8ccf30e 955aaf0b0ee1899608a#.

Milbank, John, Catherine Pickstock, and Graham Ward, eds. *Radical Orthodoxy*. London: Routledge, 1999.

More, Paul Elmer. *The Religion of Plato*. Princeton: Princeton University Press, 1921.

Muir, James. *The Legacy of Isocrates and a Platonic Alternative*. New York: Routledge, 2020.

Mylonas, George Emmanuel. *Eleusis and the Eleusinian Mysteries*. Princeton: Princeton University Press, 1961.

National Center for Educational Statistics. Table 322.10: "Bachelor's degrees conferred by postsecondary institutions, by field of study: Selected academic years 1970–71 through 2020–21." *Digest of Education Statistics*. Prepared September 2022. https://nces.ed.gov/programs/digest/d22/tables/ dt22_322.10.asp.

Nienkamp, Jean. *Plato on Rhetoric and Language*. Mahwah, NJ: Hermagoras, 1999.

Nietzsche, Friedrich. *The Gay Science*. Translated by Josefine Nauckhoff. Cambridge, UK: Cambridge University Press, 2001.

Nightingale, Andrea. *Philosophy and Religion in Plato's Dialogues*. Cambridge, UK: Cambridge University Press, 2021.

Norlin, George, trans. *Isocrates, Vol. I*. Loeb Classical Library 209. Cambridge, MA: Harvard University Press, 1961.

Norlin, George, trans. *Isocrates, Vol. II*. Loeb Classical Library 229. Cambridge, MA: Harvard University Press, 1992.

Nunn, John. *Ancient Egyptian Medicine*. Norman: University of Oklahoma Press, 2002.

Nussbaum, Martha. *The Fragility of Goodness*. Cambridge, UK: Cambridge University Press, 2001.

Orwell, George. "Politics and the English Language." In *George Orwell: Collected Essays, Journalism, and Letters*, vol. 4, *In Front of Your Nose 1945–1950*, edited by Sonia Orwell and Ian Angus, 127–40. Jaffrey, NH: David R. Godine, 2019.

Padilla, Mark W., ed. *Rites of Passage in Ancient Greece: Literature, Religion, Society*. Cranbury, NJ: Associated University Presses, 1999.

Pasqualoni, Anthony Michael. "Plato on Being, Time, and Recollection." *ΣΧΟΛΗ* 16, no. 2 (2022): 644–64.

Percy III, William Armstrong. *Pederasty and Pedagogy in Archaic Greece*. Champaign: University of Illinois Press, 1996

Philostratus. *Lives of the Sophists*. In Philostratus, Eunapius, *Lives of the Sophists. Eunapius: Lives of the Philosophers and Sophists*, edited and translated by Wilmer C. Wright, 2–318. Loeb Classical Library 134. Cambridge, MA: Harvard University Press, 1968.

Pickstock, Catherine. *Aspects of Truth: A New Religious Metaphysics*. Cambridge, UK: Cambridge University Press, 2020.

Pieper, Josef. *The Platonic Myths*. South Bend, IN: St. Augustine's, 2011.

Plato. *Apology*. Translated by Harold North Fowler. Loeb Classical Library 36. Cambridge, MA: Harvard University Press, 2001.

Plato. *Epistle VII*. Translated by Glen R. Morrow. In Cooper, *Plato*, 1646–67.

Plato. *Gorgias*. Translated by W. R. M. Lamb. Loeb Classical Library 166. Cambridge, MA: Harvard University Press, 2001.

Plato. *Gorgias*. Translated by Robin Waterfield. In Waterfield, *"Gorgias": A New Translation*. Oxford: Oxford University Press, 2008.

Plato. *Gorgias*. Translated by Donald J. Zeyl. In Cooper, *Plato*, 791–869.

Plato. *Laws*. Translated by Trevor J. Saunders. In Cooper, *Plato*, 1318–1616.

Plato. *Lysis. Symposium. Phaedrus.* Translated by Chris Emlyn-Jones and William Preddy. Loeb Classical Library 166. Cambridge, MA: Harvard University Press, 2022.

Plato. *Meno.* Translated by G. M. A. Grube. In Cooper, *Plato*, 870–97.

Plato. *Phaedrus.* Translated by Alexander Nehamas and Paul Woodruff. In Cooper, *Plato*, 506–56.

Plato. *Phaedrus.* Translated by R. Hackforth. In *Plato's "Phaedrus": Translated with an Introduction and Commentary.* Cambridge, UK: Cambridge University Press, 1972.

Plato. *Phaedrus.* Translated by Christopher Rowe. In *Phaedrus: Edited with an Introduction, Translation, and Commentary.* Oxford: Oxbow Books, 2013.

Plato. *Phaedrus.* Translated by Robin Waterfield. Oxford: Oxford University Press, 2009.

Plato. *Philebus.* Translated by Dorthea Frede. In Cooper, *Plato*, 398–456.

Plato. *Protagoras.* Translated by Stanley Lombardo and Karen Bell. In Cooper, *Plato*, 746–90.

Plato. *Republic.* Translated by G. M. A. Grube and C. D. C. Reeve. In Cooper, *Plato*, 971–1223.

Plato. *Timaeus.* Translated by R. G. Bury. Loeb Classical Library 234. Cambridge, MA: Harvard University Press, 1929.

Postman, Neil. *Amusing Ourselves to Death.* New York: Viking Penguin, 1985.

Poulakos, John. "Early Changes in Rhetorical Practice and Understanding." *Revue de critique et de theorie litteraire* 8 (1989): 307–24.

Poulakos, John. "Gorgias's *Encomium to Helen* and the Defense of Rhetoric." *Rhetorica* 1, no. 2 (1983): 1–16.

Poulakos, Takis. *Speaking for the Polis: Isocrates' Rhetorical Education.* Columbia: University of South Carolina, 1997.

215

Protagoras. *Fragments.* In Laks and Most, *Early Greek Philosophy, Vol. VIII.*

Pseudo-Dionysius. *Celestial Hierarchies*, vol. 1. Archived at *Hodoi Elektronikai*, managed by Alain Meurant, Université Catholique de Louvain, updated 20 Jan. 2010. http://mercure.fltr.ucl.ac.be/Hodoi/concordances/denys_areopagite_hier_cel/ligne05.cfm?numligne=1&mot=82#debut.

Raaflaub, Kurt A. "Conceptualizing and Theorizing Peace in Ancient Greece." *Transactions of the American Philological Association* 139, no. 2 (2009): 225–50.

Reams, Robin. *Seeming and Being in Plato's Rhetorical Theory.* Chicago: University of Chicago Press, 2018.

Reinhardt, Karl. "The Relation Between the Two Parts of Parmenides' Poem." In *The Pre-socratics: A Collection of Critical Essays*, edited by Alexander P. D. Mourelatos, 293–312. Princeton: Princeton University Press, 1993.

Ricoeur, Paul. *Being, Essence, and Substance in Plato and Aristotle.* Translated by David Pellauer and John Starkey. Cambridge, UK: Polity, 2013.

Rinella, Michael. "Supplementing the Ecstatic: Plato, the Eleusinian Mysteries and the *Phaedrus.*" *Polis: The Journal of the Society for Greek Political Thought* 17, nos.1–2 (2000): 61–78.

Robinson, Edwin Arlington. "Miniver Cheevy." In *Anthology of American Literature, II. Realism to the Present.* 2nd ed. Edited by George McMichael. New York: Macmillan, 1974.

Rowe, Christopher J. *Phaedrus.* Warminster: Aris & Phillips, 1998.

Schreiner, Megan, Mark A. E. Williams, and S. David Zuckerman. "Inspirations and Limitations: Reason, the Universal Audience and *Inspire* Magazine." *Journal of Communication & Religion* 36, no. 1 (2013): 196–210.

Scoon, Robert. *Greek Philosophy before Plato.* Princeton: Princeton University Press, 1928.

Sextus Empiricus. *Against the Logicians.* Translated by R. G. Bury. Loeb Classical Library 291. Cambridge, MA: Harvard University Press, 1989.

Sextus Empiricus. *Outlines of Pyrrhonism*. Translated by R. G. Bury. Loeb Classical Library 273. Cambridge, MA: Harvard University Press, 1933.

Shakespeare, William. *The Complete Works of Shakespeare*. Edited by David Bevington. Chicago: University of Chicago Press, 1980.

Shapiro, Teyva Turok. "'Everything Everywhere All At Once' is a Dazzling, Must-Watch, Sci-Fi Spectacle." *Daily Maverick*, March 13, 2023. https://www.dailymaverick.co.za/article/2023-03-13-everything-everywhere-all-at-once-is-a-dazzling-must-watch-sci-fi-spectacle/.

Sipiora, Phillip, and James S. Baumlin. *Rhetoric and Kairos: Essays in History, Theory, and Praxis*. Albany: SUNY Press, 2002.

Snodgrass, Anthony. *Archaic Greece: The Age of Experiment*. Berkeley: University of California Press, 1980.

Spoehr, Thomas, and Katherine Kuzminski. "Bad Idea: Relying on the Same Old Solutions to Meet the Military Recruitment Challenge." *Defense360: A Project of the Center of Strategic and International Studies*, March 10, 2023. https://defense360.csis.org/bad-idea-relying-on-the-same-old-solutions-to-meet-the-military-recruitment-challenge/.

Stiefel, Marc, Arlene Shaner, and Steven Schaefer. "The Edwin Smith Papyrus: The Birth of Analytical Thinking in Medicine and Otolaryngology." *The Laryngoscope* 116, no. 2 (2006): 182–88.

Stump, Roger W. *The Geography of Religion*. London: Rowman & Littlefield, 2008.

Suidas. *Suidae Lexicon*. Oxford: Oxford University Press, 1834. Composite authorship of Byzantine scholars.

Taylor, A. E. *Varia Socratica, First Series*. Oxford: James Parker & Co., 1911.

Thucydides. *History of the Peloponnesian War*. Translated by C. F. Smith. Loeb Classical Library 108. Cambridge, MA: Harvard University Press, 1919.

Tolkien, J. R. R. *The Fellowship of the Rings*. New York: HarperCollins, 2002.

Too, Yun Lee, ed. *Education in Greek and Roman Antiquity*. Leiden: Brill, 2001.

Too, Yun Lee. *The Rhetoric of Identity in Isocrates: Text, Power, Pedagogy*. Cambridge, UK: Cambridge University Press, 2009.

Turiacci, Mariana. "'Como la Cigarra,' la icónica canción de María Elena Walsh que se convirtió en un himno nacional." *Billiken*, February 1, 2023. https://billiken.lat/interesante/como-la-cigarra-la-iconica-cancion-de-maria-elena-walsh-que-se-convirtio-en-un-himno-nacional/.

Van Hook, La Rue, trans. *Isocrates, Vol. III*. Loeb Classical Library 373. Cambridge, MA: Harvard University Press, 1945.

Vernant, Jean-Pierre. *The Origins of Greek Thought*. Ithaca, NY: Cornell University Press, 1996.

Vitanza, Victor. *Negation, Subjectivity, and the History of Rhetoric*. Albany: SUNY Press, 1997.

Vlastos, Gregory. *Socrates: Ironist and Moral Philosopher*. Ithaca, NY: Cornell University Press, 1991.

Voegelin, Eric. *Order and History, Volume II: The World of the Polis*. Baton Rouge: Louisiana State University Press, 1986.

Walsh, Maria Elena. "Como la Cigarra" [like the cicada]. *Como La Cigarra*, track A5. CBS Records, 1973. Vinyl.

Waterfield, Robin. *The First Philosophers: The Presocratics and the Sophists*. Oxford: Oxford University Press, 2000.

Welch, Kathleen. *Electric Rhetoric*. London, UK: MIT Press, 1999.

Werner, Daniel S. *Myth and Philosophy in Plato's "Phaedrus."* Cambridge, UK: Cambridge University Press, 2012.

Whiting, Jennifer. "Fools' Pleasures in Plato's *Philebus*." In *Strategies of Argument: Essays in Ancient Ethics, Epistemology, and Logic*, edited by Mi-Kyoung Lee, 21–59. Oxford: Oxford University Press, 2014.

Williams, Mark A. E. "From Here to Eternity: The Scope of Misreading Plato's Religion." In *Communication and the Global Landscape of* Faith, edited by Adrienne E. Hacker Daniels, 13–26. New York: Lexington Books, 2016.

Williams, Mark A. E. "St. Socrates, Pray for Us: Rhetoric and the Physics of Being Human." In *Rhetoric in the Twenty-first Century: An Interactive Oxford Symposium*, edited by Nicholas J. Crowe and David A. Frank, 81–89. Newcastle-upon-Tyne, UK: Cambridge Scholars Press, 2016.

Williams, Mark A. E. "Substantive Discourse: Love, Justice, and Hierarchy as the Basis for Civility." In *Humility and Hospitality*, edited by Naaman Wood and Sean Connable, 33–46. Pasco, WA: Integratio, 2022.

Woodruff, Paul. "Why did Protagoras use Poetry in Education?" In *Plato's Protagoras: Essays on the Confrontation of Philosophy and Sophistry*, edited by Olof Petterson and Vigdis Songe-Møller, 213–27. New York: Springer, 2017.

Wotton, William. *Reflections on Ancient and Modern Learning*. London: printed by J. Leake for Peter Buck, 1698.

Xenophon. *Anabasis*. Translated by Carleton Brownson and John Dillery. Loeb Clasical Library 90. Cambridge, MA: Harvard University Press, 1998.

Yannaras, Christos. *Person and Eros*. Translated by Norman Russell. Brookline, MA: Holy Cross Orthodox Press, 2008.

Index

www.ingramcontent.com/pod-product-compliance
Lightning Source LLC
Chambersburg PA
CBHW031456120626
46545CB00005B/1622